THE EMERGENCE
OF THE
SOCIAL SCIENCES,
1642–1792

TWAYNE'S STUDIES IN
INTELLECTUAL AND CULTURAL HISTORY

Michael Roth, General Editor
Scripps College and the Claremont Graduate School

THE EMERGENCE
OF THE
SOCIAL SCIENCES
1642–1792

Richard Olson

Twayne Publishers • New York
Maxwell Macmillan Canada • Toronto
Maxwell Macmillan International • New York Oxford Singapore Sydney

The Emergence of the Social Sciences, 1642–1792

Twayne's Studies in Intellectual and Cultural History, No. 5

Twayne Publishers   Maxwell Macmillan Canada, Inc.
Macmillan Publishing Company   1200 Eglinton Avenue East
866 Third Avenue   Suite 200
New York, New York 10022   Don Mills, Ontario M3C 3N1

Macmillan Publishing Company is part of the Maxwell Communication Group of Companies.

Library of Congress Cataloging-in-Publication Data

Olson, Richard, 1940–
    The emergence of the social sciences, 1642–1792 / Richard Olson.
        p.   cm. — (Twayne's studies in intellectual and cultural
    history ; no. 5)
    Includes bibliographical references and index.
    ISBN 0-8057-8607-4 — ISBN 0-8057-8632-5 (pbk.)
    1. Social sciences—History. I. Title. II. Series.
    H51.057   1993
    300'.9—dc20   92-36978
                                                                CIP

10 9 8 7 6 5 4 3 2 1 (hc)
10 9 8 7 6 5 4 3 2 1 (pb)

The paper used in this publication meets the minimum requirements of American National Standard for Information Sciences—Permanence of Paper for Printed Library Materials. ANSI Z3948-1984.©™

Printed and bound in the United States of America.

Contents

Contents

Foreword

Twayne's Studies in Intellectual and Cultural History consists of brief original studies of major movements in European intellectual and cultural history, emphasizing historical approaches to continuity and change in religion, philosophy, political theory, aesthetics, literature, and science. The series reflects the recent resurgence of innovative contextual as well as theoretical work in these areas, and the more general interest in the historical study of ideas and cultures. It will advance some of the most exciting work in the human sciences as it stimulates further interest in cultural and intellectual history. The books are intended for the educated reader and the serious student; each combines the virtues of accessibility with original interpretations of important topics.

Richard Olson's study provides a rich account of the variety of meanings of the sciences of society in their earliest years and of the early development of the disciplines that now go under the name of the social sciences. The focus here is on economics, psychology, political science, and the philosophy of history. The book examines the various strains of social science as they emerged from the constellation of social and intellectual themes important to early modern Europe. Olson's thesis is that psychology, politics, and economics began with strong programmatic emphases, and that they developed as social sciences in ways quite antithetical to their early agendas. The social sciences eventually helped to remake the social conditions out of which they emerged. The book shows both the traditions out of which the social sciences developed and the problems that they helped to define. In this way, Olson shows how the early social sciences created a bridge between the pre-modern and the modern world.

The Emergence of the Social Sciences surveys the very different intellectual and national traditions of England, Germany, and France. It shows how the social sciences, emerging out of very different conditions, come to have strong affinities with one another. This intellectual history is richly contextual, yet it is based on a close reading of the relevant authors. Richard Olson's book points both to the traditions in religion and science within which the social sciences achieved importance, and to their very modern goals which reconfigured these traditions.

MICHAEL S. ROTH
Scripps College and the
Claremont Graduate School

1

Introduction

This book has three major objectives. First, it seeks to characterize and briefly analyze each of four major new and self-consciously scientific traditions of discourse about humans and their institutions which emerged in the seventeenth century and came to flourish in the eighteenth. It will pay special attention to methodological issues—explicit and implicit notions of how to formulate questions, structure discourse, and evaluate arguments and evidence. In this connection, it will address a variety of questions. What did the initiators of these new approaches to social knowledge expect to gain from applying scientific methods to their subjects? What did each understand the central features of a scientific approach to be? How did the differences in their answers to methodological questions lead to distinctive and sometimes contradictory conclusions about the extent and limits of human capacities to influence and consciously shape institutions and events?

Second, it seeks to explore the ways in which preexistent social, political, and intellectual conditions, interests, and beliefs shaped the emergent traditions of social science. With rare exceptions, the new social sciences inherited their principal problems and many of their initial value orientations from the traditions of discourse they sought to supplant or reform; moreover, they were all initiated to serve particular political, social, economic, or religious interests. In spite of the fact that most of the new social scientists wanted to claim that their methods freed them from biases associated with special partisan interests, it is unquestionably true that ideological assumptions were either unwittingly or intentionally incorporated into every seventeenth- and eighteenth-century attempt to formulate a scientific approach to social subject matter. Some social-scientific traditions were initiated in an attempt to stabilize or perfect existing political and social institutions; others sought to accelerate and guide political change; still others claimed to be indifferent to social and governmental forms and capable of improving the quality of human life within any social and political structure. Their initial aims had a bearing on the character of each tradition, and they must be considered if we are to understand the early social sciences.

Together, the first and second goals of this work address what recent scholars sometimes call the "social construction" of the early social sciences. They presume that these sciences, like all other human creations, are shaped by the conditions in which they emerge. New sciences, in particular, are responses to contemporary understandings of the character of science drawn from knowledge of other scientific activities, to specific social and economic circumstances and commitments, and to the special interests they are intended to serve.

The third goal of the work is quite different from the first two and is both more ambitious and more problematic. It is to explore the ways in which the emergent traditions of social science operated to *reconstruct* the intellectual and social contexts out of which they emerged. Like every other form of human creative activity, the sciences operate both as mirrors that reflect features of the culture which produces them and as lamps which illuminate features of that culture's future.

Ironically, in no case that I know of did any of the social sciences that emerged in the seventeenth century effectively serve the major interests that its earliest advocates sought to further. A *psychological* tradition was initiated by Thomas Hobbes to defend political absolutism and monarchy; yet, as we shall see, it was transformed during the late seventeenth and the eighteenth centuries into the chief buttress of radical social and political positions, including secular socialism and individualistic feminism. Similarly, a *sociological* tradition initiated by James Harrington was aimed at undermining the monarchy and promoting republicanism in seventeenth-century England; yet, by the end of the eighteenth century it had become a central prop for reactionary political platforms that sought a return to an imagined absolutist past, a system of feudal vassalage, or even, in some cases, a preagrarian primitivism. A tradition of *political economy* initiated by William Petty in order to increase the capabilities of a central government to manage resources for the general well-being of its citizens and to "level" their economic standing soon became the foundation of liberal economic doctrines that served principally to limit the role of the state to the protection of private property and rejected notions of distributive justice. Finally, a tradition of *cameralism*, intended by Ludwig von Sekendorf and Johann Becher to improve the intensely personal and paternalist rule of German princes and to increase the efficiency and productivity of their estates, contributed to generating some of the most impersonal, bureaucratic, and inefficient governmental practices of the late eighteenth and early nineteenth centuries.[1]

It thus seems that early social-scientific traditions took on lives of their own which turned their impact almost directly against the intentions of their initiators. This perversion of original intent seems peculiarly apt, for if there was a single general principle embraced by all of the social-scientific traditions by the middle of the eighteenth century it was one which is often called "the law of unintended consequences." The most widely cited and ironic expression of this general notion appeared in Bernard Mandeville's *The Grumbling Hive, or Knaves Turned Honest* (1705) which was eventually expanded into *The Fable of the Bees*. Mandeville emphasized the seemingly perverse fact that though the wealthy intended only to aggrandize themselves through conspicuous consumption, their vain habits served to stimulate commercial activity and provide jobs for the poor and industrious:

> whilst luxury
> Employed a Million of the Poor,
> And odious Pride a Million more;
> Envy itself, and Vanity,
> Were Ministers of industry;
> Their darling folly—fickleness
> In diet, furniture, and dress—
> That strange, ridiculous vice, was made
> The very wheel that turned the trade.

At the hands of such social theorists as Charles-Louis de Secondat, baron de Montesquieu, Giambattista Vico, Adam Smith, Adam Ferguson, and Edmund Burke, this notion was generalized to an assertion that the products of virtually every human design are transformed under the influence of unexpected circumstances into something quite unintended.

I hope to suggest that there were certain features linked to the particular methodological practices within each new tradition of social science that made that tradition unsuitable for achieving its initially intended goals and adapted it instead to those ideological ends which it had come to both serve and shape by the late eighteenth century. From this point of view I hope to complement the exploration of the social construction of the early social sciences with an attempt to understand the role of these social sciences in re-constructing modern European social beliefs and behaviors.

In order to accomplish these three goals in a way that is accessible to non-specialist readers and within the space limitations imposed by this series, I have adopted several strategies. First, I have focused on a very small number of representative authors, though I fully acknowledge that any comprehensive discussion of my themes would have to deal with many more major and minor figures. Second, in imputing some significant social impact to many of the texts I discuss, I have often simply *assumed* the existence of a broad and literate (or at least knowledgeable) audience interested in and capable of responding to them. Recent works by Daniel Roche, Natalie Z. Davis, David Cressy, Peter Burke, Robert Darnton, Margaret Jacob, and others have compelled a new awareness of a very large audience for the ideas of major seventeenth- and eighteenth-century intellectuals.

Finally, I have chosen to use many anachronistic terms such as class, gender, socialism, liberalism, feminism, economics, sociology, psychology, and even *science* that are familiar in late-twentieth-century American non-specialized discourse but which were unused, infrequently used, or used in quite different ways by seventeenth- and eighteenth-century European authors. Though such a practice inevitably introduces some distortion into an attempt to communicate about the past, without it the problem of communicating economically with a general audience is overwhelming.

My use of two specific terms calls for special comment. First, in speaking of *ideologies*, I use the term in the broad sense common among English-speaking and French non-Marxist scholars to indicate any sets of assumptions, values, and goals which direct the actions of members of a community. These assumptions, values, and goals need not be explicitly expressed, and they are rarely subject to critical analysis within the community that shares them. This use does not presume that ideologies are inevitably and exclusively reflections of dominant class interests in preserving the status quo; rather, it acknowledges implicitly that the sources of ideological elements may vary considerably and that ideologies may be oriented toward transforming current conditions as well as toward preserving them. Second, in speaking of early modern social science I mean any tradition of discourse regarding humans and their interactions and institutions which consciously drew its ontological, epistemological, and methodological assumptions as well as many of its guiding metaphors from mathematics, medicine, and natural philosophy. I will try to make good the claim that such a usage is consistent with ordinary modern conventions and that it distorts the intentions and ideas of historical actors no more than is absolutely necessary to convey a usable sense of the past to non-specialist readers.

2

Contexts for the Emergence of the Social Sciences: Traditions of Social Discourse and the New Philosophies of the Scientific Revolution

The social sciences were born toward the end of a century which most contemporaries understood as one of unprecedented change, instability, and crisis in every dimension of European life.[1] First, a series of economic crises brought on by population fluctuations and growth, rapid urbanization, growing international trade, the need to support large mercenary armies, and the rise of expensive court officialdoms, led to inflation, frequent local food shortages, fiscal chaos, and concentration of wealth. This raised endemic tensions between wealthy elites and the expanding middle and lower classes to the level of frequent overt rebellion and violent repression. Second, a series of political crises, most frequently pitting the growing power and interests of centralizing monarchies against the more localized power and interests of traditional landholding aristocracies, flared into full-scale civil war in almost every region of Western and Central Europe between 1567 and 1648. Third, a series of spiritual and religious crises associated with the Reformation and Counter-Reformation both intensified and focused responses to economic and political turmoil and challenged the traditional insti-

---

tutional foundations of morality. Finally, a series of intellectual crises, often closely related to religious instability, were intensified by the European contact with alien cultures and ideas that flowed from the sixteenth-century expansion of trade and missionary activity. Equally destabilizing were many of the products of the print revolution, which offered a form of surrogate travel not only through space but also across time, providing new and widespread access to Greek, Roman, and older European ideas and customs as well as to reports by contemporary travelers. All of these crises culminated during the middle of the seventeenth century in what has been called "The General Crisis of the Seventeenth Century."

The Traditional Ideology of Order and Orders

Because of the widespread sense of crisis, virtually all mid-seventeenth-century intellectuals were obsessed with restoring or creating foundations for social, economic, religious, and/or conceptual order in the face of perceived anarchic and chaotic tendencies. This demand for order went beyond the general human effort to find meaning in our lives; the dominant ideologies of late Renaissance Europe were explicitly and not merely implicitly focused on the concept of order.[2]

My goal here will be to characterize this ideological concern briefly and to focus on its expression in a place that brought it down from the high intellectual domain of theorists and poets and into the everyday life of ordinary people. In 1547 the Anglican church provided its clerics with a book of "Homilies" that set out topics to be presented through an annual cycle. The appropriate homily was to be read and then glossed in a sermon. What follows is the annually read "Homily on Obedience":

> Almighty God hath created and appointed all things in heaven and earth and waters in a most excellent and perfect order. In heaven, he hath appointed distinct and several orders and stages of Archangels and Angels. In earth he hath assigned and appointed Kings, Princes, with other governors under them, in all good and necessary order. The water above is kept and raineth down in due time and season . . . man, himself also has all of his parts within and without, as soul, heart, Mind, memory, understanding,

reason, speech, with all and singular corporal members of his body in a profitable, necessary, and pleasant order: every degree of people in their vocation, calling, and office hath appointed to them their duty and order: some are in high degree, some in low, some kings and princes, some inferior and subject, Priests and laymen, masters and servants, fathers and children, husbands and wives, rich and poor, and every one have need of the other, so that in all things is to be lauded and praised the goodly order of God, without the which no house, no city, no commonwealth can continue and endure, or last. For where there is no right order, there reigneth all abuse, carnal liberty, enormitie, sin, and Babylonical confusion. Take away Kings, princes, rulers, magistrates, judges, and such estates of God's order, no man shall ride or go by the highway unrobbed, no man shall sleep in his own house or bed unkilled, no man shall keep his wife, children, and possessions in quietness . . . and there must needs follow all mischief, and utter destruction. . . .[3]

Several features of this passage illuminate the assumptions about society which dominated European life at the time when the social sciences came into existence. First, it shows how closely notions of regularity and coherence were linked to notions of hierarchy through the concept of order. Violence and anarchy can be averted only through the acceptance of a network of deference and authority. Second, the order of society is clearly understood to be divinely ordained. Third, the hierarchical structure of society is understood to reflect a hierarchical structure that pervades the universe. In the "Homily on Obedience," the focus is on how the earthly political hierarchy reflects the hierarchy of angels on the one hand and the hierarchy within the patriarchal family on the other. But in most presentations, special attention was called to much wider ranging parallels between the hierarchical ordering of the cosmological "macrocosm" (an ordering from the superior sphere of the fixed stars, downward through the decreasingly noble outer planets, to the terrestrial locus of all "corruption" in the universe) and the political, social, or human "microcosm" whose ordering is related to that of the larger cosmos through what is often called the doctrine of correspondences.[4]

The doctrine of correspondences (see Table I) and the attendant microcosm-macrocosm analogies which shaped early modern understandings of the social domain had tremendous persuasive power. They not only bound together and reinforced knowledge across almost all subject matters, but they also bound together the cultures of intellectual elites and the common people. That cultural unity was especially indebted to a shared belief in astrological doctrines which embodied the notion of correspondences at their very core.[5]

TABLE 1

TYPICAL TABLE OF CORRESPONDENCES

COSMIC	ANIMAL	HUMAN	MINERAL	SOCIAL
SUN	LION	HEART	GOLD	KING
MOON	FOX	BRAIN	SILVER	CLERIC
MARS	BULL	ARMS	IRON	SOLDIER

If the focus on hierarchy which pervaded early modern understandings of social issues was reinforced through macrocosm-microcosm analogies, a second major feature of widespread political understandings was powerfully supported by reading the correspondences backward from the human microcosm to the social and political macrocosm. The author of the "Homily on Obedience" refers to the various parts of man as parts of a particular, profitable, and necessary order. The chief use of this notion of man as a microcosm was to call attention to the fact that the various parts of man take on meaning not independently, but as elements of an organic whole whose well-being is dependent on cooperation among the different elements. The human head, arms, and body do not and cannot exist alone and for themselves. By the same token, the believer in macrocosm-microcosm correspondences was compelled to believe that on the political plane, the king (head), military (arms), and body (common citizenry) must work together in harmony to promote the well-being of something (the state or community) which was greater than any of its parts, yet dependent for its existence upon the proper functioning of each.

The suggestive and supportive power of macrocosm-microcosm correspondences helps to explain why the Copernican revolution in astronomy had such widespread cultural repercussions. Traditional

Aristotelian cosmology formed the foundation for all early modern astrological thought, and through astrology and the related correspondences it was heavily implicated in such formal intellectual activities as the teaching of medicine[6] and in the formation of widely held notions about the social and political orders. The new astronomical system was clearly incompatible with the old Aristotelian order, so when John Donne, referring at least in part to Copernicanism, complained that "the new philosophy calls *all* in doubt," he was voicing a concern that was widely shared.

Tensions Between the Scientific and the Sacred in Early Modern Social Discourse

It is against the background of a widespread perception of crisis in economic and political life coupled with a sense that the traditional ways of relating the cosmological order to the human order had been undermined by Copernicus, among others, that a number of intellectuals who had become fascinated with new approaches to natural philosophy, medicine, and mathematics sought to extend these new approaches to understanding and managing the state and society. All of these men saw in the new philosophies of the early scientific revolution tremendous opportunities to restore or create order in an unstable human world, for the sciences seemed to them the only possible source of certainty and authority in a world in which religious, political, social, and intellectual authority had been thoroughly undermined.

We shall see later that these thinkers had very divergent understandings of the character of scientific practice and the kind or degree of confidence that one might place even in scientific knowledge. Several general attitudes, however, united the new social scientists and distinguished their efforts from those of others who had discussed social and political issues in the distant and recent past. First, they presented their attempts to understand and order human actions and institutions as superior to others because their methods of investigation transcended the ordinary conflicts of interest and passion. Such a claim to disinterestedness was crucial because it was generally assumed, following legal precedent, that any arguments made or evidence provided by interested parties tainted one's case and precluded general assent to any claims made.

Many early social scientists admitted that their works were intended to serve certain interests, but they contended (with varying degrees of success) that there was something about the nature of scientific inquiry and argument that insulated scientific truth claims from compromise and warranted assent regardless of the scientist's interests or motives.

Whether the inerrancy of science was presumed to derive from the clarity and distinctness of its concepts coupled with the logical rigor of its argumentation, as René Descartes and his followers insisted, or from the use of a form of induction from experience that had been perfected to eliminate the influence of the traditional "idols" associated with egoistic and collective biases, as Francis Bacon and his fellow travelers held, it was widely argued that scientific method, properly prosecuted, guaranteed its own conclusions. Furthermore, the new social scientists insisted, such methods were fundamentally independent of subject matter and therefore immediately transferable from discussions of the natural world to discussions about the human world. We will return shortly to discuss how strange and problematic this assumption of methodological homogeneity seemed even to most scientists during the seventeenth century, but for the moment it is enough to insist that it was a common element of social-scientific thought.

A second feature of most early social-scientific thought, closely related to the assumption of methodological homogeneity, was its aggressively secular character. Some early social scientists, such as Thomas Hobbes, were openly anti-clerical and often covertly irreligious. Others, like William Petty, were just plain insensitive to and disdainful of the intensity of commitment that most men had to religious positions. Many more were probably conventional in their religious beliefs and practices, but were nonetheless insistent that religious claims should be set aside in the formulation of our knowledge about human interactions and institutions. James Harrington expressed the views of this group when he wrote: "To hold that the wisdom of man in the formation of a house or of a government, may go upon supernatural principles, is inconsistent with a commonwealth, and is as if one should say, 'God ordained the temple, therefore it was not built by Masons.' . . . Government is of human prudence and human prudence is adequate to man's nature."[7]

Note that Harrington does not deny an ultimately divine intention or plan in connection with the building of a commonwealth. Rather, he insists that God operates through human nature and that our understanding of a commonwealth is dependent on an understanding of its *human* sources without regard for God's aims.

When Copernicanism came under attack during the early decades of the seventeenth century, one line of criticism held that Copernicus's claim that the sun remained unmoved while the earth moved must be incorrect because it stands in opposition to the inviolable word of God in Scripture. Galileo and most of his supporters responded by reviving an argument that goes back at least as far as Clement of Alexandria and Origen. The Bible, they argued, was intended as a guide to how humans should live and not as a textbook of natural philosophy. All of its passages were "set down . . . by the scribes in order to accommodate them to the Capacities of the common people who are rude and unlearned."[8] When it dealt with its central moral themes, it did so both in the form of parables which could be comprehended by even the most uneducated and in the form of direct prescriptive regulations which allowed for no misunderstanding. When it dealt incidentally with the natural world, however, it simply reflected the primitive cosmological beliefs of its intended audience. Natural philosophy was then to be understood as completely independent of any literal reading of Scripture.

In spite of the fact that complicated circumstances led to the condemnation of Galileo and his version of Copernicanism (at least in Catholic countries), the view that Scripture should control moral discourse but is itself subordinate to natural philosophy in physical matters was widely promoted during the seventeenth century, within both the religious and the scientific communities. Such a view carved out a domain in which natural philosophy could develop relatively free of religious pressures at the same time that it acknowledged and protected the moral authority of the religious community against naturalistic claims. Most natural philosophers were no more interested in rocking the boat on this issue than were most clergy, and the common feeling of both was nicely expressed by the Italian nobleman Virgilio Malvezzi in 1634 after the termination of the Galileo affair: "Whosoever explains natural events by referring them to God is a poor philosopher. But whosoever does *not* refer to God to explain political events is a bad Christian."[9]

Those who challenged this formula invited criticism, not just from clerics, but from natural philosophers as well. Thus, when Samuel Pufendorf published his *De jure naturae et gentium octi libri* (*Eight*

Books on the Law of Nature and of Man) in 1672 without reference to Scripture, his friend, Gottfried Wilhelm Leibniz, was among the first to complain of his poor judgment.

There is one important, conspicuous, and crucial exception to these arguments. As we shall see below, there was a very important natural-scientific tradition stretching through the Renaissance and early modern period in which the boundaries between the sacred and the secular, between the natural and the moral, were so permeable that its adherents simply could not acknowledge the possibility either of a natural philosophy that did not refer to God or a morality that was unconcerned with the natural world. This tradition, often associated with the term "Hermetic" and with the science of alchemy, was on the wane throughout most of Western Europe by the middle of the seventeenth century, but it continued to have a major influence on Central European intellectual life for a substantially longer period. Consequently, when German intellectuals, such as the alchemist and physician Johann Becher, sought to develop scientific approaches to the state and society, they continued to fuse the sacred and the secular.

The Late-Renaissance Traditions of Jurisprudence and Classical Political Theory

In connection with their extreme secular emphasis, early English and French social scientists almost uniformly admired at least one feature of Niccolo Machiavelli's works. In the fifteenth chapter of *The Prince* (composed about 1513 but only published posthumously in 1532) Machiavelli sought to distinguish his advice from other advice to Renaissance princes by claiming that he alone portrayed men as they are rather than as they ought to be. Aristotle had voiced an opinion that was widely held in the early modern world when he argued in the *Poetics* that poetry is a more powerful and appropriate guide to human action than history because it is free to depict truths that are higher than factual ones. Indeed, Aristotle granted Homer his greatest praise because he taught other poets to lie effectively in order to inspire men to act nobly. But Machiavelli now insisted upon a descriptive rather than a normative approach to political life:

> It has seemed wiser to me to follow the real truth of the matter rather than what we imagine it to be. For speculation has created many Principalities and Republics such as have never been known to have any real existence; for how we live is so different from how we ought to live that he who studies what ought to be done rather than what *is* done will learn the way to his downfall rather than to his preservation. A man striving in every way to be good will meet his ruin among so many who are evil. (*The Prince*, ch. 15)

The early social sciences were grounded in this conviction. They almost always did end up by exhorting people to one or another form of action, but they all agreed that such exhortation could be valuable only to the extent that it was grounded in an awareness of human weaknesses and vices as well as strengths and virtues. As Harrington pointed out, "Neither Hippocrates nor Machiavelli introduced diseases into man's body nor corruption into Government, which were before their times; and seeing they do but discover them, it must be confessed that so much as they have done tends not to the increase, but to the cure of them" (*OOW*, 514).

The Machiavellian and early social-scientific attempt at "realism" was, I suspect, like the literary realism of nineteenth-century authors such as Emile Zola, more inclined to wallow in the socially pathological side of human behavior in reaction to the overly idealistic inclinations of its immediate predecessors than to offer a reasonably balanced view of humankind. Thus, the first generation of early social scientists tended to ascribe the sources of almost all human action to the vices of greed, ambition, and lust and to virtually ignore the existence of altruistic and charitable impulses. The major focus of their concern was thus on the need to offer strategies and structures to control, manage, or somehow counter the vices.

Their sense of a need to submit to facts in the study of human affairs, as well as a related tendency to identify aspects of the study of human affairs with the study of medicine, involved the early social scientists on one side of an ongoing debate about the extent to which natural and human phenomena were susceptible to similar analyses.

In the classical Greek philosophical tradition a sense of human uniqueness was expressed by distinguishing between *physis*, or nature, which governed the non-human world, and *nomos*, or convention and custom, which governed human interactions.

Though initially interpreted as divine, the source of *nomos* gradually became associated more and more with specifically human choices. Thus, it was acknowledged that although the customs which guided different communities might be quite different, the citizens of each community were rightly governed by their own self-imposed *nomos*.

Aristotle incorporated the distinction between *physis* and *nomos* within a powerful taxonomy of knowledge which continued to dominate attempts to understand human interactions well into the early modern period, and which thus provided the framework for the forms of social discourse out of which and in opposition to which the seventeenth-century social sciences grew. So we need briefly to explore Aristotle's taxonomy and its vicissitudes into the late sixteenth and early seventeenth centuries.

Aristotle begins by offering a three-fold division of knowledge into theoretical, practical, and productive, based on the ends to which the various kinds of knowledge are aimed. The taxonomy is grounded in the assumption that the perfection of any kind of thing lies in the most complete realization of those potentials which distinguish that kind of thing from all others. Humans are distinguished in two critical ways from other "lower" animals. First, humans are "rational" animals, capable of understanding why things are as they are. Stated in a slightly different way, humans can attain knowledge of the causes of objects and events. Thus full participation in the life of the mind constitutes a form of human perfection. Second, humans are "political" animals, capable of living in a *polis*, or city-state. So full participation in the collective cultural life of the polis is also a form of human perfection.

Humans are *not* distinguished from other animals in their ability to satisfy their material and biological needs. Thus the production and distribution of commodities to enrich material life, as well as life within the household, which was primarily the locus of productive and reproductive activity, were deemed distinctly inferior to the life of contemplation or the life of *public* action. Not only did production and reproduction fail to express any uniquely human capacity; they also diverted time and energy from the higher activities which demanded leisure for their pursuit.

Aristotle's hierarchical assessment of human activities clearly reflected his own preferred philosophical activities and supported the status claims of the pre-commercial aristocracy from which his students were drawn. Whatever their sources, however, his basic views persisted within the ideologies of Europe's educated elite well into the modern era.

Given his hierarchical view of human activities, Aristotle developed a correspondingly hierarchical view of human knowledge. The productive arts depend only upon being able to follow traditional rules and patterns of behavior, without concern for why things are done as they are. The knowledge of the technician is thus mere opinion without rational foundation. At the other end of the spectrum is knowledge of nature, or purely theoretical knowledge. The key fact about natural objects and phenomena is that they cannot be changed in any way by human action. Thus knowledge of nature is sought purely for its own sake and without regard to any possible application to productive or political life. Its imperviousness to human influence gives nature a special kind of stability which allows us to produce universal, philosophically necessary, or *true* knowledge by the application of syllogistic logic to derive consequences from unchangeable and certain first principles.

Knowledge associated with political life is quite different from that associated with either productive activity or the natural world. Political life depends on the exercise of choice or will rather than on the blind and unreflective following of rules, and this distinguishes it from productive life. Moreover, the whole notion of intentionality and agency is grounded in the assumption that the agent can understand the ends to which his acts are directed and anticipate their consequences. There must therefore be some way to discover relationships between human actions and their consequences. At the same time, because public life is a creation of conscious actions rather than a product of unconscious behaviors, it must involve an element of indeterminacy, making it very different from nature. Thus, according to Aristotle, the idea of "often" guides investigation of human interactions while the idea of "always" guides the investigation of nature. Practical knowledge, or *prudential knowledge*, cannot be universal and derived syllogistically; instead it is particular and must be intuited, through a kind of pattern recognition, from the study of how different persons and groups have acted to produce their customs, laws, and institutions and of how those customs, laws, and institutions served to encourage or discourage a rich political and philosophical life.

During late antiquity this Aristotelian hierarchy of knowledge was modified in two distinctive ways. In the first place, it was Christianized. Within the Augustinian tradition the importance of the material world continued to be downplayed in comparison with the spiritual world and productive knowledge retained its low status. Contemplation of the natural world—now not for its own sake, but for the insights it might offer into the character of its divine author and for the assistance it could offer in scriptural exigesis—retained its superior place among secular forms of knowledge, becoming the "handmaiden" of theology. As a consequence, mathematics, astronomy, and natural philosophy became the foundation for Christian education in the early medieval cathedral schools and the emergent universities.

In addition, Christians generally argued that morality and ethics were more appropriately grounded in scriptural revelation than in humanly constructed codes of behavior. One key consequence of this Christianized view was that the relativism implicit in Aristotelian political, moral, and ethical perspectives was de-emphasized in favor of the assumption of universal standards of human activity grounded in the divine *logos,* or reason. The early medieval intellectual tradition did not so much deny that local and customary elements guide some aspects of human life as insist that there were higher and lower guides to human action and that divine revelation took priority over mere custom.

Between the eleventh and sixteenth centuries this notion was developed into a doctrine that posited three levels of law: divine law, expressed directly in Scripture; natural law, or the law of reason; and positive law, created as a consequence of human choice. Each level of law was presumed to be subordinate to that above it in such a way that the law of reason, while not derivable from divine law in any direct way, could not be in conflict with it. Similarly, it was argued, positive law should not violate either divine or rational laws, though it might not be derivable from them.

The second major modification of Aristotle's taxonomy of activities and knowledge flowed from the impact of Roman culture on European life. Roman writers were generally uninterested in contemplation, holding the active life of the citizen to be the most rewarding and noble of all. As a consequence, Roman intellectuals focused their attention on social and political concerns and on the creation of explicit legal codes. Most Roman thinkers would have agreed with Aristotle both that law was primarily a voluntary human creation and that public life was somehow superior to private life, but Roman jurists did not make the same radical distinction between the productive and the political that Aristotle had. Roman civil law, in particular, focused attention on individual rights, on the family, and on the regulation of exchanges of property, that is, on productive and reproductive issues.

Between 1300 and 1500, law became an important subject within the newly emergent medieval universities in response to demands for both canon and civil lawyers to help in managing increasingly complex ecclesiastical and secular institutions. The university study of law was grounded in the recovery and analysis of Justinian's codification of Roman law, and the study of Roman law naturally led to a revival of the Roman focus on the active life and to a new concern among European intellectuals in broadly social, and not merely "political" issues.

Eventually, there was a split among legal scholars based on the Aristotelian differentiation between theoretical and practical knowledge. On one side of the split were those who believed that legal studies would have greater status if they could claim to be more theoretical. For this group, it was important to argue that "the legist and canonist know through causes,"[10] just like the natural philosopher. Ultimately, some adherents of this tendency became particularly interested in regional and temporal variations in customs and laws. They began to seek the causes of local variations of positive law in geographical and climatological factors, setting the primary agenda for one important tradition within the early social sciences that I have called sociological.

On the other side of the split were those who celebrated the new "humanistic" emphasis on the active life associated with the Roman revival and who sought to differentiate themselves from what they considered a bankrupt Aristotelian naturalism. The early-fifteenth-century Florentine, Coluccio Salutati, offered a particularly important expression of this view in his *De Nobililate Legum et Medicinae* (On the nobility of law and medicine), written around 1400. Salutati's epistemological claims suggested a pattern followed by one of the most important of seventeenth-century social scientists, Thomas Hobbes.

Salutati begins by praising law as more noble than medicine because the study of law aims at the active life through which humans can regain that goodness which was lost through original sin. He goes on to link this virtue with a new kind of epistemic claim derived from late medieval nominalist attacks on traditional Aristotelian knowledge claims. It is possible to know law, he says, in a way that is superior to the way in which we know nature, because nature is ultimately a product of God's unfathomable will, while society and law are the product of knowable human actions.

Our experience of nature allows us only contingent knowledge of the facts of experience, not the kind of absolutely certain knowledge of causes which Aristotle had claimed for natural science. Positive laws, on the other hand, "have their origin, not in external things, but *in us*. They contain man's natural reason which every sound intelligence can understand by reflection and discussion. . . . Thus we know them with such certainty that they cannot escape us and it is not necessary to seek them among external facts. . . . Laws exist unshakably in the relations to human minds to each other. And they are not only certain, but also fully known."[11]

Strange as it may sound, for Salutati, and subsequently for Hobbes, law can be understood perfectly because it is created by human beings rather than by God and because we can understand human motives, perceptions, ideas, and actions directly. This notion adds an odd twist to the old claim that humans are free to choose their laws and that for this reason, laws cannot be said to be caused. According to Salutati and Hobbes, laws embody men's natural reason, and since reason is the same in all men, the same conditions must give rise to the same laws without regard to choice. Law, then, unlike nature, *does* turn out to be subject to causal, or scientific analysis. One critically important tradition in social science that I call psychological was built upon this complete inversion of the traditional Christianized Aristotelian hierarchy of knowledge.

So far, I have argued that conflicts within Renaissance legal studies provided important stimuli to both the psychological and sociological traditions of social science. But conflicts between students of law and political writers linked to Machiavelli's revival of classical political theory also had an extensive impact. The basic conflict between Machiavelli and the legal community arose because, as guardians of the legal canon and the self-appointed agents of "civilization," the lawyers were appalled when Machiavelli and his adherents claimed that there were "political" considerations that might override ordinary law, custom, and morality. The Machiavellians focused on the notion that subordination to law was less important than the voluntary exercise of the *virtues* of citizenship in the pursuit of military glory and participation in political activity. J. G. A. Pocock has shown that much seventeenth- and eighteenth-century Anglo-American political discourse was shaped by the tension between law and classical notions of virtue as they were presented by Machiavelli.[12] As we shall see, this tension was a central feature of Scottish social science in the eighteenth century. But it had an earlier impact in Germany.

To accept Machiavelli's argument was to accept the subordination of law to politics and of lawyers to politicians, and this the lawyers were understandably disinclined to do. One possible response to the situation was to offer an alternative to Machiavelli's kind of advice to princes that offered the advantages Machiavelli claimed to offer, but did so by emphasizing the absolute need to work through the creation of appropriate law rather than extra-legally. This was precisely the German Cameralists' response. They offered a self-consciously anti-Machiavellian advisory literature aimed at producing stable, wealthy, and powerful principalities through the legal regulation of social and economic life.[13]

The New Philosophies of the Scientific Revolution

Well into the seventeenth century, the term science was commonly used to indicate any well-organized and stable body of knowledge or practice. Thus, early-seventeenth-century goldsmiths were said to practice a science, even though nothing they did was governed by explicitly stated rules. The legal scholars who wanted to claim scientific status for their studies were, of course, appealing to the more restrictive understanding of the term that was derived from the Aristotelian taxonomy of knowledge and was common among university-trained intellectuals. But even this understanding was much broader than that which became dominant in the eighteenth century. Aristotle included metaphysics among his theoretical sciences, and medieval Aristotelians saw theology as the queen of the sciences, giving it a kind of paradigmatic status. But neither metaphysics nor theology belongs among the sciences as most people understand them today or as most people understood them by 1750.

Within the late-Aristotelian context, the claim that some domain of knowledge constituted a science depended almost exclusively on arguing that, in principle, assent to its propositions was forced by the use of syllogistic logic to derive its conclusions from its initial premises. By the eighteenth century, though the notion that logical argument alone might compel assent was still part of the accepted definition of science, attention had become focused on other issues which restricted the common use of the word. Chief among these were concerns about the kinds of experiential foundation admissible for the premises assumed in arguments, the kinds of "causes" that could and should be investigated, the kinds of tests—other than pure logical coherence—scientific knowledge should be subject to, and the relationship scientific knowledge had to human action. Even in the mid eighteenth century (in fact, even today) there was no unanimity on how all or any of these other issues were to be resolved, but argument centered on a very small range of alternatives. Since these alternatives came to prominence with the development of new approaches to the study of nature during what is now known as the scientific revolution, we must turn to these to discover how to understand the "science" in the early social sciences.

The first widely influential family of perspectives to challenge the many variants of scholastic Aristotelianism as a framework for understanding nature has variously been called "occult," "animist," "Hermetic," "Neo-Platonic," and "Paracelsan." Each of these terms reflects some element in a network of attitudes and habits of mind that recent historians call Renaissance naturalism. Though it flourished primarily in the sixteenth and early seventeenth centuries and died out as a major intellectual force by the early eighteenth century, Renaissance naturalism left important traces on most subsequent scientific traditions and was a major force in shaping both Cameralism and, to a lesser extent, the early political economy of William Petty.

Above all else, Renaissance naturalism was deeply and unreservedly religious, though it had extremely heterodox elements. Renaissance naturalists differed in many ways, but they agreed on a small number of key notions. Chief among these was that the highest duty of the Christian was *not* to retreat into some contemplative shell, but to act directly to improve the lives of one's fellow human beings. Charity was the great Christian virtue for the Renaissance naturalist, and the most promising path for exercising charity lay through re-establishing the knowledge of and control over nature which humankind had lost with the Fall. Natural knowledge was thus defined through its potential power to serve material needs rather than in terms of some epistemic superiority related to its imperviousness to human influence. Bacon summarized the pervasive view when he wrote: "In natural philosophy practical results are not only the means to improve human well-being, they are also the guarantee of truth. There is a true rule in religion that a man must show his faith through his *works*. The same rule holds good in natural philosophy. Science, too, must be known by its works. It is by the witness of *works* rather than by logic or even by observation that truth is revealed and established. It follows from this that the improvement of man's lot and man's mind are one and the same thing.[14]

Most Renaissance naturalists accepted the Platonic notion that the universe is a living being, animated through some kind of world soul, or *anima mundi*. Furthermore, they were almost universally committed to the parallelism of the human microcosm and the myriad planes of the natural macrocosm, as well as to the idea that knowledge of the correspondences between different planes could be used to direct the sympathetic forces animating the universe in order to attain human ends. Thus, for example, Paracelsus used his knowledge that the planet Mercury corresponded both to the metal mercury on the mineral plane and to the reproductive organs on the human plane in order to realize that venereal diseases could be treated with mercury salves. Finally, most assumed that inherent in material objects were *active* principles, often hidden, or *occult*, which might be discovered and then controlled to operate on nature. The big question, of course, was how to discover these hidden powers.

God did offer clues for the human magus to follow. God wrote into nature certain mathematical regularities which those interested in "mathematical magic" could try to discovery and exploit. Such figures as John Dee, Thomasso Campanella, Tycho Brahe, Johannes Kepler (in his early works), and even John Wilkins followed these clues into the domains of astronomy and mechanics. God also offered certain immediately recognizable signs to suggest the uses of some objects; the only way to discover these signs was to gather in masses of experiences. Paracelsus and his followers were probably the most aggressive opponents of classical authority and advocates of immediate experience and *experiment* in the search for natural knowledge. They were in excellent company, however, for a new emphasis on the primacy of experience also dominated early modern natural history and medicine.

It may seem to some twentieth-century readers that I am belaboring a totally obvious and ridiculous point, but it is critical to recognize that not all early modern scientists or natural philosophers agreed with the extreme empirical emphasis of the Renaissance naturalists. Many of the great names among the figures of the scientific revolution, including René Descartes, Christian Huyghens, and Gottfried W. Leibniz, took a completely different approach to scientific knowledge. Though they did not deny that natural science must somehow ultimately conform to experience, they argued that the starting place for the discovery of scientific knowledge was independent of experience and to be found in reason alone. Thus, for example, when Leibniz was confronted with Robert Boyle's magnificent series of experiments on air pressure, he criticized Boyle's stategy, writing: "He does nothing but draw from an infinity of beautiful experiments a conclusion which he should have taken as his first principle; that is that everything in nature is done mechanically. *This principle can be rendered certain only by reason, and never by experiments, no matter how many one does.*[15] We will return to the issue of mechanical explanations later; what is important at this point about this comment is that it denies that the first principles of science have a primarily empirical source. For practical purposes this view, which has long been called "rationalist," was made prominent by René Descartes, whose reading of Greek skeptical philosophy undermined his confidence in sensory experience.

Struggling with the question of how to discover a starting point for scientific reasoning, Descartes drew heavily on his knowledge of Euclidean geometry, which seemed to offer the only model of knowledge which escaped the skeptics' criticisms. The founding propositions of geometry were not developed by induction out of experience, he argued; rather, they were directly *intuited*. In his *Regulae ad directionem ingenii* (*Rules for the Direction of the Mind*), composed about 1628, Descartes sought to extend this notion beyond geometry, explaining just what he meant by intuition:

> By intuition I understand not the fluctuating testimony of the senses, not the misleading judgment that proceeds from the blundering constructions of the imagination, but the conception which an unclouded and attentive mind gives so readily and distinctly that we are wholly free of doubt about that which we understand. . . . *[It] springs from the light of reason alone.* . . . Thus each individual can mentally have intuition of the fact that he exists, and that he thinks; that the triangle is bounded by three lines only, the sphere by a single superficies, and so on.[16]

Well into the late eighteenth century such advocates of "rational mechanics" as Jean D'Alembert and Joseph Louis Lagrange continued to hold this Cartesian view regarding the founding principles of the sciences, and it was injected into the social sciences by Hobbes and Benedictus Spinoza.

Most of those who agreed with Descartes that the initial principles of the sciences must "spring from the light of reason alone" also agreed with him that the deductive model of Euclid's *Elements of Geometry* provided the ideal way to move from first principles to scientific conclusions. These people were said to be imbued with the *ésprit géometrique*, and they sought to cast all scientific knowledge into hypothetico-deductive form, with appropriate definitions, postulates, axioms, and theorems. Even some who did not agree with Descartes on the non-experimental character of scientific first principles accepted his emphasis on the hypothetico-deductive structure of scientific argumentation. For example, Isaac Newton's great anti-Cartesian opus, *Philosophiae Naturalis Principia Mathematica* (*The Mathematical Principles of Natural Philosophy*) (1687), was cast in this form.

There is one additional aspect of the kinds of science most frequently associated with Descartes' *ésprit géometrique* that demands comment because of its centrality to the early social sciences. When Descartes was trying to figure out why mathematicians seemed to be so successful in solving problems, he saw that they often used the strategy of breaking down a very complex problem into a series of relatively simple ones, solving those first (sometimes by breaking them into a set of even simpler ones), and then combining the solutions of the simple problems to solve the initial problem. The links between such a strategy and the Euclidean *ésprit géometrique* are obvious when one considers reading Euclid's *Elements* backwards. The complex later theorems are proved by assuming the proof of previous, more elementary ones, and this process can be carried back to the simple initial definitions, postulates, and so on. This same stategy had been widely discussed among late Aristotelians under the label of the method of resolution and composition, but Descartes' formulation was exceptionally clear, and it stimulated widespread interest in what eventually came to be called the techniques of *analysis* and *synthesis*. Analysis referred to the process of breaking an initially complex problem into its simpler elements, and synthesis to the process of recombining them to reconstitute the initial whole. It is by no means clear that all problems of interest to natural philosophers should be adapted to this approach, but it was so successful in connection with a class of problems to be discussed next that it seemed to have universal applicability.

During the seventeenth century, whether one was disposed toward an experimental and experiential emphasis drawn from Renaissance naturalism, a rationalist and geometrical emphasis drawn from Descartes, or some combination of the two, one was very likely to be influenced by the rise of the so-called mechanical or corpuscular philosophy, which cut across methodological orientations. The terms mechanical and corpuscular, which were used more or less interchangeably by Robert Boyle, reflect two different sources which came together to inform most studies of natural philosophy in the early seventeenth century.

One important source in shaping the new orientation was the revival of the ancient atomist doctrines of Epicurus and Lucretius. Carefully disengaged from their anti-religious origins by scholars such as Pierre Gassendi in France and Walter Charleton in England, these doctrines held that all objects and events in the physical universe could be understood as products of the motion and impact of solid little corpuscles of various shapes. Such particles did *not* have within themselves any active forces, so that, in Leibniz's words, "a body is never moved naturally except by another body which touches and pushes it. . . . Any other kind of operation on bodies is either miraculous or imaginary."[17] Many natural philosophers were at great pains to assert that this corpuscularism did not extend to matters of the human mind and spirit, so they could avoid conflict with orthodox Christianity. But some, such as Hobbes, refused to make the distinction. Regardless of whether they extended their corpuscularism to human issues or not, all who accepted atomist notions eventually rejected the presumptions that underlay Renaissance naturalism, of a living macrocosm and of active forces pervading the universe.

The rejection of animist notions from natural philosophy was reinforced by a second source of the mechanical philosophy, namely, the pervasive early modern experience of and familiarity with complex mechanical devices and artifacts of many kinds. Though the clock came to stand as a symbol for all machines, the ordinary urban upper- and middle-class citizen of the late sixteenth and early seventeenth centuries came into contact with a wide variety of spectacular mechanisms. If he or she went to the theater, elaborate stage devices constituted a critical and eagerly anticipated part of the entertainment. If he or she went into any major public or private garden, hydraulically driven automata sprang up to chirp and twirl when plates hidden in the paths were stepped on to activate them.

Music, especially church music, was dramatically influenced by the construction of increasingly complex and magnificent pipe organs. Emperors and minor princes were constructing museums or *Kunsthäuser* and filling them with fascinating artifacts, of which the later Fabergé eggs are among the most spectacular. For the lower classes, military engineers turned entrepreneurs built automata imitating quacking ducks and lute-playing ladies and charged a small admission for a look at these new marvels. And all of this was built upon the mechanical constructions which undergirded commercial and military technology. Massive cranes for loading and unloading ships, locks and canals to improve transportation, new forms of looms for the textile industry, trip hammers for metalworking, and most importantly, navigational and surveying instruments are among the almost endless list of new devices that provided new metaphors, analogies, and models for understanding natural phenomena.

For present purposes, one of the most important aspects of the mechanical and corpuscular philosophies was the reinforcement they provided to those who saw the analytic method of Descartes as central to the development of scientific knowledge, for the application of an analytic approach to machines was almost automatic. One could clearly be said to understand a machine if one could break it down into its constituent gears, springs, and other parts, and then reconstitute it by reassembling them. More important still, one could be said to have a complete knowledge of each part of the machine without any need to know what that part contributed to the functioning of the machine as a whole. Thus a machinist could fabricate each part of a clock from a mechanical drawing without knowing either the purpose of a clock or what each piece contributed to the clock's functioning. Imported into an attempt to understand the state by Hobbes, this notion led to the assumption that the constituent parts of the state—its individual citizens—had to be understandable in the first instance independently of their functions within the whole. Clearly, this overturned a fundamental premise of the ideology of orders, which saw the meaning of individuals as bound up with their specific functions within the community.

3

Renaissance Naturalism and Political Economy in the German Cameralist Tradition

In 1668, when the Polish throne became vacant as a result of the abdication of Johann Kasimir, several candidates from as far away as Florence, France, and Moscow sought the post. As part of the pre-electoral maneuverings, the elector of Mainz hired two free-lance intellectuals to help secure the throne for his friend Philipp Wilhelm von Neuburg, count palatine. The first of his agents, Gottfried Wilhelm Leibniz, took the intellectual high road. In a pamphlet entitled *Specimen demonstrationum politicam pro eligendo Rege Polonorum novo scribendi genera ad claram certitudinem exactum.* (An example of political demonstration regarding the election of the king of Poland according to a new kind of arguing which offers exactitude, clarity, and certainty), he purported to prove that von Neuburg should be elected. Writing in the geometrical style promoted by Descartes, Hobbes, and Spinoza, Leibniz called attention to the certainty of mathematics that had begun to spread into the other sciences and claimed to extend that certainty to civic affairs.[1] Johann Joachim Becher, Leibniz's colleague in this enterprise and a frequent competitor for court favor, took a very different tack, and this difference offers insight into scientific approaches to economic and political topics in seventeenth-century Germany.

On the face of it, Becher's efforts on behalf of von Neuburg might seem to a twentieth-century reader to have little or nothing to do with science, but I will try to show that they did typify an approach to the state and the economy which incorporated perspectives and methods drawn from Renaissance naturalist alchemy and medicine. If von Neuburg were elected king, Becher proposed to offer his talents and connections to help him establish a shareholding company for the production and sale of wool, silk, wine, and sugar in his impoverished and commercially backward Polish lands. Becher's contacts would allow him to interest wealthy investors. And von Neuburg's reputation for honorable dealings—his social "credit"—would assure potential investors of the safety of their investments, especially since he would promise to offer the company special privileges in Poland. The establishment of commerce in Poland would in turn bring fame, prosperity, and peace to the land and its ruler. Von Neuburg was the only candidate for whom such a proposal would work because most of the candidates either had little credit or already held lands which were developing commercially and would be unwilling to establish competition for their home territories' activities. Like Leibniz, Becher claimed a special kind of authority for his proposal. This, he wrote, "is the only *impartial and legitimate* means to help Poland and bring it credit, renown, prosperity, recognition, and reputation; for where there is well-being (*Nährung*) the restless spirits that promote faction and war are united in their interests" (*A C & C*, 244).

For all of their claims to certainty and impartiality, Becher's and Leibniz's combined efforts failed to gain the crown for von Neuburg. But Becher went on to play a significant role in shaping Central European court attitudes and policies on economic issues down to the time of the French Revolution through his writings, especially his *Politischer Discurs von den eigentlichen Ursachen des Auf- und Abnehmens der Städt Länder und Republicken* (Political discourse on the true causes of the improvement and decline of cities, territories, and republics). This work was published in 1668, augmented in 1673, reprinted in 1688, and revived by George Heinrich Zincke (professor of Law and Kameral-Wissenschaften at Leipzig) in 1754. Frequently reprinted during the second half of the eighteenth century, it proclaimed the foundations on which Becher's arguments for von Neuberg had been based.

The Political and Economic Context for
Kameralwissenschaft

By the end of the Thirty Years War in 1648, any pretense of unity that the old Holy Roman Empire had claimed was completely under-mined and Central Europe was broken up into some three hundred different principalities of varying size. Each of these was governed *de facto* by its own absolute monarch through a set of ministries or councils (*Kammer*) managed by dependent courtiers drawn largely from the landed but impoverished nobility. Most of the old free cities of the empire, which had dominated German international trade during the High Middle Ages and which had established indepen-dent governments ruled by their artisanal guilds, had lost their economic power and had become subordinated to the princes, who moved their courts into these urban settings.

The overwhelming fact of economic life was stagnation, brought on by crushing losses of population and wealth during the Thirty Years War. This war, the culmination of over a century of religious and dynastic conflict, had reduced the population by up to one-third in many regions and led to the removal or destruction of huge amounts of property by looting armies. As a consequence of this general impoverishment, the overwhelming preoccupation of the princes—or more accurately, of the princes' finance ministers—was to obtain ready cash. For cash was necessary to support the merce-nary armies needed to repel external aggression, maintain internal security, and finance court activities, which absorbed vast resources in lavish display.

The issue of display is critical, not only because court expenditures provided a huge sink for money that went largely to foreign musicians, actors, architects, artists, and so on, and which thus left the domain of the prince, but even more because it was symptomatic of the upper aristocracy's attitude toward money. Few princes shared the urban tradesman's and merchant's view of money as something to be put to productive use. Instead, they viewed it as a means of establishing their fame and glory through public spectacle and display. Most princes and finance ministers (who usually shared their monarch's attitudes on this issue) focused on extracting cash from their lands and subjects rather than on ensuring that there was greater wealth to tap. It was thus a major goal of writers like Becher, his brother-in-law, Philipp von Hornigk,[2] and his successor at

Leopold's court, Wilhelm Freyherr von Schröder, to explain how the economy operated and how it could be managed to maximize both the wealth of the state and the income of its prince.

When they offered advice to their princes, these men were also seeking patronage. Unlike many later economic thinkers, they did not begin by thinking of economic issues as primary and asking how governments could respond to serve economic needs. Rather, they started by taking the fiscal demands of absolutist regimes as a given and asked how the economy could be rationally and efficiently organized and managed to best meet these demands. They saw the economy as a goose that laid golden eggs, and they were concerned mostly with the eggs it laid rather than the goose itself. More than their predecessors at court, however, they focused on the need to keep the goose alive and healthy, and so extended their interests far beyond the mere process of egg collection.

The general perspective adopted by this whole group is perhaps most clearly and simply expressed in the preface to von Shröder's *Fürstliche Schatz- und Rent-Kammer* (The prince's treasury) of 1686:

> Those who rightly examine the chain by which the members of a state are bound together must acknowledge, in accordance with sound reason and experience, *that the prosperity and welfare of the subjects is the foundation upon which all happiness of a prince as ruler of such subjects is based.* . . . The common man is not satisfied with words. He wants good subsistence, cheap times and protection. I have accordingly shown in general all possible means and ways by which a prince may make his subjects or his lands rich and prosperous. In order however that a prince, in exacting tribute and ordering institutions, may make no mistake, I have advised that he make his demands where there is something to take, and where he who must pay can afford it. To that end it is necessary that a prince shall be informed about his land and his subjects, their occupations and their gains.[3]

With rare exceptions, the seventeenth-century cameralist innovators focused on the commercial sector of the economy, and the reason for this emphasis deserves some comment. Traditionally, princes had derived their income primarily from the agricultural productivity of their lands and from taxes on goods exported from the free cities. They had sought neither to invest in commercial activities nor to interfere with the activities of the urban artisans and merchants who, in effect, purchased with their tax payments the right to operate without constraint. Neither the princes nor their aristocratic advisers wished to lower themselves by becoming involved in commercial activity. But the fall-off in both agricultural productivity and artisanal production for export, combined with the growing costs of military preparedness and court life, left the princes in an impossible fiscal bind that called for extraordinary measures. Becher and his cameralist colleagues identified the commercial domain as one that offered new economic opportunities for the princes.

On the one hand, Becher and others who wrote in the early cameralist tradition had to battle the anti-commercial biases of the old landed nobility, who feared the erosion of their status as political power became more closely linked with mere wealth. On the other, they also had to battle the urban artisan and merchant guilds, who objected to the competition which court-sponsored commercial enterprises offered and even more to the state regulation of their economic activities.

In the face of opposition from almost every traditionally powerful interest group, the cameralists' success in getting the princes to promote and regulate commercial activity is impressive. These men succeeded not just because of the economic crisis, but because they were able to craft a set of compelling arguments which accomplished two things. First, they linked the interests of the prince with the common interests of society, raising these above all private and corporate interests and setting the collectivist tone which pervaded German social thought well into the nineteenth century. Second, they linked the well-being of society with the production, distribution, and consumption of manufactured goods.

To accomplish the first of these goals, they appealed to powerful religious and anti-Machiavellian sentiments that supported the princes' claims to divine right in governing and simultaneously offered them the promise—or illusion—both of wealth in this world and salvation in the next (see *The Cameralists*, 143). To accomplish the second goal they presented arguments which drew much of their language and much of their general inspiration from the medical and alchemical doctrines associated with Renaissance naturalist science. It is to these arguments and their sources of inspiration that we now turn.

Alchemy, Economic Theory, and the Promotion of Industry and Commerce

Within virtually all medieval discussions of economic life, the status and legitimacy of any activity depended on its contribution to the community's well-being. Contributions were understood to be limited to the production of goods and the provision of direct services. Agriculture was thus among the most highly valued of all pursuits because the very survival of the community depended upon adequate food supplies. Starting in the twelfth century, artisanal occupations such as carpentry and shoemaking, which had always been acceptable, were raised in status as they were increasingly seen as imitating the creative activity of God. Still acceptable, but lower in status, was work such as that of housemaids and the transporters of goods which seemed somehow less essential or creative. Within this general structure the activities of merchants and financiers were assigned very low status; indeed, the clergy were forbidden to participate in them by canon law. This was because they produced no goods and provided no direct services, and thus seemed to be fundamentally *parasitic* activities which consumed the wealth of the community without offering anything in return. As a consequence, such roles were often delegated to the marginal groups in society—Jews and foreigners—and were looked down upon by both the agricultural elites and the members of craft guilds.

In order to argue that commerce played a positive and constructive role in the economic life of the community, Becher focused on the paradigmatic commercial enterprise, the *Verlagen* (the putting-out company), and applied to it insights derived from alchemy. According to traditional economic ideas, no enterprise illustrated the parasitic nature of commerce better than the *Verlagen*. These companies bought up the natural products of the land at low prices and then sent them out to artisans to be worked up into finished goods for minimal wages. Finally, they sold the finished goods, producing huge profits for their investors. At no point in this process did the company actually produce anything or offer any obvious direct service to anyone, yet the company somehow seemed able to produce money.

Becher approached this commercial process as an alchemical problem. In general, alchemists sought to artificially accelerate or imitate natural processes of growth. Metals, for example, were understood to grow slowly to the perfection of gold within the womb of the earth through a continuous process of decay and rebirth. Base metals were believed to be consumed in a process of natural corruption just as a living seed decayed in the earth after the death of its parent plant to be reborn as a new plant. But in the case of metals the rebirth was in a new and more perfect form. Alchemists sought to speed up this process by artificially dissolving and heating imperfect metals to speed up their decay and rebirth. In some cases they used a special substance identified as the philosopher's stone that could help to "multiply" the seeds of the newborn metal, much as fertilizer enhanced the multiplication of seeds of grain. For present purposes it is critical to realize that most alchemists, including Becher, did not think that the philosopher's stone provided any *material* contribution to alchemical processes. It served rather as an animating principle, or in Renaissance terms, as a "soul" (*anima*). To use a modern chemical analogy, the philosopher's stone served as a catalyst which could speed up or drive a reaction in a particular direction without being a reactant itself.

Turning to commercial activities, Becher argued that merchants provided the same kind of animating principle, or soul, for economic processes that the philosopher's stone did for alchemical ones. It was true that in the absence of commercial enterprises like the *Verlagen* there was a natural process through which the products grown and harvested or mined by the peasant order might be purchased directly by artisans, transformed into finished goods, and sold by the artisans to consumers for cash, but the process was slow and incapable of producing money rapidly enough to meet the demands of the prince and his court. With the artificial stimulus to production provided by the investors in putting-out companies and trading companies, however, the transmutation of the fruits of the earth was accelerated tremendously and money was multiplied so rapidly that the surplus could be extracted by the state without seriously burdening its citizens.

Given this situation, Becher now identified merchants as the princes' "politician's stone" and the "nourishers" of the entire society. Moreover, among the merchants he identified the *Verlager* as "the foundation pillars of the community" (*The Cameralists*, 128). In this manner he found a way to legitimize commercial activity as central to the community and to challenge traditional court hesitancy about promoting commerce. Indeed, in 1675 he managed to get Leopold I to establish a model commercial enterprise, a *Kunst- und*

Werkhaus, outside of Vienna and to appoint him director. Becher's political enemies soon undermined his position at court, and he left in 1677 to offer his services in Holland and then in England, where he died in 1682. The *Kunst- und Werkhaus*, however, remained as a center for the promotion of commerce.

In spite of his enthusiasm and respect for both alchemy and commerce and his insistence that both offered great benefits for the state, Becher trusted neither alchemists nor merchants. He was almost certainly correct in believing that most of the first were cheats and that most of the second were far more concerned with feathering their own nests than in serving the public interests. This distrust led him to insist that alchemy and commerce alike must be regulated and controlled as well as promoted and encouraged by the state in order to ensure that public interests were not sacrificed to private ones. Becher and all of his near colleagues sought, for example, to limit the import of foreign goods that could be produced locally on the grounds that imported goods led both to the loss of money to the country of origin and to the loss of jobs and income at home. They sought to regulate guild monopolies and privileges because they discouraged the immigration of productive artisans. At the same time, however, they opposed merchant attempts to completely destroy craft guilds because that practice led to an unfair depression of wages. They thus balanced their aggressive encouragement of commercial activity with an equally aggressive insistence that the state regulate all economic activity in the public interest.

One final point made by Becher was to have major importance for subsequent economic theorizing through its adoption by Pierre Boisguilbert, among others. This point was that *consumption,* or what we now call the *demand* for goods, is what drives economic activity and maintains high employment levels. For this reason, Becher argued that traditional virtues like saving and frugality were disastrous when carried very far. In fact, Becher tells an almost certainly apocryphal story about what he argues was Elizabeth I of England's great economic wisdom in burning large stockpiles of wool cloth in order to restore demand for the work of weavers. That one man's expenditure is another man's income was a point frequently emphasized by Becher, and Joseph Schumpeter has even labeled it "Becher's Principle."[4]

4

Rationalist Mechanical Philosophy and the Psychological Tradition of Social Science

In late July of 1641, Thomas Hobbes wrote to his patron, Sir William Cavendish, from Paris. There he was working on a mammoth intellectual project in the company of Marin Mersenne and Pierre Gassendi. On an earlier trip to the Continent, Hobbes had become fascinated with both the geometrical method and with the mechanical philosophy. Now, as he worked to develop a unified mechanist philosophical system incorporating physical nature, human nature, and the nature of society and the state, he sought the encouragement and critical advice of two of the major mechanical philosophers of the age.

On the face of it, the most important part of Hobbes's letter to Cavendish had no immediate connection with his philosophical project. Instead, it sought to encourage the earl to persist in his attacks on the Anglican ecclesiastical hierarchy, whose political influence in England was growing. Hobbes was deeply disturbed by the religious sectarianism which seemed to be sweeping England under the banner of Puritanism. But he was even more perturbed by the claims of the Anglican hierarchy that it alone had the right to determine the meaning of Scripture, independent even of the will of the crown. His distress arose because in 1641 Hobbes had a deep fear of civil war and, he wrote to Cavendish, it was dissension "between the *spiritual* and *civil* power [that] has of late more than any other thing in the world, been the cause of civil wars, in all places of Christendom."[1]

For much of the next ten years Hobbes worked to craft a compelling argument to justify the concentration of all social authority, sacred and secular, in a single sovereign power. And here is where his political anxieties and his philosophical program became joined. Not only did his attempts to promote undivided sovereignty incorporate the methods and the results of his philosophical project, but his very methods were chosen in light of his attitudes toward intellectual authority.

The Political Context for Hobbesian Social Science

Just as Becher's cameralist economic theories took on their particular form in response to the political realities and economic crises of seventeenth-century Germany, Hobbes's psychological and political theories took shape in response to the economic realities and the religious and political crises of early-seventeenth-century England.

The problems facing the Stuart court were substantially different from those facing the German princes in the early seventeenth century because England's relative isolation as an island nation had allowed it to undergo a unique process of economic, religious, and political development since the mid fourteenth century. After the plagues of the early fourteenth century, the English peasantry had been more successful than those of the Continent in taking advantage of the increased demand for agricultural labor. They saw a 50 percent rise in real wages during the second half of the century, a simultaneous reduction of feudal obligations to provide services to their lords, and the growth of long-term fixed-rent leases. As a result, there was a substantial transfer of income from the nobility to the peasantry, and through the next century the most successful peasants used their new wealth to buy small farms from the less successful nobility, creating a large class of landowning yeoman farmers.

During the sixteenth century several developments accelerated the economic advances of the yeomanry and its urban counterpart, the merchants, who often used their new wealth to purchase land. This process created a relatively large class of landed "gentry," the concomitant relative shrinkage of the traditional nobility, and the creation of an even larger class of poorer wage earners. Typically, the new landowning rich of early modern England kept wage increases below their increases in rents and profits.

As population steadily increased, the prices of agricultural commodities increased even more rapidly than the general rate of inflation—600 percent between 1500 and 1640—giving farmers increasing disposable income.[2] Some of this income was used to purchase consumer goods, leading to an expanding market served by artisans and merchants. Some was used for capital investment in livestock, farm equipment, and farm buildings that increased productivity and profits even more and reduced the demand for labor, driving rural wages down. Finally, some was used for the purchase of still more land.

Early in the sixteenth century, Henry VIII had confiscated Catholic church lands. Gradually these lands (almost 25 percent of the total land area of England) were sold off to provide income for the crown. In most cases they were transferred to the old nobility, but by the end of the century most of these lands had found their way into the hands of the new gentry.

The creation of an increasingly wealthy but non-noble landed class and a rural wage-earning underclass had tremendous social and political repercussions. The Tudor monarchs sought to use the rising gentry to dilute the power of the old nobility relative to the centralized state. To do so, they granted substantial local political power to the gentry, including the right to appoint justices of the peace. In addition, they changed the structure of Parliament, increasing its size from three-hundred to five-hundred by adding seats for landowning commoners and dividing it into two houses, Lords and Commons. But in increasing the political power of the gentry, the Tudor crown had created a virtual sorcerer's apprentice. As their political power grew, the gentry increasingly saw that power as theirs by right rather than by royal grant. By the beginning of the seventeenth century, this class, whose local political power was by now well-entrenched, was challenging the crown itself through its representatives in Commons and through its control of common-law courts.

The rise of the gentry also substantially modified traditional economic and social relations. As a predominantly subsistence economy was replaced by a market-oriented rural economy, there was a growing division between wealthy landowners and prosperous tenant farmers on the one hand, and an underemployed wage-laboring poor on the other. Social tensions increased, local rebellions became more frequent, and there was a growing fear among the propertied of the possibility of revolution.

Adding to and complicating the political and social tensions in late-sixteenth-century England were religious tensions mirroring those which broke into open warfare on the Continent. The Anglican church created under Henry VIII was a reformed church which retained many Catholic rituals and an elaborate ecclesiastical hierarchy similar to that of the Catholic church. Onto these it grafted doctrines that were more Lutheran than Calvinist. After the brief reign of the Catholic Mary Tudor in the mid-sixteenth century, many Anglican clergy who had gone into exile at Calvinist centers like Geneva and Zurich came back intending to push the church in a Calvinist direction. These "Puritans," however, were opposed by the crown and by the more conservative clergy because, among other things, they sought to eliminate the hierarchical structure of the church and deprive the crown of its right to make church appointments. As a result, England saw increasing tensions among religious factions, which became intertwined with social and political issues as a few enthusiastic preachers encouraged underclass rebellions and as some parliamentary commoners saw the breakup of an ecclesiastical hierarchy controlled by the monarch as a way to increase their own political power.

For a variety of reasons Elizabeth had allowed substantial religious diversity in England, but this policy led to increasing fragmentation and tension. When James Stuart (James I) came to the throne in 1604, he faced an England that seemed to him to be threatened with both social rebellion and religious and political anarchy. This view was shared by Thomas Hobbes. No doubt the royalist fears of an imminent collapse of England were paranoid, but Stuart policies aimed at instituting an absolutist state in England by suppressing religious dissent and imposing the royal will on both Parliament and the religious hierarchy soon drove all forms of opposition into increasing intransigence, virtually guaranteeing civil war.

Ancient Atomism, the Mechanical Philosophy, and Hobbesian Psycholgy and Politics

When Hobbes left Oxford at age 19 to become tutor to William Cavendish, he had little interest in mathematics or natural philosophy. In general, his attitudes seemed to reflect those of the Italian humanist Collucio Salutati. As his concerns about the course of English politics intensified, his first major response was a typically humanist one. In 1628 he offered an English translation of Thucydides' *History of the Peloponnesian Wars*, in large part because it seemed so beautifully to demonstrate the dangers inherent in democracy. Soon after this effort, Hobbes traveled to the Continent with his student. There he underwent an intellectual transformation as he became a convert, first to geometry and then to the mechanical philosophy. He did not give up his interest in political issues, but rather added natural philosophy to them, and during the early 1630s formulated his plan to produce a complete system of philosophy in three parts. The first would deal with *Body*, or matter in motion. The second would deal with *Man* as a specific kind of body in motion. The third would deal with *The Citizen*, and how knowledge of human nature could be used to create a stable state.

Hobbes's geometrical methodology and mechanistic ontology are integrated throughout his works, but I will separate the two for simplicity of exposition and will begin with the mechanical aspects of his system, for they are more in the foreground of his considerations of psychology, while the geometrical methods come to the fore in the political discussions which follow the analysis of human nature in his masterpiece, *Leviathan* (1651).

Hobbes was by no means alone in trying to develop a mechanist interpretation of human psycholgy during the mid seventeenth century. In his *Les passions de l'âme* (*Passions of the Soul*) and *Traité de l'homme* (*Treatise on Man*), Descartes offered mechanistic interpretations of human sensation, as did Mersenne and any number of Cartesians. One, François Poullian de la Barre, even used his analysis for a clearly social purpose when he argued in his *De l'égalité des deux sexes: Discours physique et moral* (A physical and moral discourse on the equality of the two sexes) of 1673 that because women have the same sensory organs as men as well as brains that cannot be distinguished anatomically, there can be no significant intellectual diferences.[3] But Hobbes differed from these Cartesians both in seeking to extract much more extensive implications for morality and society and in insisting on a purely materialist interpretation of psychology.

Cartesians distinguished between body and spirit, or mind, and while they offered mechanistic explanations for how the sense organs worked and how impulses were transmitted from them to the brain, they abandoned their materialism when they spoke or wrote about how the mind or spirit used those sensations for its own intentional ends. Even Gassendi, the reviver of ancient atomism, insisted on the existence of an immaterial spiritual domain. But Hobbes would not back away from pure materialism, in large part because the materialist notions of unreformed atomism fit so well with his anti-clerical sentiments.

According to Hobbes, the notion of an "incorporeal substance" was literally nonsense, for the very notion of substance incorporated extension and therefore body. He argued that such a notion had been foisted upon an ignorant people by priests, who sought to exploit peoples' fears of invisible powers by claiming a special ability to intercede with those powers. "By their demonology, and the use of exorcism, and other things apertaining thereto," Hobbes wrote in *Leviathan*, the priests "keep, or think they keep, the people in awe of their power . . . [and] lessen the dependance of subjects on the sovereign power of their country."[4] Like Epicurus and Lucretius, Hobbes believed that the best way to counteract these pernicious beliefs was to offer a compelling alternative cosmology which avoided appeal to fictitious spirits or incorporeal beings.

Though Hobbes's materialist philosophy was suggested by ancient atomism, it was no mere rehash of antique doctrines. His physics, for example, denied atomist claims for the existence of void space and incorporated the latest Cartesian argument that there could be no void because extension was a defining attribute of body and where there was no body, there could be no extension. Much more importantly for present purposes, his psychology depended critically on the recent physiological studies of William Harvey reported in his *De Motu Cordis et Sanguinis* (*On the Motion of the Heart and the Blood*) of 1628.

Hobbes begins his theory of man by arguing that all living organisms are distinguished from inert matter by the existence of an internal "vital motion" which Harvey had demonstrated to be "the motion of the blood perpetually circulating in the veins and arteries" (*EW*, 1: 407). All organisms, including humans, have one dominant goal: to maintain their vital motions or to preserve their own lives. The only thing that distinguishes humans from other animals is that they have larger and more sophisticated brains which provide greater memories and imaginitive and rational capacities to help them in their fundamental task of self-preservation.

Placed in an environment of constantly moving bodies, humans interact with that environment as their sensory organs are struck and moved by those bodies. Sometimes, as with taste and touch, the contact with sensed bodies is direct; sometimes, as with vision and hearing, the bodies being sensed set up a vibration in the aerial fluid which surrounds them, and this vibration is transmitted to the eye or ear. Once the sense organs are activated, their motion in turn is transmitted through the nerves to the brain where part of these motions produce "phantasms," thoughts or ideas, which are nothing but "some internal motion in the sentinent, generated by some internal motion of the parts of the object, and propagated through all the media to the innermost part of the organ" (*EW*, 1: 391). We will return shortly to what happens to the phantasms in the brain, but first we have to consider what happens to that part of the motions coming in through the senses which do not affect that organ, for they are even more important.

These motions are conveyed to the heart, where they either add to or subtract from the vital motions by "quickening or slackening, helping or hindering the same" (*EW*, 1: 406). At this point, Hobbes takes a step that was to have tremendous moral and political implications. He claims that whenever such motions augment the vital motions they produce what we call *pleasure* and when they decrease the vital motions they produce what we call *pain*. Since all humans are motivated principally to maintain their vital motions, humans must inevitably act to increase their pleasures and decrease their pains. Finally, Hobbes insists, whatever produces pleasure in us we call *good*, and we say that we *love* or desire it. Whatever produces pain, we call *evil*, and we say that we hate it or *fear* it (*EW*, 1: 410).

For Hobbes, the question of whether humans avoid pain and seek pleasure is *not* fundamentally an empirical one. We do not discover it by observing what people do; rather, we deduce that they must act in this way from their very nature as life-preserving organisms. When they appear to violate this principle—as do persons who commit suicide, martyr themselves for their religion, or offer their lives for their country—we must conclude that some pathological condition is present. Either there is some internal breakdown in the body, or some external agent such as the priesthood has introduced fraudulent notions that distort normal mental functioning.

The Hobbesian reduction of moral notions of good and evil to psychological ones of pleasure and pain—and ultimately to the physical ones of increased or decreased motion—had tremendous influence on seventeenth- and eighteenth-century moral and political discourse. Few accepted his reduction of pleasure and pain to mere changes in motion. But the claim that humans were fundamentally pain avoiders and pleasure seekers and the concomitant interpretation of good and evil as fundamentally rooted in pleasure and pain were not only seriously discussed and debated, but even became the foundation of the dominant eighteenth-century theories of morality.

One of the most important implications of Hobbesian psychologically based morality is that good and evil are properly related only to individuals. It is impossible to speak of a social or common good which is not simply an aggregation of the goods of individual persons, for the "body politick" has no way of feeling its own pleasures or pains. To speak, as Johann Becher did, of the need for individuals to sacrifice their own interests for the common good made no more sense then to talk about incorporeal substances. Individuals had to be understood in the first instance in purely egoistic terms, as seeking nothing but their own self-preservation.

How then was one to understand the relation of the individual to the social order and to the state? Hobbes argued that the instinct for self-preservation drove humans into a potentially endless attempt to acquire power: "I put for a general inclination of all mankind, a perpetual and restless desire of power, that ceases only in death. And the cause of this is not always that a man hopes for a more intensive delight than he has already attained to; or that he cannot be contented with moderate power; but because he cannot assure the power and means to live well, which he has at present, without the acquisition of more."[5]

No matter how strong, smart, and "vital" a human might be, no individual can ever be strong enough to prevail in a conflict with several others acting in collusion to deprive him or her of life or property. In order to provide for their security people must enter into social alliances, or civil societies.

Through all of his writings Hobbes insisted that states, or civil societies, come into existence solely to provide security for people and property. In doing so he had venerable precedent in the traditions of legal discourse, for most early modern jurists argued that the laws were intended not so much to do good as to keep people from doing evil to one another. But by focusing on the notion of justice, Hobbes rejected the rich tradition of political discourse from Plato and Aristotle onward, in which the polis was intended to offer the *good* life and not mere life itself. Moreover, he consciously abandoned the tradition of Christian morality which insisted that humans accept a positive responsibility for the well-being of others. He was perfectly willing to allow for people to enter into limited arrangements to promote various good works, subject to limits established by the laws of the civil society. But he insisted that justice in the narrow sense was the only legitimate function of the state. An amazing number of English political theorists were influenced by Hobbes on this issue. As late as Jeremy Bentham (1748–1832), English political theory still focused more on criminal law and penology than on issues of social welfare, and English theories had a substantial impact on political practice. For example, although the German state accepted responsibility for public elementary education early in the eighteenth century, and the French state did the same during the period of the French Revolution, the English insisted that education was a private matter until 1870.

Hobbes finally went on to argue that there is only one way in which civil society can be made sufficiently strong to enforce the peaceful co-existence of its members. All individuals must invest all of their power and authority, except for that of immediate self-defense, in a single, undivided sovereign who alone can create and enforce rules of acceptable behavior. Nothing less will do; for without a stable civil society, humans have little hope of living to enjoy the fruits of their own labor, and without an undivided sovereign no civil society can be stable. If power is shared between king and nobility, civil wars like the revolt of the Netherlands and the Fronde occur. If power is divided among religious factions, civil wars like those in the Germanies result. And if power is shared between the monarchy and the gentry, as in early-seventeenth-century England, civil war is inevitable.

Just as the traditional moral concepts of good and evil found new meanings through Hobbes's materialist psychology, the traditional political notions of liberty and freedom were also redirected. Within the classical tradition, notions of liberty were predominantly associated with positive privileges to engage in activities. Political liberty, for example, was first associated with the right of Roman citizens to take part in their own governance, and civil liberties were associated with the right to engage in economic, religious, and other social activities. In Hobbes's mechanistic interpretation of man, however, such notions of liberty or freedom made little sense. Hobbes insisted that the term liberty was used properly only to indicate the absence of external impediments to motions. In this sense, anyone who is not in "chains and prison" is free to do anything he or she might wish. (*EW*, 3: 199). Thus, laws cannot in any meaningful sense "grant" liberties or freedoms. Liberty or freedom are only meaningful with reference to what the sovereign's laws do not restrain or regulate: "The liberty of a subject, lieth therefore only in those things, which, in regulating their actions, the sovereign hathe praetermitted [omitted]: such as the liberty to buy, and sell, and otherwise contract with one another; to choose their own abode, their own diet, their own trade of life, and institute their children as they themselves see fit." (*EW*, 3: 199).

Hobbes thus used his mechanistic understanding of human nature and the state to suggest that liberty is not so much tied to what governments involved themselves in as to the domains in which they refrained from interference. For much of the subsequent English tradition of liberalism, the notion that liberties are protected primarily by limiting government involvment in economic and social activities became commonplace.

Geometry, Rationality, and the State in Hobbes

The Hobbesian depiction of human nature and the relationship of humans to the state drew heavily from both the ancient atomic philosophy and from the more recent mechanistic physiology of William Harvey. But Hobbes rejected the experimental approach to natural philosophy taken by Harvey in favor of the geometrical and "rationalist" approach usually associated with Descartes. In fact, as Steven Shapin and Simon Schaffer have shown in great detail, Hobbes waged a one-person war against the experimental philosophy of Boyle and the early Royal Society for decades (*LAP, passim*). It was not that Hobbes denied the importance or utility of experience and the knowledge which it provided. Indeed, Hobbes was perfectly willing to admit that philosophical or scientific knowledge is grounded in experience. Experience alone, however, is an uncertain guide to action. It produces what we call prudence, which is extremely important and often the best kind of knowledge that we have, but it cannot offer certainty.

Until Hobbes discovered Euclidean geometry around 1630 he was pessimistic about the possibility of attaining any certain knowledge. But like Descartes, Hobbes found in geometry a new cause for optimism, for it provided both evidence that certainty was possible and insight into the way it can be achieved. Taking mathematics as his model, Hobbes defined philosophy, or science, as "such knowledge of effects or appearances, as we aquire by true *ratiocination* from the knowledge we have first of their causes or generation [or], of such causes or generations as may be from knowing first their effects" (*EW*, 1: 3).

One key to the success of geometry was the precise and unambiguous character of its terms. The definitions of geometry were purely denotative, carrying with them no fuzzy connotations, and Hobbes demanded the same of all scientific language. The second key to the success of geometry was the rigidly restricted way of reasoning that it allowed in moving from its definitions and initial axioms to its conclusions.

Hobbes discussed his definition of reason in many places, but nowhere was it more clearly or concisely stated than in *Leviathan*, where it was approached in connection with a problem that I left hanging above: What happens to the "phantasms" or motions of the brain when some of the incoming sensory motions proceed to the heart? These motions are left, gradually decaying in the brain, where they constitute what we call "memories," which are the objects the brain operates on when we say that it thinks, or reasons. The brain can do a very limited number of things with these memories. It may return its attention to them, which we say is to imagine them. It may attach words, or linguistic signs to them. And it may combine and compare them. If the combinations are not subject to any special rules, as sometimes occurs in dreams, we do not get knowledge, but rather some kind of fantasy. But if we restrict the combination of ideas in a certain way, we say we "reason" about them, and this reasoning produces certainty about their connection.

Hobbes is very clear about what precise mental activities constitute reasoning. They are just those kinds of activities, and those kinds of activities alone, which are allowed in mathematics:

> When a man reasoneth, he does nothing else but concieve a sum total from the addition of parcels; or concieve a remainder, from subtraction of one sum from another. . . . These operations are not incident to numbers only, but all manner of things . . . For as arithmeticians teach to add and subtract in numbers; so the geometricians teach the same in lines, figures (solid and superficial), angles, proportions, times, degrees of swiftness, force, power, and the like. . . . Writers of politics

add together pactions to find men's duties; and lawyers, laws and facts, to find out what is right and wrong in the actions of private men. In sum, in what matter soever there is a place for addition and subtraction, there also is a place for reason; and where these have no place, there reason has nothing to do. (*EW*, 3: 29–30)

If we reason correctly in this way, our conclusions must be *true*. Thus, any science, including the science of politics which Hobbes purports to develop in *Leviathan*, that is constructed through reasoning about unambiguous and meaningful terms should command assent.

In general, the natural sciences are open to challenges that address neither the mathematical sciences nor the science of politics because we can never be absolutely sure that our experiences of natural objects encompass all of their attributes. But geometry and the state are both artificial creations of human beings. As such, they can contain nothing which was not put in them by their human creators, and they can be known in their entirety. Just as Salutati had claimed two centuries earlier, Hobbes argued that "geometry is demonstrable, for the lines and figures from which we reason are drawn and described by ourselves; and civil philosophy is demonstrable because we make the commonwealth ourselves" (*EW*, 7: 184).

Hobbes, however, did not accept the assurances developed by Descartes and others that intuition could establish the correctness of definitions, even in mathematics, or that every normal human being would automatically reason correctly if he or she simply made an effort to follow appropriate rules. In attempting to understand how to establish that correct definitions and correct reasoning had been used in the development of any scientific argument, Hobbes showed how closely his notions of mathematical method were related to his ideas of undivided political sovereignty.

Agreement among geometricians does not arise because such terms as line, plane, and circle are intuitively obvious to all persons and because there is only one inborn form of natural reasoning whose conclusions will always be correct. Instead, it arises because all geometricians agree to accept the meaning of the terms laid down by Euclid and to use the conventions of rationality established by him. Euclid thus stands as a kind of sovereign authority who simultaneously creates the objects of geometry and establishes the laws through which they are related. The same kind of sovereign is needed to create and judge the laws of the state. As Hobbes writes after discussing mathematics, "when there is a controversy in an account, the parties must by their own accord, set up, for right reason, the reason of some arbitrator, or judge, to whose sentence they will both stand, or their controversy must either come to blows, or be undecided, for want of a right reason constituted by nature; so it is in all debates of what kind soever" (*EW*, 3: 30–31).

For this reason, Hobbes opposed the claims of experimental philosophers that the truth of some propositions could be established by the testimony of *any* number of witnesses. And for this reason he also argued that "the skill of making, and maintaining commonwealths, consisteth in certain rules, as doth Arithmetic and Geometry: not (as in Tennis-play) in practice. . . ." (*EW*, 3: 195-96).

The notion of reason expressed by Hobbes, and shared with minor variants by Descartes, Leibniz, Spinoza, and many other seventeenth-century developers of social "sciences," was of tremendous importance. It not only seemed to legitimize a new form of discourse about moral and political issues, but it also focused attention on quantification and thus led to the highly problematic assumption that what can be counted or measured is uniquely significant or important. Hobbes, for example, was led by this notion to suggest that the value of a human life could be established by estimating the future earnings that would be lost by the death of the person. His close friend, William Petty, carried out this calculation for an average Englishman, and we continue to use this notion for policy purposes even though it does violence to all prior religious and moral traditions, for which value was a moral rather than a merely economic concept.

The Radical Tendencies in Hobbesian Psychology and Politics

Hobbes's aims in *Leviathan* were conservative. He was trying to shore up a monarchical government that he saw as under attack by groups who were seeking to usurp power that he believed belonged to the king. It is true that England had never had an absolute monarchy, so Hobbes was not, strictly speaking, seeking return to some status quo ante, but he was trying to block the continuing erosion of monarchical power and authority. Nevertheless, the strategies which he adopted to serve these ends were radical. They challenged almost all long-standing assumptions about political life and grounded those challenges in an insistence that every term of political discourse be analyzed at the most fundamental level. In the process, Hobbesian analyses undermined virtually every available alternative for justification for monarchical government and for traditional social hierarchies and provided critical materials for the construction of increasingly egalitarian social and political theories.

His thoroughgoing materialism certainly undermined all divine-right theories of monarchy. In fact, his opposition to mind-body dualism seemed to many opponents to put him in the same camp as Levelers like Richard Overton, who also drew from ancient atomist notions to insist that "man is a compound wholly mortal, contrary to that comon distinction of Soule and Body,"[6] and who linked that notion to purely democratic political programs. Perhaps even more importantly, his psychologically grounded individualism also undermined those Christianized Aristotelian theories that argued that people become significant only as part of a cooperative community whose well-being stands above that of its members. Finally, and perhaps most importantly, that same individualism undermined all claims that there was a natural aristocracy of birth, for within the Hobbesian scheme, every person was born with roughly the same physical and mental structure and stood in precisely the same relation to the sovereign as all others. Such implications were not lost on other Royalists such as the earl of Clarendon, who complained of Hobbes's "extreme malignity to the nobility, by whose bread he hath been always sustained."[7]

Spinoza and the Exploration of the Radical Implications of Mechanism and Mathematicism

Elements of the mathematical and mechanical philosophy explored by Hobbes were appropriated by a few radical sectarians such as Overton during the English Civil War, but the first widely distributed attempt to exploit them wholesale in support of democratic doctrines was made by Benedict de Spinoza. Born into a wealthy Jewish merchant family in Amsterdam in 1632, and given a taste for scholarship by his early teacher, Manasseh ben Israel, Spinoza turned to study Latin with the lapsed Jesuit freethinker and Cartesian, Francis van den Ende. Van den Ende was not only an excellent teacher who introduced his young students to mathematics and Cartesian philosophy, but also a political radical who was executed in 1674 for his participation in an attempt to establish an egalitarian commonwealth in northern France. Though he never accepted his teacher's advocacy of violence, Spinoza did develop a strong commitment to egalitarian principles. As a result, he resigned his position as head of the family firm, began to work as a lens maker, and participated in the activities of a group of liberal republican followers of Jan de Witt, who was also an advocate of the mathematical and scientific study of political issues.

At this point, in 1656, Spinoza was excommunicated from the Jewish community of Amsterdam. Nominally, Spinoza was excommunicated for his theologically heretical beliefs. As a result of his mechanist philosophical commitments he had come to insist on the absolute equality of all peoples and to deny that the Jews had a special status as the chosen people of God. In addition, two of his Jewish "friends" reported that he had told them that "since nothing is to be found in the Bible about the non-material or incorporeal, there is nothing objectionable about believing that God is a body" (*SRL*, 34). But theological heterodoxy was common within the Amsterdam Jewish community, and few were punished for it. The real reason for his punishment was almost certainly for his support for liberal republican political activities that threatened to upset the favorable but fragile position of Amsterdam's Jewry.

As a result of the revolt of the 1580s, the northern Netherlands had come under the control of a small oligarchy of wealthy Calvinist merchant families. Within this political context, as in others throughout Europe, Jews were excluded from public positions and from membership in the powerful guilds and were pushed into menial labor or into commerce. Thus, when Spinoza's teacher, Manasseh ben Israel, was forced out of his position as rabbi, he had to become a merchant, complaining, "I am engaged in trade, what else is there for me to do" (*SRL*, 6). But in the Netherlands, as elsewhere, their commercial activities offered the Jews substantial economic opportunities. In spite of their small numbers, Jews owned about 25 percent of the shares in the Dutch East India Company and the Dutch West India Company, and their average taxable property was almost double that of the gentile population of Amsterdam. (*SRL*, 6). Of course not all Amsterdam Jews were wealthy, but the wealthiest controlled the synagogue; they had developed close business ties with the membership of the elitist Calvinist party, and the last thing they wanted to see was a disruption of the political status quo. Spinoza's radicalism was both an embarrassment and a threat, so the leadership of the community first sought to bribe him into silence. When he refused to conform, they excommunicated him.

The young Spinoza tried to fight his excommunication by appealing to the civil authorities with an argument taken directly from Hobbes's *Leviathan*. There can be only one sovereign power, he argued, and since his civil rights were established by virtue of his status as a member of the Jewish community, that community could only reject him if it had been granted the authority to do so by the Provincial Estates, in which sovereignty rested. The Estates had not granted such power to the judges of the synagogue; so they had no right to excommunicate him. Futhermore, it would be a terrible mistake for the sovereign to grant such powers to any religious body, for it would give that body leverage to exert "the most complete sway over the popular mind" (*SRL*, 24).

Not surprisingly, Spinoza lost his appeal, and he retired to the Mennonite village of Rijnsburg, where he began composing his major political and ethical tracts grounded in the geometrical method and mechanical philosophy. The first of these, the *Tractatus Theologico-Politicus* (*A Treatise on Religion and Politics*), published anonymously in 1670, seems to have been the only writing of Spinoza's that was widely disseminated, but it struck fear into the hearts of conservative political and religious leaders everywhere. Among other things, it advocated democratic political institutions and openly undermined the claim that revealed religion could have any authority as a legitimate foundation for morality. Leibniz claimed that such ideas "dispose all things to the general revolution with which Europe is threatened," and that Spinoza's followers would be capable "of setting on fire the four corners of the earth" (*SRL*, 256). Conservative fears were to some extent justified, for Spinoza's ideas had a major impact on the anti-clerical and anti-monarchical writings of the French Enlightenment. "The greatest single influence exerted upon the writers of the period," writes Ira Wade, "is that of Spinoza. So great is his impact, in fact, that one is tempted to see in the whole movement a gigantic manifestation of Spinozism triumphant over other forms of thought."[8]

The very close similarities between Spinoza's and Hobbes's strategies in approaching political issues show up almost everywhere, but they are nowhere clearer than in Spinoza's most fundamental statement of his aims. "My object in applying my mind to politics is not to make any new or unheard of suggestions, but to establish by sound and conclusive reasoning, and to deduce from the real nature of man, nothing save the principles and institutions which best accord with practice."[9]

In some cases Spinoza and Hobbes arrive at different conclusions simply because Spinoza is more rigorous in following out the implications of common assumptions. But in one absolutely critical case Spinoza makes a clear break with Hobbesian assumptions, leading him to advocate a radically different kind of political organization. Hobbes had made clear that the driving force of all human behavior was the need to conserve vital motions, but Spinoza adds a second major consideration. "A truly human existence," he argues, "is characterized, not by the mere circulation of the blood and other vital processes common to all animals, but primarily by reason, the true virtue and life of the mind" (*PW*, 311). Any acceptable state must not only serve to preserve the lives of its citizens, but must also offer them an opportunity to exercise their rationality. "A commonwealth whose peace depends on the apathy of its subjects, who are led like sheep so that they learn nothing but servility, may more properly be called a desert than a common-wealth" (*PW*, 311).

Spinoza's addition of the exercise of reason to the preservation of vitality as fundamental to human existence is not simply a gratuitous assumption grounded in old Aristotelian notions, though it is doubtlessly in part just that. It is rooted in his agreement with Descartes that our most primitive and fundamental experiences are those of our own intellectual activity and that these experiences cannot be reduced in any credible way to the mere motion of parts of the brain. At the same time, Spinoza agrees with Hobbes that there are absolutely no grounds for believing in the existence of souls, or spirits, or minds, *independent* of material bodies. Spinoza's way of accounting for this set of circumstances is to argue that neither mind nor body have a separate and independent existence, but are simply two different ways in which we apprehend the same thing. In his terms, they are different *modes* of existence, each of which is necessary. From this point of view, humans can no more stop thinking before death than their hearts can stop pumping. Moreover, as Hobbes had insisted, reason has a key role to play in self-preservation, for it is only through the use of reason that people can recognize the need to enter into a civil society with a single sovereign power.

Hobbes had argued that once under the control of a sovereign, humans can and must give up the right to decide for themselves what is in their best interest, that is, they must abdicate their reason. On the contrary, Spinoza argues, people with enough reasoning ability to recognize the need to submit to the authority of a sovereign for some purposes could not turn off their reasoning and submit blindly to the sovereign will on all things. The kind of absolute sovereignty demanded by Hobbes is simply inconsistent with human nature. Spinoza thus recasts Hobbes's problem of the creation of the sovereign. The trick for Spinoza is to figure out how to establish a sovereign authority with enough power to do its job without asking people to do something which they could not possibly do.

This problem is approached by Spinoza from two quite different directions, one in the *Tractatus Theologico-Politicus*, and the other in the *Tractatus Politicus* (*Treastise on Politics*), published in 1676. In the first case Spinoza asks how a sovereign would be constructed in the absence of any external constraints, if people came together with no history of established customs and laws, but in a "state of nature." In the second case, he seeks to analyze how peoples accustomed to either monarchical or aristocratic governments should behave in order to maximize both their safety and liberty.

The distinction between these two approaches in Spinoza is important for several reasons. First, it is self-consciously grounded in a particular understanding of the mechanical philosophy as it was developed by Galileo and Descartes, and so illuminates the ways in which strategies from the natural sciences shaped approaches to human and political issues. Second, the two approaches virtually define the methodological distinctions between the "psychologically" driven social sciences of the eighteenth century and those associated with terms like philosophical history, or sociology. Third, by looking at Spinoza's two approaches to sovereignty we can recognize how different methodological approaches to a problem, perceived or at least promoted by the investigator as purely descriptive or "objective," can lead to different normative implications. While acknowledging the existence of both strands in Spinoza's writings, it is important to recognize that he became best known through the *Tractatus Theologico-Politicus* and its vernacular translations. Spinozism was almost exclusively psychological in its orientation, though Spinoza was not.

Every entity in the universe, including each individual human being, can be considered as a body, and every body can be considered both in terms of its internal constitution and laws independently of its interactions with other bodies, or in terms of its interactions with external bodies and the laws of those interactions. A complete understanding of any body must include both knowledge of how it would act independent of others and how it does interact with others. For Spinoza, as for Hobbes, there is a clearly preferred order in which these two kinds of considerations should be addressed. We never experience bodies except through their interactions with one another, so it might seem plausible that we should begin from the point that is closer to our immediate experience and focus first on the external relations of bodies. But Galileo's approach to falling bodies and Descartes' discussions of the method of analysis seemed to demonstrate the vastly greater power of the alternative strategy which begins by abstracting the body—isolating it in thought—from all others and dealing first with its behavior in this counter-factual, or hypothetical isolation. After Galileo dealt with how bodies would fall in a vacuum, he could then deal with modifications to that idealized motion produced by the interaction of the falling body with a viscous medium. By the same token, both Spinoza and Hobbes argued that we should first analyze human nature as it could be imagined to exist outside of civil society or in a counter-factual state of nature. Neither argued that the state of nature was historical, only that it was a device for stripping socially constructed accretions from some core. Thus, while Spinza admits that some groups exhibit characteristics different from others, he insists that "it is individuals, not peoples that nature creates" and that there is a common human nature which can be modified but not created by variations of languages, laws, and customs (*PW*, 181). This is why both Spinoza and Hobbes begin with a study of individual human psychology before they move on to their analyses of social and political interactions.

Both thinkers agree that the law of conservation of vital motions or of self-preservation is the primary natural law governing the individual and both concur in seeing the passions as driving most human activity. Moreover, both agree that though human passions aim at pleasure, or increased vitality, when they are not directed by reason they are often so misguided that they lead to pain instead. But Spinoza and Hobbes diverge radically on the relationship between reason and the passions, for as we have seen above, Spinoza believes that the exercise of reason is itself a source of pleasure which, in some sense, competes with the other passions for control over actions, whereas Hobbes sees the role of reason as purely instrumental.

We can best understand the special role of reason for Spinoza by refocusing our attention on the isolated individual from the point of view of its existence as a mode of thought rather than as a body. Seen from this perspective, the drive for self-preservation manifests itself as an active drive for self-determination. Stuart Hampshire gives a particularly clear summary of Spinoza's complex argument on this issue. "The conatus [vital motion] of an individual, conceived as a thinking being, . . . is the essential and natural tendency of the mind to assert active thinking and knowledge against the passive association of ideas in imagination. The more the sequence of a man's own ideas can be explained without reference to causes outside his own thinking, the more active and self determining he is."[10]

Other passions guide human actions through the imperfect, inadequate, and often erroneously interpreted "association" of ideas in imagination. Pleasure, for example, is associated in our minds with the consumption of food, so we eat. But we also tend to overeat, inadvertently producing pain, unless we actively guide our eating through a rational analysis of the consequences of our actions which takes into account long-term as well as short-term effects. The exercise of fully informed rationality alone must always produce the pleasures it seeks, and when humans are allowed to act in accordance with their rationally determined goals, they are said to be "free."

When Spinoza comes to consider the political implications of this analysis, he ends up arguing that the only kind of government consistent with the simultaneous needs to protect people from the predations of the merely passionate and to retain a domain for freedom is democracy, for in a democracy, while each citizen agrees to act according to the common decisions, each also retains the right to think, express his views, and vote his conscience on matters of substance. "This method of government is undoubtedly the best," Spinoza argues, "because it is best suited to human nature. . . . [In it], because all men cannot think alike, they agree that the proposal which gets the most votes shall have the force of decree, but meanwhile retain the authority to revoke such decrees when they discover better" (*PW*, 239).

Focusing on human nature without concern for the complicated social and historical contexts into which every human in born thus leads Spinoza into the claim that one particular political arrangement, democracy, is better than any other because it alone can simultaneously meet the "objectively" determined human needs for both security and freedom.

As we shall see, whether they knew of Spinoza's arguments or not, virtually every eighteenth-century author who attempted to ground social and political arguments in any individualistic account or analysis of human nature ended up supporting republican or democratic institutional structures. Looked at from a slightly different perspective, after the works of Hobbes and Spinoza, virtually everyone who sought to justify republican or democratic institutions found that arguments grounded in individualist theories of human nature were more compelling and convincing than any alternatives.

When Spinoza returned to analyze issues of sovereignty in the *Tractatus Politicus*, he retained the notion that the security and liberty of citizens were the most important aims of any government. But now he focused attention on how those aims could be accommodated within social and political institutions that are already established and that have so shaped the attitudes of people through existing laws and customs that they *cannot* either recognize the privileged status of democratic institutions or hope to establish them in the face of traditional practices.

In the *Tractatus Theologico-Politicus* Spinoza had already acknowledged the power of tradition in sustaining any particular government. Following a discussion of why a people accustomed to democracy cannot accept a king or tyrant, he went on to argue, ". . . it is equally dangerous to remove a king, even although it is perfectly clear that he is a tyrant. For a people accustomed to royal rule, and kept in check by that alone, will despise and make mockery of any lesser authority; and so, if it removes one king, it will find it necessary, as the prophets of old, to replace him by another. . . . This is why peoples, though often able to change their tyrants, have never been able to abolish them and replace monarchy with a different form of constitution" (PW, 201). In the *Tractatus Politicus* he completely surrendered his preference for democracy and in the subtitle to the book he acknowledged the need to operate within given forms. The subtitle is, "Wherein it is shown how a monarchy and an aristocracy must be organized if they are not to degenerate into tyrrany, and if the peace and freedom of the citizens is to remain intact." Seemingly retreating from the idealized and admittedly counter-factual assumption of a state of nature which shaped the discussions of his earlier work, Spinoza heaps praise on Machiavelli's realism and even acknowledges that there are circumstances when people are well advised to simply submit to the will of a tyrant because tyranny is inevitable (*PW*, 313). Spinoza does not abandon hope for political reform; indeed, almost every passage of the *Tractatus Politicus* is intended to show how imperfect governments can be modified to more nearly meet the citizens' desires for security and freedom. But he does insist that traditions of custom and law constrain reform within basic patterns or forms which cannot be transcended by particular peoples. In insisting on the inviolability of certain traditional forms within which limited modifications might be made, Spinoza anticipates the "philosophical-historical," or sociological approach to society which was fully developed by people like Montesquieu and Edmund Burke and which was often seen by later psychological theorists as fundamentally conservative because it accepted as inevitable some elements of the *status quo ante.*

5

Experimental Mechanical Philosophy, Political Arithmetic, and Political Economy in Seventeenth-Century Britain

During the 1620s England experienced a dramatic economic depression, caused primarily by the virtual disappearance of its major international markets for both raw wool and finished textiles as the Thirty Years War disrupted the Continental economy. Several years of poor harvests coupled with population growth forced the British to import grain at a time when exports were dropping, so the declines in employment and productivity were accompanied by a massive inflation which reduced most people's standard of living and drove up the crown's need for income to meet expenditures. As in Germany, traditional understandings of moral economy offered few insights into the causes or solutions of England's economic problems. The intellectual responses to the situation in Britain were quite different from the cameralist responses to a similar set of conditions, however, for several reasons.

First, the dilution of royal power and the growing power of Parliament set up a situation in which open debates over economic policies were not only possible, but inevitable. Furthermore, within Parliament there were different factions with quite different economic interests. In particular, there were members of Commons engaged in commerce as well as landowners, and these two groups had quite different attitudes regarding state regulation of commercial activities. Finally, throughout the seventeenth century British literacy rates grew very rapidly, especially in regions with high levels of commercial activity, and with this literacy grew a tremendous appetite for political and economic information. England consequently saw an explosion of literature on economic issues beginning in the 1620s and accelerating through the seventeenth century.[1]

Some of this literature was produced in response to either crown or parliamentary requests for expert advice. For example, Thomas Mun's *England's Treasure by Forraign Trade*, which was published only in 1664, had been written in connection with an investigation into "the true causes of the decay of trade and scarcity of coin in this realm" begun within the king's Privy Council in 1623 (*ETI*, 37–38). John Locke's *Some Considerations of the Consequences of the Lowering of Interest and Raising the Value of Money* of 1691 was written at the request of an MP, Sir John Somers, to inform debate on a bill to change legal interest rates.[2] Much of the literature was either open or thinly disguised special pleading on behalf of mercantile interests, or it was, like Becher's *Politischer Discurs*, unsolicited advice offered to the crown or Parliament by men who were interested in gaining patronage and power. Whatever the aims and audiences, however, as the century progressed economic writers increasingly sought to justify their claims by arguing that their approaches were scientific and therefore disinterested and true. As William Letwin has argued, "The needs of rhetoric brought forth the method of economic theory" (*OSE*, 105).

Among the many who sought to wrap their special pleading in the cloak of science or to offer what they understood to be genuinely scientific analyses of economic issues, far and away the most important and persuasive were the brilliant and eccentric William Petty and his close associate, John Graunt. No less interested than others in the policy implications of economic theorizing, both Petty and Graunt seem to have been genuinely concerned not only to appear but actually to *be* disinterested. As Petty wrote in a letter to his cousin, Robert Southwell, it was his goal to argue "without passion or interest, faction or party; but, as I think, according to the eternal laws and measures of truth."[3] In fact, Petty's insistence on dispassionate analysis often made him seem so cold and insensitive that his audiences were repelled rather than drawn in. Thus, in spite of the fact that his *Political Anatomy of Ireland* (1672) supported policies intended to improve the condition of the underclasses of Ireland, the callousness of its language made it a perfect target for bitter satirical treatment in Jonathan Swift's *A Modest Proposal* . . . of 1729.

Petty and the Incursion of Experimental Mechanical Philosophy into Policy Considerations

Born in 1623, the son of a clothier in the southern English port town of Romsey, Petty claimed later in life that he was fascinated in his youth by the work of craftsmen and that he haunted the local smiths, watchmakers, and carpenters "until he could have worked at any of their trades."[4] After a brief stint as a cabin boy on an English merchant ship, Petty was left in France at age 14 when he broke a leg. During the next couple of years he attended the Jesuit college at Caen and supported himself tutoring French naval officers in mathematics. In 1641 he joined the Royal Navy, but in 1643 left for Holland where he began medical studies with the Cartesian anatomist, Cornelius van Hoogelande, from whom Petty seems to have developed a special interest in experimental anatomy, both dissection and vivisection. The experimental cast of his medical training was particularly important during the next phase of his intellectual development.

In late 1644 or early 1645 Petty arrived in Paris, where he became involved with the circle of natural philosophers around Mersenne and Thomas Hobbes.[5] When he left Paris in 1646, Petty, while retaining his experimentalist orientation, also carried with him a set of literal and metaphorical gifts from Hobbes. Physically, he carried away a magnificent microscope. Intellectually, he carried away both a thoroughgoing commitment to the mechanical philosophy and an enthusiasm for egoistic-individualist interpretations of human behavior.

Back in England, Petty associated with a group of London intellectuals led by Samuel Hartlib and John Dury. Drawing heavily from the Hermeticist writings of Johann Andreae and from the programmatic writings of Francis Bacon, the Hartlib group encouraged numerous inventors and educational reformers. In Hartlib's

circle Petty developed a friendship with Robert Boyle and a fascination with invention and entrepreneurship, patenting a mechanical
device for producing multiple copies of written documents in 1647.[6]
The ever-restless young scholar left for Oxford in late 1647. Here
he ceased to be a young accolyte to other scientists and became their
intellectual leader. He was granted his doctorate in medicine in 1648
and was hired as deputy to the professor of anatomy, Thomas
Clayton, Jr., in 1649. During the same year, the Oxford Experimental
Philosophy Club, one of the principal precursors of the Royal Society
of London, began meeting in Petty's lodgings under his leadership.

In 1650, at age 27, Petty became both vice-principal of Brasenose
College at Oxford and the Tomlin reader in anatomy. He was well
launched on a comfortable academic career in the company of a
group of very able scientific colleagues who offered both stimulation
and admiration. His anatomy lectures, which were among the first to
integrate Harvey's insights on the circulation of the blood and
explanatory theories grounded in the new French mechanical philosophy into British medical education, seemed to be drawing
students into medicine, and his prospects for a lucrative medical
practice at Oxford were outstanding.

Within little over a year, however, Petty moved again, this time to
become professor of music at Gresham College in London at the
invitation of the trustees, including the merchant John Graunt. Less
than a year later, while retaining his Gresham position and salary,
Petty left London for Ireland with a new title and position as chief
medical officer to the English army that had been sent to regain
control of Ireland for the English, now Parliamentary, government.

In Ireland, Petty's career took a new twist that would eventually
lead him to apply the scientific perspectives he had picked up in his
travels to issues of governmental policy-making and finance. The
English armies in Ireland drew both financing and personnel with
the promise that loans and salaries would be paid off through the
grant or sale of lands forfeited by the Irish rebels. But no sale or
distribution of land could be undertaken without a massive land
survey, and the surveyor-general for Ireland anticipated that such a
survey would take nearly 13 years to complete. In the face of
impatient creditors and a restless and unpaid soldiery, this was a
hopelessly long time to wait. Petty saw an opportunity to exploit his
mathematical knowledge and analytical skills for both public benefit
and private gain. The managerial challenge also fascinated him. He
proposed to the governor-general to organize and carry out a land

survey that would be completed within 13 *months* if he were given authority to train and use some of the army to do the job. Reflecting a few years later on his decision to undertake the Down Survey, he wrote: "I hoped thereby to enlarge my trade of experiments from bodies to minds, from the motion of the one to the manners of the other, thereby to have understood passions as well as fermentations, and consequently to have been as pleasant a companion to my ingenious friends, as if such an intermission from physic had never been."[7]

Taking his strategy from the Cartesian method of analysis, Petty broke down the complex surveying process, from the initial construction of instruments to the production of the final maps, into literally hundreds of simple tasks for which suitably chosen workers were trained. Using an extreme division of labor as well as a variety of innovations in management and quality control, Petty completed the Down Survey between 11 December 1654 and 1 March 1656, in under 15 months. It still stands as a model of surveying accuracy and precision. For his efforts Petty personally gained over 9,000 pounds, with which he promptly bought up choice pieces of Irish land for a small fraction of their value. By late 1657, Petty owned over 70,000 acres of Irish estates and was one of the most wealthy commoners in Britain. In the meantime his position in Ireland had drawn from Petty the first of a number of economic writings.

A decision was made by the military government in Ireland to set aside the entire county of Connaught as a de facto concentration camp for all of the Catholics who had been displaced from their lands. In 1655 Petty co-authored a pamphlet entitled *A Discourse Against the Transplantation into Connaught*, which argued that this was an unwise move. First, he and his co-author, Sir Vincent Gookin, MP, argued with marvelous foresight that by separating the Catholic and Protestant Irish populations into two isolated and hostile camps, the English would be creating a permanent source of tension. Equally important from Petty's perspective, by removing the Catholic peasantry from regions of English land ownership, the government was depriving landowners of a critical source of cheap labor and the Catholics of job opportunities (*P*, 5–6). Such a policy would hurt everyone. As was true of virtually all of Petty's shrewd policy suggestions, the government ignored his advice.

Within just a few years Petty himself became an MP, and for the remainder of his life spent most of his time in London, where he fought litigation against his Irish claims, bought and developed land, served for a time as commissioner of the navy, and was active in the Royal Society and Parliament. Increasingly, from about 1660 to the end of his life in 1687, his major intellectual efforts were given over to scientific analyses of economic policy issues. Most of these efforts remained unpublished until 1691, but some had fairly wide circulation within the government and among scientific intellectuals.

The clearest statement of Petty's theoretical perspective appears in the preface to *Political Arithmetic* (completed about 1676, and published posthumously in 1691). After stating his goal, to demonstrate that the English state is in a strong position relative to its two major competitors, Holland and France, for wealth and power, Petty writes:

> The method I take to do this, is not yet very usual; for instead of using only comparative and superlative words, and intellectual arguments, I have taken the course . . . to express myself in terms of number, weight, or measure; to use arguments only of sense, and to consider only such causes as have visible foundations in nature; leaving those that depend upon the mutable minds, opinions, appetites, and passions of particular men, to the consideration of others: really professing myself as unable to speak satisfactorilly upon those grounds (if they may be called grounds), as to foretell the cast of a dye or to play well at tennis, billiards, or bowls (without long practice) by virtue of the most elaborate conceptions that ever have been written *De projectibilus et missilibus*, or of the angles of incidence and refraction. (*EWSWP*, 1: 244)

The first thing to note about this statement is that it openly rejects the Hobbesian notion that one needs to understand human nature ("the mutible minds . . . of particular men") in order to gain important knowledge about issues of political economy or policy. There are quantifiable regularities in aggregate behaviors (we now call these statistical laws) which can be empirically discovered even if we cannot know precisely how each individual event is caused. Christian Huyghens, whom Petty met at the Royal Society, had written on such regularities in dice and card games in his *De ratiociniis in ludo aleae* (Rationality in games of chance) of 1657. Petty sought to exploit them for political ends.

The second thing to note is Petty's insistence that quantification offers a more compelling foundation for policy than any form of merely verbal argument. As early as 1660, Petty was urging Charles II to establish a registry of lands, commodities, and population (an extension of the Dutch *Kadaster*, which registered lands only) on the grounds that it is from the want of information "whose foundations are sense and the superstructure mathematical reasoning . . . [that] so many governments do reel and stagger, and crush the honest subjects that live under them."[8]

One of the criticisms often leveled at Petty's work by historians of economic thought is that for all of his claims about the importance of quantification and mathematical reasoning, Petty was extremely casual about the sources of his numbers, often apparently picking them out of the air, and that he developed no new mathematical techniques for handling the numbers that he did use (see *OSE*, 123, 144–45). Though perhaps true, such complaints are irrelevant to an understanding of his role as a promoter of a quantifying view of the world and as a stimulus to the development of statistical techniques by others. Petty was very clearly aware both of the limitations of his own sources of information and of his own mathematical techniques. He saw himself as the initiator of a method that others would have to refine.

This self-perception comes through most clearly in his prefatory and concluding passages to John Graunt's *Natural and Political Observations . . . Upon the Bills of Mortality* (1662). Petty emphasizes the fact that the Bills of Mortality for London are an extremely limited and unpromising source of information, calling them "poor and despised";[9] furthermore, he acknowledges that nothing but mere "Shop-Arithmetique" has been used in their analysis (*OBM*, 7). The whole point of Graunt's work and, by implication, his own is to serve as an illustrative model of how much can be accomplished with his method even with such limited sources and mathematical techniques. Thus Petty ends his conclusions to Graunt by pleading once again for the systematic collection of statistical information to provide much more secure policy guidance (*OBM*, 778–79).

In a very important sense, Graunt's work did accomplish what he and Petty hoped for it, although it took much longer than they could have expected. Its third edition was reviewed by the French *Academie des Sciences* in 1666, leading immediately to the creation of a bureau to collect vital statistics for the Paris region and soon to the collection of agricultural, social, and economic statistics compiled in the *Memoires des intendents* of 1697–1700.[10] In the Germanies it almost certainly stimulated the initially abortive attempts by Cameralists like Becher to initiate commercial statistical collections. And in England it provided the direct model and stimulus for Gregory King's magnificent *Natural and Political Observations and Conclusions Upon the State and Condition of England* (1696), which remains even today the chief source of demographic and economic information about late-seventeenth-century England.

Self-styled political arithmeticians attempted to get an official governmental registry of statistical information established in Britain several times during the eighteenth century, but these attempts were effectively blocked by both conservative and radical groups who quite correctly saw that the collection of such information would increase the power of the centralized state.[11]

One of Petty's chief goals in several of his works was to emphasize the importance of labor relative to land for the wealth of a state. In *Verbiem Sapienti and on the Value of People*, written around 1665, he found an ingenious quantitative way to establish his point. He first estimated the population of England and Wales to be approximately 6 million persons. Then he showed that for all purposes these people spent approximately 40 million pounds sterling each year, and called this the annual expenditure. Next he estimated the total stock (we would say capital assets) of England and Wales to be 144 million in land, 30 million in housing, 3 million in ships, 36 million in livestock, 6 million in money, and 31 million in durable goods, totaling 250 million pounds in assets. Rents, interest on loans, and income from investments in joint stock companies all returned around 6 percent per annum, so Petty calculated that the annual return on the use of all assets must be approximately 15 million pounds. The difference between this number and the annual expenditures of 40 million pounds amounts to 25 million pounds that must come from the labor of the people; labor therefore accounts for almost two-thirds of the annual income of England and Wales.

Not only did this discussion provide the direct stimulus for analyses of the relative importance of land, labor, and capital in the creation of wealth undertaken by Richard Cantillon, and thus by the Physiocrats and Adam Smith, it also became the model for virtually all subsequent treatments of human beings as commodities, whose value can be determined in purely monetary terms. For Petty went on to argue that if humans, like other forms of stock, were assumed to return about 6 percent per annum, then the human stock of England and Wales was worth about 416.66 million pounds. Since he calculated that only 50 percent of all persons actually work for a living, each productive laborer was worth about 138 pounds. A quick check of the sales price of young adult slaves sold at auction confirmed Petty in his estimates (*EWSWP*, 1: 105–8).

The objectification of human beings which shows up so clearly in the above example is just one aspect of a general characteristic which Petty's works exemplified, encouraged, and passed on to subsequent students of political economy. Traditional moral economic ideas embedded economic discussions in a broad context of moral and political discourse focused on the cooperative exchange of services aimed at providing social stability in a hierarchically structured community. Moreover, as we saw in chapter 3, even the cameralist economics of the Continent, though it reinterpreted certain social roles, treated economic topics within a broad moral context. But the new emphasis on quantification and the analytic strategy pursued by Petty and those who followed him tended to divorce economic considerations from their broader context. In the short run, Petty's insensitivity to context limited the impact of his work, but in the longer term the predictive success that quantification and the isolation of economic factors from their broader context made possible tended to override such concerns and increase the dependence of policymakers on narrowly construed economic analyses.

The methods adopted by Petty for political arithmetic and subsequent political economy had interesting implications. On the one hand, by emphasizing aggregated data and statistical averages, political arithmetic made it difficult to deal with individual differences, so in a sense it assumed what Joseph Schumpeter has called the analytic identity of economic actors. This assumption was often made explicitly in other economic works in order to simplify analyses; political economy thus unquestionably encouraged a certain kind of leveling which ignored issues like social status. At the same time, the emphasis on aggregated data tended to focus the attention of early political economists on maximizing quantities like the total wealth of a nation and made it difficult to deal with issues of distributive justice within the larger entity. Even Petty occasionally considered the redistribution of assets within the larger aggregate, but the overall tendency of early political economy was to simply assume that if the wealth of the nation were increased, all of its inhabitants would be better off.

In one crucial case, however, Petty's analysis did exploit the fact that the economic behavior of rich and poor differed in an important manner. This case involved an analysis of the optimal amount of money in a society. Unlike his German contemporaries, Petty did not see the endless accumulation of money as the major goal of the state. Though he has many things to say about money, he insists upon two central considerations. First, money's primary function is to ease the production and consumption of other commodities like food and consumer goods. Second, there is a cost associated with producing money itself. A shortage of money must lower productivity levels, so it is very important to have enough. At the same time, because there is a cost associated with producing money, it is wasteful to have too much, for the expense of producing extra money might have been allocated to producing consumable commodities. In order to figure out how much money is "enough," Petty invented a new concept, the "velocity of circulation," or "vent" of money (*EWSWP*, 1: 112–13).

The amount of money needed in a society with a certain total annual expenditure will depend upon the number of times that money is used to purchase goods; the amount of money needed, therefore, will depend upon its velocity of circulation. A given amount of money does more work in a given period of time if it passes through several hands than if it passes through just a few, and poorer artisans and laborers are paid more frequently and expend their income more rapidly than wealthy landowners. Thus, looked at from one point of view, there will be a smaller need for money where the ratio of poor to wealthy is greater; looked at from another point of view, there will be greater productivity in a society with limited amounts of money when that money is in the hands of artisans and laborers rather than in the hands of wealthy landowners. For this reason Petty advocated the "leveling" of incomes, or the transfer of wealth to the lower classes.

In spite of his claim that political arithmetic should be independent of any theory of individual motives, Petty did make one important assumption about human nature and psychology. In fact, he adopted the Hobbesian notion that humans act solely in their own self-interest and he attributed to them a purely Hobbesian calculative rationality in determining what their interests are. These ideas were taken directly and self-consciously from Petty and Hobbes by Charles Davenant, John Graunt, Pierre Boisguilbert, and Richard Cantillon, taking their place among the fundamental assumptions of subsequent political economy through their incorporation in the writings of Adam Smith.

One of the most fascinating applications of such notions in Petty's *Treatise on Taxes* (written about 1662) occurs in an analysis of the economic aspects of criminal justice. Given his assumption that people represent a valuable economic resource, Petty violently opposed capital punishment and unproductive imprisonment. For those who must be imprisoned for the protection of others, he proposes a form of enforced "slavery" which would enrich the nation rather than deprive it of its human stock (*EWSWP*, 1: 68), but for those who can safely be left free, he proposes a series of fines that draws on his assumption of egoistic calculative rationality. Criminals, especially thieves, must engage in their anti-social behavior because they expect to gain by their acts. According to Petty, we can stop this kind of activity or turn it to social benefit by establishing a series of fines that will produce a net loss in connection with their calculations of gain. First, we determine the expected gain from any given type of crime. Then we determine the probability that a criminal will be caught. The inverse of this probability multiplied by the expected gain determines the break-even point for a thief. If we set fines a bit higher than this figure for any given class of crimes, criminals will stop because they realize that they are more likely to lose than gain by their criminal activity. Even if they miscalculate and act anyway, the fines can be set to more than compensate the victims for their losses and the state for its expenses (*EWSWP*, 1: 69). In this crude form, Petty's notions of criminality were quite rightly ridiculed, but they did become the starting place for the subsequent utilitarian penal reform movements initiated by Cesare Beccaria in Italy and Jeremy Bentham and his followers in England. More importantly, the assumption of an egocentric rational actor implicit in this argument became the common starting point for virtually all economic analysis.

Petty's Medical Model and Economic Liberalism

Almost as important as his notion of the rational actor for subsequent economic analyses was Petty's understanding of the constraints within which governmental attempts to manage economic phenomena should be exercised. Petty, like all seventeenth-century aspirants to the title of social scientist, rejected the Aristotelian distinction between practical and theoretical knowledge and insisted that human activities, like those of inanimate matter, were governed by natural laws. The assumption that economic activity is governed by natural law created something of a paradox, however, for if it were true, it would suggest that attempts to intervene in the economic sphere to modify economic behavior are hopeless. At this point, a set of ideas derived from medicine played a central role in guiding economic theorizing, and Petty played a pivotal role in making these ideas explicit.

It is not at all accidental that many of the most powerful economic theorists of the seventeenth and early eighteenth centuries— including Petty and Locke in England, Becher in Germany, and François Quesnay in France—were all trained in medicine and active medical practitioners. In fact, the difference between the medical tradition of Paracelsus in which Becher was trained, and the tradition of Cartesian anatomy, which dominated the training of Petty, Locke, and Quesnay, may account for some of the significant differences between cameralist approaches to economics and the "liberalism" of the other three.

The basic presumption of all medical theory and practice during the seventeenth century was that health was normal and natural and that, in most cases of disease, natural processes would lead to healing. It was the function of the physician to assist and encourage those natural processes, most frequently by intervening to block or remove abnormal, or pathological, conditions. The Paracelsan tradition focused predominantly on the use of proper diet and medication to assist natural forces; thus Becher's emphasis was on the active encouragement of commerce, which was understood to accelerate normal economic processes. Petty and Locke both trained under Petty's friend, Thomas Willis. Their analyses, influenced by their anatomical studies of pathology, focused on removing pathological conditions.

When he turned his attention to political economy Petty constantly appealed to medical metaphors. For example, he titled his analysis of the economic condition of Ireland a *Political Anatomy* and he spoke of the work as establishing a basis for the *political medicine* which must be applied to that country. Moreover, in his *Political Arithmetic* he spoke of his recommendations as being intended "to remove the impediments to England's greatness." But the most interesting appeals to medical notions appear in the *Treatise on Taxes*, where he uses them to emphasize the need to remove inappropriate regulations that cannot work because they try "to persuade water to rise of itself above its natural spring." Furthermore, he argues that when interference is necessary, it should be done only in the least intrusive way. "We must consider in general, that as wiser physicians tamper not excessively with their patients, rather observing and complying with the motions of nature, than contradicting it with vehement administrations of their own, so in politics and economics the same [care] must be used" (*EWSWP*, 1: 60).

Given their medical notion that what we now call homeostatic mechanisms function naturally to keep people healthy, Petty and the other medically trained political economists tended to sympathize with the admittedly self-interested claims of merchants that governments should not interfere in the free exercise of trade and sought to discover the nature of the homeostatic mechanism for governing economic activity. Though Petty never did offer a general discussion of this problem, his self-professed follower in political arithmetic, Charles Davenant, offered one of the first accounts of how market competition among self-interested economic actors automatically establishes prices for commodities (*ETI*, 187). Henceforth Davenant's claim that "trade is in its own nature free, finds its own channel, and best directeth its own course" (*ETI*, 191) became one of the dogmas of liberal economics.

This perspective was given its most general expression by Josiah Tucker, whose *Essay on Trade* (1749) and *Elements of Commerce* (1755) were among the most important British contributions to political economy between those of Petty and Adam Smith. In the *Elements of Commerce*, Tucker wrote, ". . . the physician to the body politic may learn to imitate the conduct of the physician to the body natural, in removing those disorders which a bad habit, or a wrong turn of treatment hath brought upon the constitution; and then leave the rest to nature, who best can do her own work. For after the constitution is restored to the use and exercise of its proper faculties and natural powers, it would be wrong to multiply laws relating to commerce, as it would be for ever prescribing physic."[12]

In France, François Quesnay's training as a surgeon made him even more inclined to see the functions of medicine *and* economics in terms of the removal of obstructions to normal functioning. Like his British predecessors, he frequently talked of the need for "recourse to our medical knowledge" in connection with economic issues, and when he sought governmental intervention in economic affairs, it was almost always "to remove causes prejudicial" to economic growth.[13]

In spite of the fact that virtually all of the works of Petty and his followers in political arithmetic and political economy were intended to shape governmental policies, it would seem that their scientific methods and assumptions led many into a "liberal" bias which stressed the intrinsically rational behavior of individual economic actors and the extremely limited domain within which positive legislation could hope to control economic behavior.

6

Natural History, Historical
Jurisprudence, and the
Emergence of Traditions of
Philosophical History to the
Time of Montesquieu

Of the four approaches to social science that became identifiably
distinctive by the early eighteenth century in Europe, three had fairly
well-defined origins during the middle decades of the seventeenth
century. During the period between 1640 and 1670, cameralism,
political economy, and psychologically grounded political discourse
each saw the creation of several model investigations linked to clear
programmatic statements, which in turn led to persistent traditions
of discussion and analysis. The fourth approach, which I have called
sociological and anthropological and which went under the name of
philosophical history in the eighteenth century, is more complex. It
too was represented by at least one model investigation linked to a
methodological program during the 1650s, James Harrington's
Oceana. But the subsequent development of philosophical history
was not as tightly structured by the Harringtonian paradigm as the
other traditions were by the model investigations of Hobbes and
Spinoza, Petty and Graunt, and Becher and von Schröder. When the
first inclusive and widely distributed model of philosophical-histor-

ical investigation, Montesquieu's *L'esprit des lois* (*Spirit of the Laws*), finally appeared in 1749, it incorporated important elements from at least two categories of sources that preceded *Oceana*. One of these consisted of the accounts of the customs and institutions of non-European peoples by travelers, traders, and missionaries which had been organized as a form of natural history by the late seventeenth century. The second contributing element was a naturalistic and historical tradition in jurisprudence that was widespread during the late sixteenth and the seventeenth centuries and was given a special impetus by the works of the French jurist Jean Bodin.

Travel Literature, Noble Savages, and the Growth of Ethnography

The rising popularity of travel literature and the initial debates regarding whether indigenous American and African people should be understood as "noble savages" or "ignoble savages" lies outside the scope of our present discussion, but the importance of mid-sixteenth-century debates over the moral character of savages played such an important role in seventeenth- and eighteenth-century philosophical history that they demand brief consideration.

The earliest reports of such travelers as Columbus and Amerigo Vespucci already tended to assign Native American populations to classically derived categories of nobility and bestiality. This dichotomous classification was intensified and solidified during the middle decades of the sixteenth century through a series of conflicts between Bartolemé de las Casas and Gines Sepulveda. Las Casas, a Dominican monk who eventually became bishop of Chiapa, had been involved in New World colonization as a plantation owner on Hispaniola before he became appalled by the Spaniards' treatment of indigenous Americans in the Caribbean and gave up his land to become a spokesman for the rights of the Indians.

In numerous reports and in two major works, *Brevissima relacion de la destruccion de las Indias* (*The Devastation of the Indies: A Brief Account*) published in 1546, and *Apologias y discursos de la Conguistas Occidentals* (translated in 1656 as *The Tears of the Indians: Being an Historical and True Account of the Cruel Massacres and Slaughters of above 20 Millions of Innocent People by the Spaniards*) published in 1552, Las Casas emphasized the viciousness and corruption of the Spanish colonists and officials, contrasting their actions with the gentility and true nobility of the Indians, whom he depicted as ". . . people very gentle, and very tender . . . which can sustain no travail, and do die very soon of any disease whatsoever, in such sort as the very children and Noble men brought up amongst us, in all commodities, ease, and delicateness, are not more soft than those of that country: Yea, although they be the children of laborers. They are also very poor folk which possess little, neither yet do so much as desire to have much worldly goods, & therefore neither are they proud, ambitious, nor covetous."[1]

Against this highly positive vision of the Indians, supporters of the colonial slave owners and *conquistadores*, led by Las Casas's opponent in debate, Phillip II's court historian Gines Sepulveda, portrayed the Indians as "barbaric, uninstructed in letters and the art of government, and completely ignorant, unreasoning . . . sunk in vice, cruel, and . . . of such character that, as nature teaches, they are to be governed by the will of others."[2]

The portrayal of Indians as either the most noble or the most degenerate of humans was thus a product of political conflict over the Spanish treatment of Indians in their colonies, and this dichotomous portrayal was kept alive because of its political utility. Numerous Dutch authors of the 1570s focused on Spanish viciousness perpetrated on an innocent and noble people in order to justify their own rebellion against Spain. On the other side, under Phillip II of Spain, colonial brutality toward Indians increased, justified by the portrayals of filthy and devil worshiping Indians by José de Acosta and others.

In 1703, Louis Armand de Lom d'Arce, baron de Lahontan, who had fought and traveled in Canada for nearly 20 years, ushered in a new and ever more popular use of the "noble savage" paradigm when he used an Indian wise man as a vehicle for violent attacks on European society and culture in his *Supplement aux Voyages du Baron de Lahontan ou l'on trouve des dialogues curieux entre l'auteur et un sauvage de bon sense qui a voyagé* (Supplement to the voyages of Baron Lahontan in which one finds curious conversations between the author and a wise savage who has traveled). The view of savage nobility promoted by Las Casas and Lahontan probably peaked in Rousseau's *Discours sur l'origine et les fondements de l'inégalité parmi les hommes* (*Discourse on Inequality*) of 1755 before it was eclipsed by Buffon's theory of degeneracy, which both built upon and gave new credence to negative interpretations of native life.[3]

While it is true that political literature kept alive the caricature savages of the earliest depictions, it also served to sustain interest in non-European peoples on a more scholarly and discriminating level. In parallel with the polemics there thus emerged an important tradition of serious ethnography which focused on comparative studies of marriage practices, religious rituals, clothing, kinship structures, governance, male and female roles in economic and ceremonial life, and so on. This tradition, especially in the English-speaking world, was given its most general organizing principles in 1692 with the publication of Robert Boyle's *General Heads for the Natural History of a Country, Great or Small, Drawn Out for the Use of Travellers and Navigators*. Though primarily interested in the commercial potential of the material products of newly discovered lands, Boyle and his scientific colleagues did initiate some detailed ethnographic work.

Much more important for our present purposes were the reports of Jesuit scholars, who sent back detailed intelligence intended to provide their order with information that might allow them to exploit native customs in their missionary activities. Much of this material was published between 1702 and 1776 in the 34 volumes of *Lettres édifiantes et curieuses, écrites des missions étrangères par quelques missionnaires de la Compagnie de Jesus* (Edifying and curious letters written at foreign missions by missionaries from the Company of Jesus). These letters in turn provided much of the detailed ethnographic information incorporated by Montesquieu and other philosophical historians into their work during the eighteenth century.

Historical Jurisprudence and the Environmental Determinism of Jean Bodin

If the printing press gave early modern Europeans access to a bewildering variety of cultures from around the world, it also gave them a new kind of access to their own history and an awareness of the wide variety of local and regional customs among European peoples. This new awareness had an especially profound impact on legal thought, since it fed into long-standing debates over the relative significance of universal legal principles and local customs. Such debates were closely tied to the parallel question of whether law was really a science or an art. Both of these interlocked questions attained a new level of importance in early modern Europe as the rise of centralized monarchies led to conflicts over the extent to which monarchs had the right to change laws in violation of customary usage and the authority to violate what were taken by some jurists to be the more fundamental principles of natural law.

One consequence of these legal debates was the rise of a kind of legal nationalism which claimed precedence for local traditions over the hegemonic and universalist claims of Romanist lawyers. Thus, for example, the French jurist Bernard Autome wrote in his *La Conference du droict françois avec la droict romain* (Comparison of French law with Roman law) of 1610, that "Justinian never set foot in France . . . on the contrary he was defeated by the Franks".[4] By implication, French legal customs should not be subordinated to Roman law. Wherever legal nationalism took hold there was a move to explore the historical development of local and regional customs and rights, and the search for historical grounding for legal tradition spread rapidly to the Romanists as well, for their humanistic and philological training led them naturally to seek the roots of the Justinian code in the pre-Christian traditions of Rome.

One of the most important writers on historical jurisprudence was Jean Bodin, who advanced the unusual position that law should be a science, but that Roman law did not embody natural reason. Instead, he insisted that laws could be different in different localities and, at the same time, be scientifically explicable. Moreover, it was from the comparative historical study of "the character and customs of all known societies" alone that one could discover truly universal legal principles.[5] In his *Methodus ad facilem historiarum cognitionem* (*Method for the Easy Comprehension of History*) of 1566 and *Les sex livre de la république of 1576* (translated in 1604 as *The Six Bookes of a Commonweale*), Bodin first offered a method of creating an historical science of the law and then began to implement his plans.

Bodin's works had a major impact on political and legal thought, especially in England. He linked the notion of sovereignty to legislative authority (monarchical authority had traditionally been understood in judicial terms) and he advocated absolute and undivided sovereignty (Hobbes undoubtedly borrowed heavily from Bodin on this issue). But Bodin explicitly argued that the form of government which is best in the abstract may not be the best in particular situations, and it is the way in which he justifies the need to adapt law to particular places and peoples that will concern us most.

Bodin argues, as Spinoza would nearly a century later, that while governmental action can modify dispositions and customs, there are limits to what a sovereign can hope to accomplish. Unlike Spinoza, Bodin sought to explain precisely how such limits come to exist, and to do so he appealed to knowledge drawn from the natural sciences and medicine. Thus, in seeking to understand the inviolable character of particular peoples he proposed to get beyond how their attitudes are shaped by institutions to something more fundamental. "Let us seek characteristics drawn, not for the institutions of men, but from nature, which are stable and never changed unless by great forces or long training, and even if they have been altered, never the less eventually they return to ther pristine character. About this body of knowledge the ancients could write nothing, since they were ignorant of regions and places which not so long ago were opened up."[6]

Bodin's discussions drew predominantly from recently translated classical works, but they also exploited many recent discussions of European history, and they depended heavily on a few sixteenth-century travel accounts and encyclopedic works. Most critically, they incorporated material from all of these sources into a single comprehensive theory that accounted for the differences in mental characteristics of different peoples in terms of the impact of the physical environment on the balance of the humors.

According to the classical theory of humors, derived from the Hippocratic *On the Nature of Man*, the universe is composed of four basic elements—fire, which is hot and dry; air, which is hot and moist; water, which is cold and moist; and earth, which is cold and dry. The human body is also composed of four basic substances, or humors: blood, which is hot and moist; yellow bile (choler), which is hot and dry; phlegm, which is cold and moist; and black bile (melancholy), which is cold and dry. Health consists of an appropriate balance of these humors and disease results from their imbalance. In *Airs, Waters, and Places*, Hippocrates linked humoral theory to climate in a simple and direct way. Temperate climates are healthiest because they offer a balance of heat and cold as well as wet and dry. Hot, dry climates will tend to increase choleric humors; hot, wet ones, sanguine humors; cold, wet ones, phlegmatic humors; and cold, dry ones, melancholic humors.

As early as Aristotle and Galen this whole network of notions had been linked with psychological concepts by identifying human temperaments with the various humoral excesses. By the Renaissance a well-developed humoral psychology was in place. Phlegmatic persons were slow witted but strong and persistent; sanguine persons were sociable and pleasant but impatient and lustful; choleric persons were quick witted but shallow and weak; and melancholic persons were intellectually profound and vigorous but subject to fits of depression and unable to follow others.[7]

As a consequence of the different mixtures of humors produced in different locations, different peoples will necessarily have different temperaments; and customs and laws must be adjusted to them.[8] In general, Bodin writes, "One of the greatest, and it may be the chiefest foundation of a commonweale, is to acommodate the estate to the humor of the citizens; and the laws and ordinances to the nature of the place, persons, and time" (*SBC*, 547). Thus the Roman emperors made a great error when they sought to impose a single law on all nations, without distinction (*SBC*, 558).

While the particular humoral theory used by Bodin was dropped by the early eighteenth century, his general argument that locally specific customs and laws can be explained in terms of some kind of environmental determinism became one of the formative features of philosophical history in the works of Montesquieu, lasting well into the nineteenth century through the influence of Johann Herder. In no other author is the conservative character of this tradition more in evidence than in Bodin, for every one of Bodin's appeals to enviromentalism is aimed at explaining why long-standing customs cannot be changed to bring them in line with arrangements that are openly taken to be superior in the abstract.

James Harrington and the Economic Determinist Thrust of Philosophical History

If there is a single pre-Montesquieu source more important than any other in the establishment of philosophical history, it is almost certainly James Harrington's *The Commonwealth of Oceana*, first published in 1656. Bodin had taken a long-standing tradition of natural-law jurisprudence associated with studies of the Justinian code and transformed it by trying to give a scientific account of local variations of law and custom grounded in a particular theory of environmental determinism. In much the same way, Harrington took a long-standing tradition of prudential political discourse associated with republican and imperial Rome and transformed it by trying to give a scientific account of temporal variations of governmental forms grounded in a particular theory of economic determinism.

Before explaining why and how Harrington came to revise notions of classical republicanism as they had been articulated by Polybius and Machiavelli, in particular, it is critical to understand some of the major features of republican theorizing. According to republican theorists, within any polity there exists a mixture of three different principles associated with different groups of people and different political virtues and modes of action. The three principles can be capsulized as the one, the few, and the many. They corresponded in Rome to the consuls, the senatorial class, and the people (*plebes*) and in the early modern world to the princes or monarchs, the nobility, and the common citizens. Just what virtues were associated with each principal or group varied from author to author. Generally speaking, leadership was the principal virtue and mode of operation of the one. Wisdom or prudence, honor, and ambition were the principal virtues of the few and legislative activity was its dominant political mode of action. Honesty and reverence for custom were the chief virtues of the many, while the bearing of arms was considered its chief political mode of action.

Much as the health of a body depended on appropriately balancing its humors, the stability or health of a republic (meaning in this case any polity, whatever its governmental structure) depended on maintaining a proper balance of its three principles. It was both inevitable and necessary that one of the groups of principles should be dominant in any state, but in a healthy republic the dominant principle was always checked and balanced by the other two. Thus legitimate governments might have the form of a monarchy (dominated by the one), aristocracy (dominated by the few), or democracy (dominated by the many), but in each of these cases, the exercise of their appropriate virtues by the other two groups ensured that the government would continue to serve the interests of the whole polity rather than those of the dominant group alone. Harrington labeled the three major forms of government in a different and slightly misleading way, calling them absolute monarchy, mixed or feudal monarchy, and commonwealth, respectively; but even in what he called in absolute monarchy, Harrington believed that some balance existed among the three principles.

Unfortunately, every balance of principles was, according to

Polybius, ultimately unstable. Some accident of *fortuna* (chance or fortune) might at any time lead to the deterioration of one of the desirable forms of government into a degenerate form in which the two subordinate principles were so weakened that the dominant principle came to oppress the other two in the interests of its associated group. Under these conditions the class representing the dominant principle would abandon its efforts on behalf of the common good. Monarchy would degenerate into tyranny, aristocracy would deteriorate into oligarchy, and democracy would degenerate into anarchy.

Within this general scheme, the fulfillment of its appropriate political role by each group was important for two related reasons. First, in exercising their specific virtues, humans perfected themselves in the old Aristotelian sense (see chapter 2). Second, and equally importantly, if any group failed to exercise its particular virtue, the balance of principles would be lost and legitimate government would be impossible. For Machiavelli and subsequently for Harrington and his followers the greatest threat to legitimate governments in the early modern world was the creation of mercenary standing armies to replace citizen armies. This development deprived the many of their rightful participation in the political world and opened them up to the oppression of the one or the few.

One of the great aims of Machiavelli's works had been to discover how to extend the stable lifetime of legitimate governments forms, but he admitted that, in the long run, every legitimate government would become corrupted. One key question was how any state could move out of a degenerate form back to a legitimate form of government. According to Machiavelli, this could only be accomplished when some other stroke of *fortuna* made it possible for some unusually wise legislator to establish a legitimate form, and no reason could be given for this legislator to choose one of the legitimate forms over another.

The immediate stimulus for Harrington's *Commonwealth of Oceana* seems to have been the attempt of Oliver Cromwell during the early 1650s to transform the Protectorate into a monarchy by another name with himself as monarch. Though Harrington had seen personal service to the king and may have had early monarchical sympathies, by 1654 he had become associated with a group of men who had been part of the New Model Army and who were trying to preserve some of its democratic and leveling ideals against Cromwell's apparent attempt to seize authority.[9] *Oceana* attempted to appropriate republican theory, which had been used by Royalists and Parliamentarians in the debates leading up to the outbreak of civil war, for democratic ends during the Protectorate by showing that the dominant principle of a legitimate government must reflect the distribution of wealth in the relevant society. In seventeenth-century England, because wealth (land in particular) was widely distributed, only a democratic form could be successful, and attempts by either Cromwell or Royalists to reinstate any regime in which a monarch (or any other representative of the one) was dominant was doomed to failure. Even the restoration of Charles II did not upset Harrington's faith in his theories, and he continued to argue during the 1660s that in time, whatever it may be labeled, England's government was bound to become a de facto commonwealth ("The Art of Lawgiving" in *PWJH*).

In the process of justifying his modifications of classical republicanism, Harrington felt compelled to directly address and rebut the arguments which Hobbes had made in *Leviathan* and *De Cive* in favor of undivided sovereignty, and he chose to do this on methodological grounds based upon recent developments in the natural sciences.

What most differentiated Harrington's approach from Hobbes's and linked him to the radical empiricism of Bacon and the alchemical tradition was his absolute insistence that scientific knowledge had to be drawn from extensive experiences of nature, and that geometrical reasoning of the Hobbesian sort was positively pernicious in both natural and political philosophy. Harrington writes in *The Mechanics of Nature*, "Nature can work no otherwise than as God taught her, nor any man than as she taught him."[10] To the Hobbesian claim that men create the state by some human conventions, Harrington responds, "To make principles or fundamentals, belongs not to men, to nations, or to human laws. [But] to build upon such principles or fundamentals as are apparently laid by God in the inevitable necessity or law of nature, is that which truely appertains to men, to nations, and to human laws. To make any other fundamentals, and then build on them, is to build castles in the air."[11] And to the Hobbesian complaint that prior theorists derived the rights of citizens "not from the principles of nature, but transcribed them into their books out of the practices of their own commonwealth," Harrington responds almost with disbelief. "[It] is as if a man should tell famous Harvey that he transcribed his circulation of the blood not out of the principles of nature, but out of the anatomy of this or that body" (*OOW*, 38). For Harrington, experience is the only legitimate source of knowledge about both natural and social phenomena. This means that in studying social and political issues one must constantly appeal to comparative historical examples from as wide a range of contexts as possible.

In order to explain the character of his comparative historical method, Harrington talks about it as a method of political "anatomy" which, unlike Hobbes's political geometry, is capable of dealing with the complex details of political reality (*OOW*, 429). Furthermore, he argues that a Hobbesian monarch could only survive with "a parliament of mathematicians" (*OOW*, 514). Though Harrington did not go outside of the European tradition to consider Asian or New World experiences, he did explore in great detail the histories of the Hebrew nation, Rome, Sparta, Venice, and England.

Harrington disagreed with Hobbes on methodological grounds and on many specific issues, but he was impressed with Hobbes's argument that the capacity of any government to enforce its laws depends on its ability to command military force. And he built his own system on this Hobbesian insight. Harrington begins his basic argument with Hobbes's conclusion, that without the threat of military force, the law is nothing but a piece of paper. Harrington continued, "But an army is a beast that has a great belly and must be fed; wherefore this [the control of the military] will come unto what pastures you have, and what pastures you have will come unto the balance of property, without which the public sword is but a name or mere spit frog" (*OOW*, 41).

From Francis Bacon's *History of Henry VII* Harrington drew the conclusion that the military and hence the political power of the English feudal nobility was broken when the Tudor monarchs managed to transfer control of land from the traditional nobility to the gentry. From Aristotle's discussion of the constitutions of Athens, in which Solon's redistribution of property led to an increasingly democratic governmental structure, Harrington concluded that when land is widely distributed a democratic government must follow. In general, whichever of the three traditional orders controlled the bulk of the property in any state inevitably became the dominant political order. In Florence, where most of the "property" was in money, rather than in land, the merchant order, which had the most money, was dominant. In seventeenth-century England, commoners owned nearly three-fourths of the land, so Harrington concluded that a commonwealth was the only possible stable form of government for England.

Subsequent political thinkers constantly linked Harrington's name with the general claim that the governmental superstructure of a society must reflect the more fundamental distribution of economic resources. John Adams argued that this discovery of Harrington's was "as infallible a maxim in politics as that action and reaction are equal in mechanics."[12] Subsequent Republican theorists, such as John Toland, the eighteenth-century editor of Harrington's political works, claimed that "this plain truth . . . is the foundation of all government" (*OOW*, xvii).

Harrington went on in *The Commonwealth of Oceana* and other political writings to work out detailed mechanisms for guaranteeing the stability of democratic governments by ensuring that no special factions could gain control, and these arguments made him one of the most popular political authorities among eighteenth-century English commonwealthmen,[13] or country Whigs, and among Americans during constitutional debates in the decades of the founding of the United States.[14] For our present purposes, however, it was Harrington's interjection of economic determinist arguments into early modern political discourse that is most important.

7

Newton, Locke, and Changing Ideas About the Character of Science

During the eighteenth century, interest in the natural sciences and in the application of scientific approaches to social and economic issues exploded.[1] Though the expanding interest in science and its extension into many domains of human interest had many sources, it was certainly stimulated by the writings of two Englishmen, Sir Isaac Newton and John Locke, who together transformed our ways of knowing so that they became both more powerful and more extensive in their respective domains of application. Margaret Jacob, among others, has argued that their works found a peculiarly receptive audience because they served the needs of a rising commercial bourgeoisie.[2] Much more important, I suspect, is the fact that Newton's and Locke's works resonated with widespread millenarian hopes that had been raised during the period of the English Civil War, but which sectarian religious movements had been unable to fulfill. Each promised anew the coming of an age when human knowledge should be adequate to human needs, and these promises were linked in Newton's case to the successful solution of a series of long-standing astronomical and physical problems, and in Locke's to the justification of the immensely popular Glorious Revolution of 1688.

While Newton, Locke, and their followers showed how much could be learned in some domains, they also insisted that there were definite limits to any scientific attempts at understanding, which meant for them that there were limits on all understanding. In what follows we will be concerned with the sources of both the new intellectual optimism which permeated Enlightenment approaches to social science and the new admissions of impotence. Paradoxically, it was the abandonment of unrealistic expectations regarding human knowledge that freed Enlightenment thinkers to accomplish so much.

Sergio Moravia has argued that the social sciences benefited more than any other domain of inquiry during the eighteenth century from what he calls the "epistemological liberalization" stemming from the writings of Locke and Newton.[3] In order to understand how they consolidated this epistemological liberalization, the features of which had advocates before them, and to explore in more detail some of the plurality of cognitive strategies they encouraged, let us turn directly to the writings of Locke and Newton.

Locke's Philosophy of Science

Newton's most famous work, *Philosophiae Naturalis Principia Mathematica* (*The Mathematical Principles of Natural Philosophy*), appeared in 1687, three years before Locke's *Essay Concerning Human Understanding*. But it became widely known only through a series of eighteenth-century popularizations. Furthermore, his more widely read *Opticks* did not appear until 1704. As a consequence, when Newton's ideas were confronted and discussed, it was most often against a background already prepared by Locke's *Essay*. We therefore begin with Locke.

The *Essay Concerning Human Understanding* (1690) was much more important than Locke's *Two Treatises of Civil Government* (1690) for the development of the social *sciences*, even though the latter had a greater immediate political impact, so I will limit consideration to the *Essay*. In it, Locke claimed to be content with "clearing away some of the rubbish that lies in the way of knowledge."[4] But Voltaire, one of his great admirers, stated the more common perception of eighteenth-century readers when he wrote that "such a multitude of reasoners, having written the romance of the soul, a sage at last arose, who gave, with an air of the greatest modesty, the history of it."[5]

Born in 1632, the son of a modest country lawyer, Locke entered Oxford in 1652 and received his master's of divinity in 1658, remaining as a tutor and turning to medicine, which he studied with Petty's close friend, Thomas Willis. Though he retained his interests in divinity and developed strong political concerns as a result of his association with the Whig politician, Lord Ashley, later the first earl of Shaftesbury, his primary interests during the 1660s and 70s were in scientific, especially medical, topics.

In 1668, he was elected a Fellow of the Royal Society of London and soon came to serve on its governing council. From 1675 to 1688, Locke spent most of his time in Holland with Shaftesbury. Before he left Holland, he wrote the first major French-language summary of Newton's *Principia* for Jean le Clerk's *Bibliothèque Universelle* while he was simultaneously completing his *Essay Concerning Human Understanding, Two Treatises of Civil Government,* and *A Letter Concerning Toleration,* all of which were published in 1690. Locke's glowing review of Newton not only stimulated continental interest in Newton's work, but also cemented a friendship between the two men which lasted until Locke's death.

When Locke returned to England upon the ascension of William and Mary to the throne, he devoted increasing amounts of time to political and religious issues, but his scientific activities never completely ceased. He was chosen by Robert Boyle's executors to edit Boyle's *General History of the Air* in 1691, and in 1698 he completed a work entitled *The Elements of Natural Philosophy,* published after his death in 1704.

In a fragmentary manuscript on the art of medicine composed around 1670, Locke had previewed the major thrust of his later *Essay,* arguing that the greatest problem faced by those who hoped to systematize medical knowledge was the presence of so much false knowledge cluttering up the field. Because previous workers were ignorant of their own limitations, it was as if a surveyor trying to draw a map had to work "in a thick wood, overgrown with briars and thorns" (*Essay,* editor's introduction, xxiv). Locke's early thoughts on the extent and limits of natural philosophy did not lead directly to his *Essay,* however. Instead, the latter emerged as a result of a series of discussions with some friends on the principles of morality and revealed religion, subjects that seemed at first "very remote" from the epistemic problems of science. (*Essay,* "Epistle to the Reader," 9). In the process of trying to write out some of his ideas on these topics for his friends to discuss, Locke drew from his thoughts on the sources of natural philosophy, gradually arriving at the conviction that the way we discover knowledge about morality and religion is ultimately the same as the way we discover knowledge about the natural world. By fits and starts, and over a period of nearly 20 years, Locke developed these initial ideas into *An Essay Concerning Human Understanding*, the Enlightenment's first answer to Aristotle's *Prior* and *Posterior Analytics*.

In the introduction to the *Essay* Locke defines the term *idea* to signify "the object of the understanding when a man thinks." (*Essay*, Introduction, section 8, 32). After showing in book 1 that ideas cannot be innate to the mind, he turns in book 2 to the question of how we *do* come to have ideas to think about. He answers that experience alone provides ideas and that this experience is of two kinds and two kinds only—sensation and reflection. "First, our senses, conversant about particular sensible objects, do convey unto the mind several distinct perceptions of things, according to the various ways wherein those objects do affect them. . . . Secondly, the other fountain from which experience furnisheth the understanding with ideas is,—the perception of the operation of all our own minds within us, as it is employed about the ideas it has got . . . I call this *REFLECTION*. . . . The understanding seems to me not to have the least glimmering of any ideas which it doth not receive from one of these two" (*Essay*, 2: 1: 3–5).

Locke explicitly claims that he does not want to present the kind of physiological theory of mental functioning which Descartes and Hobbes had offered or to speculate about whether ideas "do in their formation, any or all of them, depend on matter or not" (*Essay*, Introduction, section 2, 26). Indeed, he proceeds to demonstrate that there is no possible way of knowing precisely how sensations produce ideas. Nonetheless, his whole theory of knowledge depends on accepting that the mind is spatially separated from the external world and that sensations are somehow produced in us by the motions of external objects. Both of these are fundamental presumptions of the mechanical philosophy, and Locke's most extended account of sensation might have come directly from Descartes, Hobbes, Gassendi, or Boyle (*Essay*, 2: 8: 12).

Locke openly begged to be pardoned for his "little excursion into natural philosophy," but he justified himself on the pragmatic, though intellectually dubious grounds that it was necessary in the course of his injury into the relationship between our ideas and "really existing" things (*Essay*, 2: 8: 22).

Locke's version of sensation and perception was grounded in mechanical philosophy and simultaneously denied that the mechanism by which motions are transformed into ideas can ever be known with certainty. As such, and with only minor modifications, it became the basis on which all major eighteenth-century psychological theorists built their arguments.

Having discussed the sources and limited extent of our ideas in book 2, Locke goes on to explore problems associated with the use of language in book 3. Then in book 4, he proceeds to analyze how we combine ideas into "knowledge" and assesses the levels of confidence that we can reasonably expect to have in different kinds of knowledge.

Knowledge is, for Locke, nothing but a perception of the agreements and disagreements among our ideas, and these can be reduced to four specific types. They are either about identity or diversity; relation; co-existence or necessary connection; or real existence (*Essay*, 4: 1: 3). For example, we can know that white is not red, which is knowledge of identity or diversity; that two triangles with equal bases and altitudes are equal to one another, which is knowledge of relation; that iron is both capable of being magnetized and of rusting, which is knowledge of the co-existence of two different properties in one substance; and that God exists, which is knowledge of real existence.

In this series of examples, it should be fairly obvious that the grounds we have for saying we "know" are somewhat different in each case, leading to differing levels of confidence in our knowledge. For Locke, the first and most certain degree of knowledge is grounded in immediate intuition. As soon as we recognize the meanings of "red" and "white," for example, we know that they do not represent the same idea. Such direct and unmediated knowledge, Locke calls intuitive (*Essay*, 4: 2: 14). Locke's second degree of knowledge is demonstrative. This kind of knowledge is produced when the agreement or disagreement of two ideas cannot be discovered except through the mediation of others. In the case of two triangles with equal bases and altitudes, for example, we cannot immediately recognize their equality. Instead, we first establish the notion of "area" which is given for any triangle by one-half the product of the base and altitude; then we relate the two triangles through the mediation of the idea of area. In this case a *proof* or demonstration is accomplished through a sequence of steps, each of which must have intuitive certainty (*Essay*, 4: 2: 2–10).

Sensitive knowledge is less certain then intuitive and demonstrative knowledge; but it is extremely important because of its uses. We say we have sensitive knowledge of some external object when we perceive the idea of that object immediately present in our mind. In this case, while we have intuitive knowledge of the *idea*, it is not, strictly speaking, possible to demonstrate the existence of the external object from our intuition of the idea alone; nonetheless, no normal person seriously questions the existence, for example, of the fire that burns him or her. Sensitive knowledge is thus "as great as our happiness or misery [demands], beyond which we have no concernment to know or to be" (*Essay*, 4: 2: 14). Since natural philosophy purports to be about an actually existing world, the highest degree of knowledge we can possibly have about it is sensitive, rather than intuitive or demonstrative.

Our knowledge of co-existence and necessary connection, which constitutes the most important category for science, is almost always even less certain than this, however, because it involves an extrapolation from the sensitive knowledge gained from one or a few experiences to future expectations. Thus, in discussing the co-existence of various properties in a substance like gold, Locke writes, "though we see the yellow color, and, upon trial, find the weight, malleableness, fusibility, and fixedness that are united in gold; yet because no one of these has any evident dependence or necessary connexion with the others we cannot know certainly that where any four of these are the fifth will be there also, how probable soever it may be, because the highest probability amounts not to certainty" (*Essay*, 4: 3: 14).

This mention of probability is absolutely critical for the liberalizing of epistemology. Since very little natural science can have the kind of certainty associated with intuition, demonstration, or immediate sensation, Locke insists that almost all scientific knowledge is merely probable. On the one hand, this may lower confidence in the sciences, but on the other hand, it opens up new strategies for generating assent to propositions which could not possibly have met the demands of many earlier theories of scientific knowledge.

When someone hopes to establish that some proposition is probable, that person must offer an argument which is "enough to induce the mind to judge the proposition to be true or false rather than the contrary" (*Essay*, 4: 15: 1). Exploring just what might constitute *enough* support for probable judgments, Locke suggests that there are several descending degrees of probability that might justify assent.

The first and highest degree of probable knowledge belongs to claims which are fully consistent with the direct "knowledge, observation, and experience" of the person(s) to whom the claims are addressed. Suppose, for example, that someone claims to have observed people walking on frozen water. If the person to whom that claim is addressed has seen people walking on ice in the past and has no special reason to doubt the claimant, then they must judge the probability to be very high. If the intended audience has had some experience of frozen water and its ability to support weight, but has never seen a person walking on ice, they should consider the probability to be high because the claim bears a similarity or analogy to their relevant experiences. But if someone from a hot climate who has never experienced frozen water hears the claim, he or she should rather assume the claimant to be a liar than to assent without further evidence, for the claim would be contrary to his or her accumulated relevant experience (*Essay*, 4: 15: 4).

In many cases we must assess the probabilities of propositions which are unsupported by any of our direct experiences. This, for example, is the condition we find ourselves in when evaluating the probability of the mechanical philosophy or any other hypothesis that purports to explain natural phenomena by invoking the existence of entities which are not directly accessible to our senses. While Locke was insistent that we "should not take doubtful systems for complete sciences" (*Essay*, 4: 12: 12), he was also absolutely insistent that the careful use of probable hypotheses was of immense value in the development of the sciences in at least three ways. First, hypotheses were crucial aids to memory because they allowed for a mental connection of masses of otherwise disconnected experiences; second, they were valuable in suggesting experiments which could lead to new discoveries; and third, they provided intermediate ideas that "may show us the agreement or repugnancy of other [non-hypothetical] ideas, which cannot be immediately compared" (*Essay*, 4: 12: 14).

Given the potential utility of hypotheses, the key question became what kinds of "further evidence" are relevant in granting or withholding our provisional assent to them, that is, what makes some speculative hypotheses more probable than others? One obvious consideration is the internal coherence of the system of propositions which the hypothesis generates. Another is the consistency of the hypothesis with multiple phenomena, or its explanatory scope (*Essay*, 4: 12: 13). More important than either of these demands for Locke, was the requirement that any hypothetical non-sensed entity or relationship have some clear resemblance to an entity or relationship about which we do have independent and non-hypothetical knowledge. *"Analogy* in these matters is the only help we have," wrote Locke, "and it is from that alone we draw all of our grounds of probability." Thus, for example, he argues that we are warranted in hypothesizing that "the violent agitation of imperceptible parts of burning matter" constitute heat and fire; because heat and fire can be produced by the violent rubbing of observable bodies (*Essay*, 4: 16: 12).

From our current point of view, Locke's discussion of scientific knowledge accomplished two basic things. It established limits on the domains within which humans can hope to establish scientific knowledge without the use of hypotheses, focusing on the centrality of empirical description within those limits. In addition, it authorized the controlled use of speculative hypotheses within science, emphasizing the importance of analogical reasoning for suggesting probable hypotheses. In this connection, Locke's work most clearly encouraged the development of a relative plurality of cognitive strategies to enrich the repertoire of rationalist, purely empiricist, and philosophically necessary causal explanatory strategies that dominated early modern approaches to science.

Newtonian Natural Philosophy as a Validation of Locke's Epistemology

In 1672, when he was 30 years old, Isaac Newton submitted his first scientific paper, "A New Theory about Light and Colours," to the Royal Society of London. His talent had been recognized earlier by Isaac Barrow, Lucasian professor of mathematics at Cambridge and the young Newton's most important scientific teacher. When Barrow resigned his professorship to accept a church appointment in London in 1669, he arranged for his student to assume his professorship. Indeed, after only two years as an undergraduate at Cambridge during 1665–66, Newton undertook a brilliant series of studies that formed the basis for his three most widely admired scientific accomplishments. Working on his own and with virtually no scientific contacts except through Barrow, he had discovered the binomial theorem and invented both the differential and integral calculus (independently of Leibniz, and using his own "fluxional" notation); he had initiated his optical studies and had already theorized that white light was composed of a mixture of all other colors; and he had discovered that a single law could account for the motions of the planets about the sun, the moon about the earth, and the fall of ordinary bodies near the surface of the earth. This last discovery he would eventually formulate as the universal law of gravity. It took nearly 40 years for Newton to work out the complete details of the optical, gravitational, and mathematical theories based on his youthful insights, but by late in 1666, Newton, though virtually unknown, was already well on his way to becoming the most celebrated scientist of all time.

Newton's optical paper of 1672 was not well received, and the dispute between Newton and his critics is worth exploring because it illuminates their different attitudes toward hypotheses and the nature of scientific knowledge in an extremely simple case.

The centerpiece of Newton's first paper is a set of experiments in which a narrow beam of sunlight was allowed to fall on a prism, creating a spectrum, or rainbow-hued pattern of illumination, on a wall on the side of the prism opposite the incoming beam. Similar experiments had been done frequently since the late Middle Ages, but what distinguishes Newton's approach is the way in which he chooses to follow up the initial production of the spectrum. Newton focuses attention on the empirical fact that the spectrum is produced because the rays of some colors emerging from the prism are bent farther from their initial path than those of other colors. Red rays are deflected least, orange slightly more, and so on, down to violet rays which are bent the most.

Speculating about the trajectory of the rays after they had emerged from the prism Newton writes, "I began to suspect whether the rays, after their trajection through the prism did not move in curved lines, and according to their more or less curvity, tend toward different parts of the wall. And it increased my suspicion when I remembered that I had often seen a tennis ball, struck by an oblique racket, describe such a curved line."[6] Newton clearly hypothesizes that rays of light might be composed of globular bodies, analogous to tennis balls. If such bodies somehow obtain a rotation in passing through a prism, they should move in curved paths like their analogues, with the more rapidly rotating bodies curving more. To test this hypothesis, Newton changed the distance between the prism and wall, discovering that the spread of the colored image was proportional to the distance from the prism and thus that there was no differential curvature to distinguish the more from the less bent rays. This result suggested to Newton not a new hypothesis, but a new set of experiments through which he was able to demonstrate that once they had been refracted by the prism, different rays moved in straight lines, that the spectrum was created because different colors have different "refrangibilities" (indicies of refraction), and that the index of refraction of each color was constant. From these experiments he further concluded that "Light itself is a *Heterogeneous mixture of differently refrangible Rays*" (*NTLC*, 51) and that whiteness is produced by "a confused aggregate of rays induced with all sorts of colors as they are promiscuously darted from the various parts of luminous bodies."

Finally, near the end of his paper, Newton deduced a critical conclusion about the nature of light and offered a crucial methodological comment:

> These things being so, it can be no longer disputed whether there be colors in the dark [there cannot be], nor whether they be the qualities of the objects we see [they are not], no nor perhaps whether light be a body [it must be]. For, since colors are the qualities of light, having its rays for their entire and immediate subject, how can we think those rays qualities also, unless one quality may be the subject of and sustain another, which, in effect is to call it a substance. . . . But to determine more absolutely what [kind of substance] light is, after what manner refracted, and by what modes or actions it produces in our minds the phantasms of colors, is not so easy. *And I shall not mingle conjectures with certainties.* (*NTLC*, 57. Emphasis mine.)

In many ways this paper might have been a model for Locke's discussion of appropriate scientific procedures. First, Newton began with an experiment. Based on the results of this experiment (the bending of light rays), he proposed a probable hypothesis grounded in an analogy (the tennis ball analogy) to suggest a new experiment. But when the results of that experiment were inconsistent with the expectations produced by the hypothesis, he abandoned it. In the remainder of the paper, Newton concentrated on describing the results of subsequent experiments and inferring aspects of the character of light directly from those experiments. Finally, though he felt confident in inferring that light was some kind of substance from his experimental results, he refused to claim more knowledge than his experiments warranted, admitting that he could not discover precisely how light was refracted or how it produces the ideas of colors in our minds.

When Hooke accused him of supposing that light was composed of globular bodies and insisted that other hypotheses could equally account for his experimental results, Newton angrily responded that his doctrine of light was not dependent on any hypothesis at all. And in response to a more generally favorable, but still guarded, review by the Frenchman F. Pardies, Newton clarified his views about the nature of his scientific claims and the appropriate role of hypotheses in the natural sciences. First, he insisted that those claims regarding light and colors which constituted his scientific doctrine "consist only in the observation and description of certain properties of light, without regarding any hypothesis, by which those properties might be explained." Then he went on to write, "the best and safest method of philosophizing seems to be first to enquire diligently into the properties of things, and establishing these properties by experiments, then to proceed more slowly to hypotheses for the explanation of them. For hypotheses should be *subservient only* in explaining the properties of things, but not assumed in determining them; unless so far as they may furnish experiments. For if the possibility of hypotheses is to be the test of the truth and reality of things, I see not how certainty can be obtained in any science."[7] Two simultaneous claims are being made here. First, hypotheses are useful only for their heuristic value; and second, the description of the properties of things constitutes adequate and reliable scientific knowledge even in the absence of any explanation for why those properties should be what they are determined to be.

Newton insisted that the major consequences presented in his *Opticks* of 1704 were also of independent hypothesis, but he concluded the first edition of the *Opticks* with a series of 16 "Queries" that suggested topics other scholars might want to investigate. In the 1706 Latin edition, this list was extended to 23, and in the third edition of 1717, it was extended to 31.

These queries, some of which ran to several pages in length, contained literally dozens of suggestive hypotheses about the causes of a wide range of natural phenomena, and their exploration virtually made the careers of innumerable eighteenth-century natural philosophers and chemists. Indeed, I. B. Cohen has compellingly argued that the Queries to the *Opticks* had a greater impact on Enlightenment experimental philosophy than the more intimidating and prestigious *Principia*.[8] Not only did the existence of the Queries suggest specific research projects, they also served more generally to authorize the widespread use of suggestive hypotheses throughout the sciences, including the social sciences—always subject to the requirement that they be based on significant analogies and subject to tests of coherence and to revision or abandonment in the face of negative evidence.

Newton's *Principia* and It's Emphasis on Universality and Simplicity

If the Queries to Newton's *Opticks* encouraged the exploration of heuristic hypotheses in scientific investigations during the Enlightenment, his *Principia* and its many popularizations focused attention on at least three other features of science. One of these, the integration of quantification and mathematical reasoning into *experimental* philosophy, was relatively unimportant for the social sciences, except in political economy where it simply reinforced previously existing tendencies. The other two—the demand that scientific theories be valued more highly as they incorporated more phenomena within their explanatory scope, and the demand that scientific theories be valued more highly as their explanatory schemes were more simple—had a much greater impact within the social sciences, especially among those who hoped to ground all social phenomena in an understanding of human psychology.

Newton's *Principia*, for all of its mathematical sophistication, tight logical structure, and secure empirical foundations, would have had relatively little impact, I suspect, except for the fact that it managed to solve a host of problems in astronomy, mechanics, and general physics through the establishment of one extremely simple and universal law. After hundreds of pages of mathematical proofs and appeals to numerous phenomena, in proposition 7 of book 3 of the *Principia*, Newton concluded his demonstration that every pair of bodies in the universe attract one another with a force that is proportioned to their masses and inversely proportional to the square of the distance separating them. Then he proceeded to demonstrate that this one simple law accounted for all celestial motions and natural motions of bodies on the earth.

This was a breathtaking and triumphant accomplishment. It led

D'Alembert to write that "the true system of the world has been recognized." It led Alexander Pope to write an epitaph to place on Newton's tomb in Westminster Abbey:

> Nature and nature's laws lay hid in night:
> God said, "Let Newton Be" and all was light.

And it led numerous investigators, including Etienne Condillac, Jean-Antoine-Nicolas Caritat de Condorcet, and even Adam Smith, to insist that there must be one or a few simple keys to understanding the nature of all human interactions.

When they appealed to the Newtonian precedent for such a search, most eighteenth-century authors directly cited or paraphrased a few sentences from the beginning of the third book of the *Principia*, where Newton set out what he called the "Rules of Reasoning in Philosophy." Because of their importance, I conclude this chapter with the first three of Newton's four rules, for these rules contain his explicit injunctions to seek simplicity and universality:

> Rule I. We are to admit no more causes of natural things than such as are both true and sufficient to explain their appearances. To this purpose the philosophers say that nature does nothing in vain, and more is in vain when less will serve; for nature is pleased with *simplicity*, and affects not the pomp of superfluous causes.
>
> Rule II. Therefore to the same natural effects we must, as far as possible, assign the same causes. . . .
>
> Rule III. The qualities of bodies which admit neither intension nor remission of degrees, and which are found to belong to all bodies within the reach of our experiments, are to be esteemed the *universal* qualities of all bodies whatsoever. (*Principia*, 397–98. Emphasis mine.)

8

Associationist and Sensationalist
Psychologies, Political Radicalism,
and Utilitarianism, 1700–1790

In the fourth edition of his *Essay Concerning Human Understanding*
(1700), John Locke added a new chapter, "Of the Association of
Ideas," in order to address an issue which he had initially ignored,
but which had played an important role in the psychological
speculations of both Hobbes and Spinoza. For both of the earlier
thinkers knowledge is constructed by creating linkages between
ideas through reason. But there is a second, almost accidental, way
in which ideas come to be connected with one another through what
Spinoza simply identified as "association." When two different ideas
are produced in our minds simultaneously or in an unbroken
sequence simply because our initial sensations of them are simultaneous or sequential, then when one of those ideas is recalled to the
mind, the other reappears as well.[1] For Spinoza, such accidental
connections of ideas could interfere with our attempts to construct
rational trains of thought (see chapter 5), and they thus constituted
a problem to be acknowledged and confronted.

In approaching the association of ideas, Locke focuses on two
considerations. First, he emphasizes the notion that chance associations are not very strong until they have been reinforced by
repetition; once associations have been made by *chance*, they must be

strengthened by *custom* (*Essay*, 2: 23: 6). Second, like Spinoza, Locke saw the association of ideas as a primarily negative phenomenon which was so apt "to set us awry in our actions, as well moral as natural" that we should constantly be on guard against its effects. Indeed, he argued that nothing was more misleading and dangerous in our mental operations than association (*Essay*, 2: 33: 9). He therefore exhorted those in charge of children "diligently to watch, and carefully to prevent the undue connexion of ideas in the minds of young people. [For] this is the time most susceptible of lasting impressions" (*Essay*, 2: 33: 8).

For virtually all of the psychological moralists of the eighteenth century, Locke's sense of the importance of the association of ideas and his linkage of that importance to childhood education became central themes. But his almost uniformly negative attitude toward associations was transformed into a predominantly positive view in Britain by the two most important figures to attempt to develop scientific psychological foundations for human society and politics, David Hume and David Hartley.

Two major factors link the basic approaches of Hume and Hartley to human nature and morality. First, each was led to his revaluation of the association of ideas by the Reverend John Gay's "Dissertation Concerning the Fundamental Principles of Virtue or Morality" which had been published as an introduction to William King's *De Origine Mali* (On the origin of evil) in 1731. In this short essay, Gay sought to appropriate Hobbesian notions of good and evil for religious purposes. In doing so, he insisted that "private happiness is the proper and ultimate end of all of our actions," and that happiness, or pleasure, is linked to certain objects or actions solely through association. It is the association of certain acts with pleasure and others with pain that makes those acts virtuous or vicious. Consequently, a particular set of associations becomes the very foundation of all morality.[2] Neither Hume nor Hartley accepted Gay's claims blindly; instead, each used them as a stimulus to investigate more extensively the roles of the association of ideas both for human knowledge and for human action.

Second, when Hume and Hartley approached the question of how the association of ideas operates to motivate and inform human actions, each self-consciously modeled his investigation on Newtonian natural philosophy. Hume particularly admired the cautious experimental and non-hypothetical approach of Newton's *Principia*;

Hartley favored the analogical method of suggesting heuristic hypotheses in Newton's Queries to the *Opticks*.

David Hume's Associationist Psychology

Applying Newtonian methods and expectations in his first major work, *A Treatise of Human Nature: Being an Attempt to Introduce the Experimental Method of Reasoning into Moral Subjects* of 1739, Hume insisted on seeking "those few simple principles" upon which human nature, and thus all human interactions, are founded.[3]

Of the simple principles that Hume arrives at in the course of the *Treatise*, he argues that the association of ideas is the most important, for while we cannot explain how or why the mind produces "a secret tie or union among particular ideas," it is an empirical fact that it does so. Moreover, such associations constitute the true and sufficient causes for a huge range of human thoughts, passions, and actions. In fact, insofar as our knowledge and passions are concerned, "these are the *only* links that bind the parts of the universe together or connect us with any person or object exterior to ourselves" (*Abstract*, 198).

For the history of the social sciences what Hume had to say about our knowledge is far less important than what he had to say about our passions, because the major implication of his analysis was that morality and social institutions have relatively little to do with rationality and understanding and a great deal to do with our passions or emotions. In connection with this claim, Hume and his associationist colleagues in England turned psychologically grounded social theories in a vastly different direction from that taken by Hobbes and Spinoza.

For the earlier thinkers, civil society was grounded in a rational analysis of the problems of self-defense and intellectual freedom. For the group of social theorists following from John Gay and Francis Hutcheson (whose 1725 *An Inquiry into the Original of our Ideas of Beauty and Virtue* and 1728 *An Essay on the Nature and Conduct of the Passions and Affections and Illustrations of Moral Sense* also provided major stimuli for Hume and Hartley), who reached their maturity with Hume and Hartley, civil society emerged instead out of the non-cognitive, passionate character of human beings. At bottom, we associate with others and regulate our behavior not primarily because we calculate some benefit, but quite literally because it makes us feel good.

For Hume and most of his colleagues, the question of why certain kinds of actions make us feel good and others make us feel bad is ultimately unanswerable. The best we can do is to study empirically what objects, events, and actions are associated with what kinds of pleasures and pains in order to guide us in shaping institutions to increase the first and diminish the second. Social structures and policies must then be judged in terms of their "utility" in producing happiness and reducing pain.

In order to judge the utility of social institutions, Hume argues that we must take into account a whole range of human passions, not just a need for self-preservation or even for self-preservation and self-expression. He shows that humans are moved by intense direct passions like grief, joy, hope, fear, despondency, and security; by intense indirect passions, including pride, humility, ambition, vanity, love, hatred, envy, pity, malice, and generosity; and by such calmer passions as an appreciation of beauty and distaste for deformity.[4] Every one of these passions must be considered in judging the overall goodness or badness of actions and social structures. Because reason has so little to contribute on these matters, we must fall back on habits and customs as our most reliable guide.

In its distrust of reason and reliance on habit and custom, Hume's psychology had a basically conservative thrust which was consistent with his own Tory political leanings. But Hume was almost alone among psychologically grounded social theorists in his conservatism, and his psychology contained within it a suggestion of how others would soon shape associationist doctrines into the foundation for very liberal and even radical ideologies.

Hume's distinction between direct and indirect passions underlies this move, for it suggests a distinction between what we might call immediate, instinctual, or natural responses to things, which cannot be changed no matter how hard we might try, and responses that are *learned* through habit and custom. For example, in trying to understand the origins of civil society, Hume argues that people could initially have had no realization of the many benefits in terms of security and economic well-being that they might gain from living in mutually dependent large groups. But there was a natural motive for bonding grounded in sexual attraction. And sexual attraction initiated a process which ultimately led to a more generalized but artificial social attraction:

. . . there is conjoined to those necessities whose remedies are remote and obscure, another necessity, which having a present and most obvious remedy, may be justly regarded as the first and original principle of human society. This necessity is no other than the *natural* appetite between the sexes, which unites them together, and preserves their union, till a new tie takes place in their concern for their mutual offspring. This new concern becomes also a principle of union betwixt the parents and offspring, and forms a more numerous society; where the parents govern by advantage of their superior strength and wisdom, and at the same time are restrained in their exercise of that authority by that *natural* affection which they bear their children. In a little time, *custom and habit*, operating on the tender minds of children, make them sensible of the advantages they may reap from society, as well as fashions them by degrees for it, by rubbing off those rough corners and untoward affections, which prevent their coalition. (*Treatise*, 2: 1: 5)

Hume does not make much of the distinction between such primary or natural passions as those between the sexes and between parents and offspring and the learned or artificial passions. But for associationists such as Hartley, who did not share Hume's extreme distrust of reason, the possibility of manipulating artificial associations offered a hope that one could produce a society vastly better able to increase human happiness than any which had come into existence through undirected historical processes.

Hartley, Priestley, and English Radicalism

The most widely read and admired of eighteenth-century British psychological moralists was unquestionably David Hartley, whose *Observations on Man, His Frame, His Duty, and His Expectations*[5] appeared in 1749. Though Hartley's moderate religious views made him seem less threatening than the atheistic Hume, he nonetheless produced a psychologically grounded morality which had much more radical political and economic implications. In fact, Isaac Kramnick argues that Hartley's *Observations on Man* became a kind of "holy book" for radical reformers during the late eighteenth century.[6] Joseph Priestley, for example, who was eventually driven from Britain to America because of his support for the American and French Revolutions, wrote, "I think myself more indebted to this one treatise, than to all the books I ever read beside, the Scriptures excepted," and "Dr. Hartley has thrown more useful light upon the theory of the mind than Newton did upon the theory of the natural world."[7] The young and still radical Samuel Taylor Coleridge named his first son David Hartley Coleridge. And most of the other major political radical writers of late-eighteenth-century England, including James Mill, William Godwin, James Burgh, and David Williams, affirmed Priestley's judgments. The most important early-nineteenth-century English socialist, Robert Owen, was deeply dependent on Hartley's psychology, and as we shall see, Hartley's associationism even provided major underpinnings for the arguments of such early English feminists as Catherine Macaulay and Mary Wollstonecraft.

The basic difference between the goals of Hume's descriptive and ultimately conservative approach to associationist psychology and Hartley's more activist and interventionist approach was already clear in Hartley's early preliminary sketch, *Various Conjectures on the Perception, Motion, and Generation of Ideas* (1746). Here he argues that "the principle use of the doctrine of associations must be considered to be the *amendment* of ethics and morals." Once we understand the origins of our desires and aversions in associations, then we can discover our power to modify them and, what is most important, we can discover "the ways by which good motivations . . . may be fostered, the bad restrained, . . . and, what is particularly noteworthy, by what precepts the tender minds of children can be best formed for virtue and piety."[8] Thus Hartley entered into his discussions of human psychology from the perspective of a moral and social reformer.

Like Hume, Hartley draws his methodology from Isaac Newton. But unlike Hume, Hartley proposes to follow the hypothetical method suggested by the Queries to Newton's *Opticks*, because the complexity of mental phenomena make the more certain "proper" method of the *Principia* unworkable.

In order to explore the phenomena of association, he adopts the hypothesis (suggested in Queries 12, 23, and 24 to the fourth edition of Newton's *Opticks*) that vibrations of particles of a subtle ethereal fluid within the white medullary substance of the brain correspond to the presence of ideas in the mind, so that when the vibrations change in frequency, direction, place, or intensity, our ideas change in some related way. Following Locke and Newton, Hartley insisted that the hypothesis of vibrations was to be understood solely as a heuristic device to suggest relationships within the theory of associations, so the descriptive doctrine of associations which followed from exploring the hypothesis of vibrations would be true whether or not the hypothesis was adopted (*OOM*, 261).

Hartley suggests initially that when the amplitudes of medullary vibrations increase they give greater pleasure until they get so big that they produce a tear or a "solution of continuity" in the medullary substance (*OOM*, 23). This explains why pleasure and pain seem to be so closely connected with one another and why in many cases, as with heat and sound, increasing the intensity of an experience increases the pleasure up to a point, after which pain ensues. Furthermore, it accounts for the pain we feel when we are cut, producing a "solution of continuity" in some tissue.

Next, he suggests how the hypothesis of vibrations can explain associations in general and how associations of simple ideas can create complex ideas. Suppose that each experience leaves a feeble set of miniature vibrations in the brain, constituting a memory. Frequent repetition of the same experience will deposit identical vibrations, creating a stronger residual vibration. This is why we generally learn by repetition (*OOM*, 37–41). Two experiences which occur together frequently will leave vibrations which are strongly linked to one another, so if one of the two experiences is recalled, it will naturally bring back not only the memory of the one but also of the other that was initially attached to it (*OOM*, 41–46). Finally, it follows that complex sequences of ideas can be linked in this way in much the same way that words are composed of letters (*OOM*, 48). But in the case of the creation of complex ideas, the vibrations are not merely linked by placing them next to one another in the brain; they may be constructed by superimposing parts of two different vibrations at a single location.

It follows that complex ideas—which we call intellectual rather than sensory—are likely to produce greater pleasure than simpler ones, but with less chance that they might produce pain. Hartley reasons that while the compounding makes them bigger, the fact that they are more spread out in the brain also makes them less likely to have those sharp edges that would produce a solution of continuity. This fact explains the long moral tradition which advocates intellectual pleasures over mere bodily ones.

Most important for Hartley, if we can analyze how our complex affections and passions are produced, "we may learn how to cherish and improve the good ones, and root out such as are mischievous and immoral, and how to suit our manner of life, in some tolerable measure, to our intellectual and religious wants." Knowledge of associations thus becomes the foundation for a kind of moral engineering through which humans can be perfected. Through appropriate manipulation of associations Hartley even suggests that fallen humans might be returned to that "paradisiacal" state "in which pure pleasure alone would be perceived" (*OOM*, 53). When it is taken up by the socialist Robert Owen, this argument is extended to the claim that "any character, from the best to the worst, from the most ignorant to the most enlightened, may be given to any community, even to the world at large" by providing the appropriate experiences.[9]

Because Hartley believes that humans are what they are almost exclusively because of the experiences they have, he finds that all humans are inherently equal and that no individual or group of individuals deserves to be happier than any other. But it is clearly the case that there are at least some circumstances in which the pursuit of pleasure by one individual interferes with the pursuit of pleasure by some other individual. This is certainly true in connection with the pleasures of sense derived from the enjoyment of food, sex, and so on. It is also true of the closely associated enjoyment of money, for at least in the short run, "whatever riches one man obtains, another must lose" (*OOM*, 289). The pursuit of selfish, or "gross," self-interest is thus ultimately self-defeating, because it deprives others of happiness and turns them into enemies. "Gross self-interest, has a manifest tendency to deprive us of the pleasures of sympathy and to expose us to its pains. Rapaciousness extinguishes all sparks of good will and generosity, and begets endless resentments, jealousies, and envies. And indeed a great part of the contentions and mutual injuries we see in the world arise, because either one or both of the contending parties desire more than an equitable share of the means of happiness" (*OOM*, 492).

How, then, is the "greatest happiness and least misery" to be provided for an entire society (*OOM*, 504)? One implication of the above passage, later developed by continental associationists into a justification for socialism, is that happiness cannot be maximized except in a society in which economic resources are relatively evenly distributed. Hartley offers a more comprehensive argument that gives English associationism a more liberal twist, making it consistent with both his millenarianism and his medical background.

If people are not exposed to inappropriate (we might say pathological) experiences, they will naturally develop in such a way that their notions of self-interest become more "refined" through higher-order pleasures. People find a new source of pleasure, the approval and admiration of others, when they act out of sympathy with others and treat them with kindness rather than exploitively (*OOM*, 291). Gradually, Hartley argues, through associations we transcend even refined self-interest to discover that our greatest pleasures and those of the entire society are provided when we act through a purely selfless benevolence guided by what Hartley calls our moral sense. (*OOM*, 309–13). This sense (initially posited by Francis Hutcheson) allows us to judge which actions are truly beneficial for others and not merely valuable in producing self-satisfaction or the admiration which a reputation for charity might bring.

Given his assumption that a natural psychological development will lead people to interact with one another to produce a society in which the greatest happiness and least misery is present, Hartley, like Petty and the liberal political economists of the seventeenth century, argues that government interference in private and social life should be limited to the protection of private rights and the removal of impediments to natural developments. Dissenting ministers, like Priestley, found such doctrines particularly useful in opposing the imposition of a state religion in England. For much the same reason, although Hartley, Priestley, and almost all of their followers emphasized the critical importance of education, they bitterly opposed state involvement in education and promoted private educational schemes.

The Origins of French Sensationalist Psychology

Just as the mid eighteenth century saw important extensions of Lockean psychology in Britain, it saw parallel extensions in France, beginning with the works of Etienne Bonnot, abbé de Condillac. Beginning in 1746 with the publication of his *Essai sur l'origine des connaisances humaine (An Essay on the Origin of Human Knowledge)*, Condillac wrote a series of influential commentaries and corrections of Locke's doctrines in his *Traité des systèmes (Treatise of Systems)* in 1749, his *Traité de sensations (Treatise of Sensations)* of 1754, his *Traité des animaux* (Treatise of animals) of 1755, and his *La logique: ou les premiers développemens de l'art de penser* (*Logic, Or the First Developments of the Art of Thinking*) of 1782.

On many issues Condillac's development of Locke's theories of knowledge are either virtually indistinguishable from those of Hartley or differ in ways that had little or no social scientific importance. In connection with two particular issues, however, they deviated in ways that had a major bearing on the eighteenth-century development of the social sciences in France.

In his first work on the origins of human knowledge, Condillac offers a new grounding for the older Cartesian and mechanistic strategy of resolution and composition through a discussion of the mental processes of abstraction and composing and decomposing ideas. In later works, especially in *Logic*, he uses the single term *analysis* to signify the dual process of decomposing (resolving) and composing. "In distinguishing the mind's ideas," he argues, "we sometimes consider its [*sic*] most *essential* qualities divorced from their subject. This is known as *abstraction*. . . . This operation is absolutely necessary for limited minds who can consider only a few ideas at a time. . . ."[10]

The crucial point here was made much earlier by Descartes. Because we get confused by too much complexity in our experiences, when we want to understand them we must first break them apart and focus on their most salient features. This operation, which depends on our ability to abstract, we call decomposition. When it comes time to reintegrate the ideas which we have studied in isolation, Condillac offers the following advice: "To compose our ideas correctly, we should note which ones are simplest, and how and in what order they are connected with the remaining ones" (*PWC*, 464). Very soon we shall see how important this notion of abstraction and analysis was for the subsequent application of psychological methods to moral and political issues in France through the works of Claude Adrienne Helvetius and Marie-Antoine-Nicolas Caritat de Condorcet.

The second feature of Condillac's theory of knowledge which is of importance for our discussion is closely connected with his emphasis on abstraction and its role in the construction of *systems* of thought. Though Condillac's *Treatise of Systems* was largely an attack on the kind of metaphysical systems of thought preferred by Descartes, Spinoza, Hobbes, and others, Condillac tolerated hypothetical systems as long as they were properly used, and he argued that the best possible way of ordering knowledge was through systems, like that of Newton's *Principia*, grounded only in principles well established by experience (*PWC*, 1–3).

With respect to the character of all *systems*, which are nothing but "the arrangement of different parts of an art or science in an order in which they all lend each other support and in which the last ones are explained by the first ones," Condillac argues, following Newton, that "the fewer principles a system has, the more perfect it is. It is even desireable to reduce all principles to a single one" (*PWC*, 1). For this reason Condillac criticized Locke for positing *two* sources of knowledge, sensations and reflections, and he directed the whole of his *Treatise of Sensations* to demonstrating that all ideas can be traced to a single source, sensation (*PWC*, 159). Not only did this emphasis on simplicity in systems of thought play a significant role for Helvetius, Condorcet, and the so-called *Ideologues*, it also seems to have been a major source for Adam Smith's understanding of the drive for simplicity in scientific theorizing. Drawing from a mechanical analogy, Smith writes:

> Systems in many respects, resemble machines. A machine is a little system, created to perform, as well as to connect together, in reality, those different movements and effects which the artist has occasion for. A [philosophical] system is an imaginary machine invented to connect together in the fancy those different movements and effects which are already in reality performed. The machines that are first invented to perform any particular movement are always the most complex, and succeeding artists generally discover that, with fewer wheels, with fewer principles of motion than had originally been employed, the same effects may be more easily produced. The first [philosophical] systems, in the same manner, are always the most complex, . . . but it often happens, that one great connecting principle is afterwards found to be sufficient to bind together all the discordant phenomena that occur as a whole species of things.[11]

Both Condillac and Smith viewed Newton's system, grounded in the principle of gravitation, as the first great philosophical system of the modern world. Condillac saw his theory of ideas, grounded in sensation alone, and his theory of knowledge, grounded in the connection of ideas through signs alone, as two excellent examples of Newtonian simplicity in the social sciences. And Smith clearly understood his system of economics, grounded in the operation of the free market, as yet another example of a model philosophical system.

Not all French Enlightenment thinkers jumped on Condillac's bandwagon. Some, including Buffon and Diderot, saw Condillac as engaging in just the same kind of "spirit of system" that he himself criticized in Descartes, Spinoza, and others.[12] But virtually all of those who engaged in psychological theorizing began from Condillac's works and views.

Claude-Adrienne Helvetius and the Links Between Sensationalist Psychology and Socialism

Of all those who extended Condillac's sensationalist psychology into the domain of morality and politics, the most influential was undoubtedly Claude-Adrienne Helvetius. Judgments about Helvetius's intellectual sophistication and originality vary tremendously. Both Condorcet and Anne-Marie Turgot were disturbed by what they considered to be his "crude utilitarianism."[13] Ernst Cassirer calls his thought "weak and unoriginal" and argues that he followed some of Condillac's methodological ideas so rigidly and mechanically that Helvetius's works constitute a virtual "parody" of those of Condillac.[14] Yet Montesquieu, who disagreed with him on virtually every major issue, wrote, "I don't know if Helvetius is aware of his own superiority; but for me he is a man above all others."[15] In my own reading and in that of many socialist thinkers, including Karl Marx and G. V. Plekhanov,[16] Helvetius's two major works, *De l'esprit (On the Mind)* of 1758 and *De l'homme (Treatise on Man)* of 1774, stand among the most insightful and original as well as influential Enlightenment attempts at social-scientific understanding.

In 1758, at age 42, after a privileged and extremely dissolute early adulthood, Helvetius published his first work, *De l'esprit*, largely as a critical response to Montesquieu's *L'esprit des lois*. In part because it was more overtly anti-religious and critical of the government than any prior books which had sought official government approval, and in part because a 1757 assassination attempt on Louis XV's life had made the government unusually sensitive to works that might in any way be deemed disrespectful of authority, *De l'esprit* produced a violent response from the censorship apparatus. It was retroactively condemned along with a number of previously approved works by such authors as Voltaire, Diderot, and D'Alembert.

One consequence of the condemnation of *De l'esprit* was the initiation of a major split between Voltaire, Turgot, and other moderate philosophes, who still felt that an enlightened monarchy offered the greatest opportunities for implementing their reform ideas, and Helvetius, d'Holbach, Rousseau, and others, who were increasingly radicalized by what they felt was unjust government repression.[17] Thus, for example, while Helvetius had condemned despotic governments in the first work, he took pains to argue that the French government was not despotic. But when *De l'homme* appeared (clandestinely) in 1774 after Helvetius's death, it not only argued that France "has at length submitted to the yoke of despotism," but also that France's ills were incurable by legal means. This was one of the first major explicit calls for a violent overthrow of the monarchy.[18]

In order to understand the direction taken by Helvetius's works we must begin by recognizing the deeply felt anti-clericalism which he shared with his colleagues Fontenelle, d'Holbach, and Voltaire, his Rousseau-like sympathy for the oppressed French peasantry, and his commitment to Condillac's understanding of proper scientific method.

Looking over the religious landscape of Europe, Helvetius sees no evidence of Christian love, but only carnage resulting from the attempts of clerical elites to impose their authority.[19] Looking over the economic map of France he sees a mass of people "more unhappy than the savage nations, which are held in such contempt by the civilized . . . [because] seven or eight millions of people languish in misery so that five or six thousand can riot in an opulence which renders them odious" (*DE*, 17–18).

In light of the widespread misery to be found in almost all times and places, Helvetius was appalled by Montesquieu's *L'esprit des lois*. For Montesquieu argued that a historical-empirical survey of how laws actually function in existing societies must be the first step in discovering how laws *should* function. He further argued that laws must be accommodated "to the religion of the inhabitants, their inclinations—their manners and their customs."[20] Helvetius fired off an angry letter to his personal friend, whom he now perceived as an intellectual traitor: "Our Aristocrats and our petty tyrants of all grades, if they understand you, cannot praise you too much, and this is the fault I have ever found with the principles of your works . . . *L'esprit des corps* assails us on all sides; it is a power erected at the expense of the great mass of society. It is by these hereditary usurpations that we are ruled" (*SL*, xxvii).

What was needed in approaching the problem of legislation was the analytic approach developed by Condillac and illustrated by the works of such scientists as Galileo. When Galileo approached the problem of falling bodies, he first analyzed the complex problem and isolated its most essential elements. Thus he began by calculating how bodies fall without regard to the resistance of surrounding fluids. Similarly, when students of mechanics analyze the effects of pulleys, they first consider motions without considering the friction in the bearings of the pulleys. Helvetius argues that precisely the same analytic approach must be taken when we approach such complex social issues as legislation. In the first instance, "we should . . . pay no regard to the *resistance* of prejudices [read religious beliefs], or the *friction* of contrary and personal interests, or to manners, laws, and customs already established."

To discover those laws "proper to render men as happy as possible and consequently to procure them all the amusements and pleasures compatible with the public welfare" (*TOM*, 2: 279), we must begin, like Hume, Hartley, and Condillac, with a basic understanding of humans and what produces their pleasures and pains. Only after we have discovered what the best laws grounded in human needs might be can we then turn to investigate "the means by which a people may be made to pass insensibly from the state of misery they suffer to the state of happiness which they might enjoy" (*TOM*, 2: 279).

Helvetius agrees with his associationist predecessors that passions govern all human behavior, but unlike Hartley, he cannot see any evidence that passions can be anything but self-oriented. "Social" passions like friendship and patriotism are ultimately grounded in our wish to be admired and obeyed. Helvetius insists that "all men tend only toward their happiness; that is a tendency from which they cannot be diverted; the attempt would be fruitless, and even the success dangerous" (*DE*, 124). Lacking Hartley's belief in a benevolent deity to arrange for a natural accommodation between the pleasure of a single individual and that of society at large, Helvetius insists that the general happiness or the public welfare (the aggregate happiness of all individuals in the society) will be maximized only when society is organized in such a way that people find it more pleasurable to act in ways that promote the general welfare than to act in ways that diminish it. The function of legislation is thus to establish rewards for appropriate behaviors and punishments for inappropriate ones, such that private interests are served only when a person acts to serve the public interest (*DE*, 289).

Through a series of long but very straightforward arguments Helvetius demonstrates that in the long run, the general happiness can be maximized only in a society in which there are no extremes of wealth, in which each family can meet its basic material needs by seven or eight hours of moderate labor in a day, in which all citizens are adequately educated, in which all adult inhabitants share in the management of public affairs, and in which no priesthood can impose a morality not based on public utility (*DE*, 15, 126, 146; *TOM*, 198, 434–35). Knowing what kind of a society must be sought in order to maximize happiness, we can then ask how things have come to be so far from the ideal and how the ideal might be implemented.

Since humans get pleasure from the friendship and admiration of others, and since people in the same families and the same occupations naturally associate with one another and share similar concerns, they soon come to realize that they are more admired and accepted within groups of their own kind than in mixed groups or in groups of people whose normal activities are quite different. In his usual acerbic way Helvetius writes, "There is scarcely a man so stupid, but if he pays a certain attention to the choice of company, may spend his life amidst a concert of praises, uttered by sincere admirers; while there is not a man of sense, who, if he promiscuously joins in different companies will not be . . . treated as as fool" (*DE*, 71). People's needs for approval are thus met primarily within private societies, or classes, which even develop their own languages grounded in common experience. As a consequence, people within the same class come to think the same as one another and differently from those in other groups. The interests shared within such groups even come to supersede individual interests in the gratification of needs for food, shelter, and sex as motivators for members, for the shared interests are constantly being affirmed by other members.

Helvetius focuses attention on three specific groups which have managed to gain sufficient power to be able to impose their ideas and aims on other groups and on society as a whole. These three groups are the priesthood, the wealthy, and the courtiers. Each of these groups has sought to serve its own interests by establishing laws to preserve and extend its privileges and powers in opposition to the common good. Moreover, they have colluded in keeping the bulk of humankind in ignorance, for they have been "very sensible that their power had no other foundation than the ignorance and weakness of mankind" (*DE*, 172). It follows that if reform is to be successful, it must depend on an unmasking of these groups' claims to be serving the public and on a demonstration that they have instead been "the most cruel enemies of human beings" (*DE*, 177).

In his first work, Helvetius viewed the clerical elite as the greatest threat to human happiness. But by the time he wrote the second, he had come to see the conflict between the wealthy and the "common citizens" as vastly more important. Furthermore, he had come to identify the interests of common men with those of the public as a whole because of their vast numerical superiority. Thus he argued that "there is no country where the order of the common citizens, always oppressed, and rarely oppressors do not love and esteem virtue. Their interest leads them to it." On the other hand, it has always been in the interests of the wealthy "to be unjust with impunity [and] . . . to stifle in the hearts of men every sentiment of equity" (*TOM*, 2: 88). The history of humankind is thus the history of a conflict between two classes, the rich and the poor, or the exploiters and the exploited, and it is always the case that the public interest is expressed by the exploited class. This argument would be taken over virtually unchanged by the socialist, Count Claude Henri de Rouvery de Saint-Simon, and through him by Karl Marx.

In connection with his discussion of what came to be called class conflict, Helvetius argued that there were some private societies "of an academical kind," whose principal goal was to detach themselves from powerful interests and to develop an appropriate language and method for the pursuit of disinterested social discourse (*DE*, 126). In fact, Jean D'Alembert had tried to argue in 1753 that the *Academie des Sciences* in Paris was just such a body in his *Essai sur la société des gens de lettres et des grands* (Essay on the relationship between academic societies and the powerful). Helvetius extended D'Alembert's discussion to claim that if ever there was to be an attempt to transform society peacefully through educating citizens to recognize and work for the public interest, the impetus would have to come from these disinterested scientific intellectuals (*TOM*, 2: 423–34). Saint-Simon incorporated the Helvetian claim that it would be through the guidance of the "have-nots" by the classless scientific intellectuals that the work of the French Revolution would ultimately be completed[21]; and this idea too became a central feature of early-nineteenth-century socialist thought.

Sensationalist and Associationist Psychology and Feminist Ideology

During 1790 and 1791, three of the most important founding documents of modern liberal feminism, Catherine Macaulay's *Letters on Education: With Observations on Religious and Metaphysical Subjects*, Condorcet's *Sur l'admission les femmes au droit de cité* (*On the Admission of Women to the Rights of Citizenship*), and Mary Wollstonecraft's *A Vindication of the Rights of Woman*, were written. Each of these appropriated the doctrines of sensationalist and associationist psychology in order to attack what was perceived as an intensifying movement to subordinate women to male authority and to deny them those rights which they should share with men as equally rational and sentient beings.

The Renaissance had seen the rise of a substantial feminist literature attacking traditional notions of women as naturally inferior to men and justifying women's education and their intellectual equality (sometimes their superiority).[22] Moreover, the mechanical philosophy of Descartes had undermined the traditional Aristotelian justification for believing in women's intellectual inferiority. During the mid seventeenth century, a whole spate of Cartesian defenses of women's equality appeared, insisting that males and females were identical in respect of their soul or intellect.[23] Moreover, especially in France, the tradition of the learned lady flourished, leading gradually to a major role for women *salonnieres* in Parisian intellectual life.

This movement never lacked opponents, but by the mid eighteenth century a major reaction was underway, spurred by a variety of male fears that the entire intellectual and social world was being disrupted by women's attempts to take on inappropriate roles and abandon their procreative, nurturing, and family responsibilities (*TMHNS*, 214–37). French economic thinkers, incorrectly believing that population was declining, decried the supposed tendency of learned women to neglect their children. With the help of medical men, they launched programs to promote breast-feeding and the virtues of motherhood and to discourage women's intellectual and professional ambitions. Perhaps most importantly, the immensely popular Jean Jacques Rousseau launched a bitter attack on the public pretensions of women, which he attributed to misguided "maxims of modern philosophy" that tended toward a "confounding of the sexes" (*TMHNS*, 220).

In book 5 of *Emile, or On Education* (1762) Rousseau prefaced his discussion of the education of women with a powerful new doctrine of the relationship between the sexes which provided the most widely accepted grounds for the anti-feminist mood. According to Rousseau, it is not necessarily the case that one sex is superior or inferior to the other. They are simply not comparable, so each has its own form of perfection which complements that of the other. "In the union of the sexes each contributes equally to the common aim, but not in the same way. From this diversity arises the first assignable difference in the moral relations of the two sexes. One ought to be active and strong, the other passive and weak. One must necessarily will and be able; it suffices that the other put up little resistance. Once this principle is established, it follows that woman is made specially to please man."[24] It is also the case that the proper purposes of women are to bear children and to limit all of their concerns to their households and their families. "This," insists Rousseau, "is the way of life that nature and reason prescribe for the fair sex" (*Emile*, 362, 366).

Every serious late-eighteenth-century attempt to rebut this reactionary sexual ideology was grounded in the reform-oriented tradition of associationist psychology, which insisted that all humans, male and female alike, were the same in so far as they were sensitive beings capable of reasoning and capable of experiencing pleasures and pains. It seemed to follow that they should be subject to exactly the same rules of law and justice and that they should enjoy identical rights. Any differences between males and females, except those directly related to childbirth and lactation, were thus seen as grounded in customary practices which were fundamentally unjust.

Catherine Macaulay stated these ideas with extreme clarity in her *Letters on Education*:

> It ought to be the first care of education to teach virtue on immutable principles, and to avoid that confusion which must arise from confounding the laws and customs of society with those obligations that are founded on correct principles of equity. . . . There can be but one rule of moral excellence for beings made of the same materials, organized

after the same manner, and subjected to similar laws of nature. . . . [It follows] that all of those vices and imperfections which have been generally regarded as inseparable from the female character, do not in any manner proceed from sexual causes, but are entirely the effects of situation and education.[25]

In the same way, Wollstonecraft insisted, "there can be but *one* rule of right" for all reasoning beings and that women therefore deserve to be treated as men's equals rather than their subordinates.[26] Similarly, Condorcet argued, "either no member of the human race has real rights, or else all have the same; he who votes against the rights of another, whatever his color, religion, or *sex*, thereby abjures his own."[27]

All of these writers were willing to acknowledge the greater physical strength of males—though Macaulay thought that even physical differences were at least partially a result of the greater freedom granted to boys to develop their bodies through play (*LOE*, 47)—and all were willing to admit the *present* intellectual and moral inferiority of most women; but all insisted that this was a product of misguided customs and that it was reversible through appropriate education.

Some modern authors, including Londa Schiebinger, have argued that the associationist feminists privileged masculine values in their arguments, unwittingly following Rousseau in ignoring the universally positive aspects of some traditionally feminine virtues, including their ability in nurturing and their relatively non-aggressive character. To some extent this complaint is undoubtedly legitimate, but Macaulay, in particular, argued that men could and should be reeducated to be more caring parents to their children (*LOE*, 10–11). In this sense, she was inclined to see gender issues more symmetrically than most early liberal feminists.

Cesare Beccaria, Jeremy Bentham, and Utilitarianism

On the Continent outside of France, the earliest and most important application of Helvetian ideas was Cesare Beccaria's *Dei Delitti e della Pene* (*On Crimes and Punishments*), published in 1764. In this work, which was central to penal reform throughout Europe, Beccaria followed Helvetius in arguing that lawmaking has almost everywhere been the preserve of those who have every interest in opposing laws that promote universal justice.[28]

Starting from the pure utilitarian and associationist position, Beccaria advocated the elimination of torture in trials, the abolition of the death penalty, the limitation of judicial latitude in interpreting law and assigning punishments, the simplification and publication of laws, the right to cross-examine witnesses, and the allocation of punishments proportional to the seriousness of offenses and adjusted to account for mitigating circumstances. Most of these reforms, with the exception of the elimination of capital punishment, were gradually incorporated into European and American legal codes during the following century; but only after they had been adopted and explicated by Jeremy Bentham and his followers.

The most important and extensive application of associationist doctrines to political purposes occurred through Utilitarianism, a movement initiated by Jeremy Bentham and ably promoted by such disciples as James Mill in England and Etienne Dumont in France. As a popular political movement, Utilitarianism was instrumental in numerous nineteenth-century reforms. It provided the major impetus for the Great Reform Bill of 1832, which dramatically extended voting rights in England, and self-styled Utilitarians were responsible for virtually all of the public health legislation and the reforms of prisons, court procedures, and criminal law during the first half of the nineteenth century in Britain.

Although Utilitarianism did not become an effective public force until the second decade of the nineteenth century, its major doctrines had all been laid out by Bentham before 1790. Bentham incorporated a number of ideas from continental thinkers, especially from Helvetius and Beccaria. Indeed, he admired Helvetius so much he argued that "what Bacon was to the physical world, Helvetius was to the moral."[29] His basic orientation, however, came from reading Hume's *Treatise of Human Nature* in the early 1760s when he was a 14- or 15-year-old student at Oxford and from his subsequent study of Priestley's abridgement of Hartley's theories. From Hume, Bentham drew his notion that all moral science "is an attempt to extend the experimental method of reasoning from the physical branch to the moral" (*EW*, 101) as well as his insistence that every action should be judged by its impact on the public utility. From Hartley, he drew a peculiar privatistic orientation, an insistence that virtually all public services should be privately delivered and that the government should only step in to regulate private activities to make sure that they do not violate public interests. Thus Utilitarianism generally encouraged private education, private hospitals, private insane asylums, and even private prisons. All were to be monitored by parliamentary commissions, whose function was to protect the public by recommending regulatory legislation when absolutely necessary. In their individualist emphases Utilitarianism and liberal political economy reinforced one another, amplifying the authority that each might have been able to exercise independently, though in its advocacy of regulation Utilitarianism challenged the laissez-faire bias of liberal political economy.

Bentham continued to refine his ideas throughout a long career, but like Hume, he expressed his basic ideas very clearly in his earliest major work, *An Introduction to the Principles of Morals and Legislation*, which was completed by 1780 though not published until 1789. Starting from the common notion that humans seek pleasure and avoid pain, Bentham begins his modification of these notions by asking how we can measure, or quantify, pleasures and pains so as to compare one with another as effective motivators. Since we are interested in anticipated pleasures and pains, rather than past ones, Bentham argues that there are six different measures which act to make an anticipated pleasure or pain more or less effective as a determinant of behavior. First is its simple intensity, which is easily understood even if not very easily quantified. Second is its duration. Pains or pleasures which we expect to last longer will operate more powerfully than those which we expect to be brief when they are of the same intensity. Third is their certainty or uncertainty. Especially in connection with criminal acts, if one is certain of being punished, a given pain will have greater force in tending to discourage the act than if one is relatively certain of escaping capture and punishment. Fourth is the "propinquity or remoteness" of the anticipated pleasure or pain. If we can expect immediate reward or punishment for an act, that reward or punishment is a more effective motivator.

The fifth and sixth measures are slightly different in that they are more strictly related to the act being considered than to the quality of any particular pleasure or pain associated with it. Fifth is what Bentham calls "fecundity," or the likelihood that the act will be followed by others which produce more pleasures or pains of the same kind, and sixth is the "purity" of the act, or the assurance that it will *not* lead to others which will produce the opposite experiences of pain or pleasure. Finally, in order to understand the measure of pleasure or pain connected with any act for an entire community, we must consider its *extent*, or the number of persons affected.[30]

When we evaluate any act in terms of its goodness or badness for some particular individual, we must take the first six factors into account; then we must do the following: "Sum up all the values of all the *pleasures* on the one side, and those of all the pains on the other. The balance, if it be on the side of pleasure, will give the *good* tendency of the act upon the whole, with respect to the interests of the *individual* person; if on the side of pain, the *bad* tendency of it upon the whole" (*PML*, 31). And when we want to evaluate the act in terms of its goodness or badness for a community, we must repeat the calculation for each individual, sum up all of the good tendencies and bad tendencies, and find the difference in order to determine whether it is good or evil on balance.

Bentham is perfectly well aware that there are immense problems with carrying out this calculation in any particular case and that humans rarely even begin to approximate such an analysis in their ordinary actions. "It may, however, always be kept in view," he argues, "and as near as the process actually pursued on these occasions approaches to it, so near will such process approach to the character of an exact one" (*PML*, 31). In a very important sense, every attempt to undertake a cost-benefit analysis in modern public choice economics is an attempt to approximate just such a Benthamite calculation.

The problem facing governments, whose function is to promote the happiness of an entire community, is to get individuals to act in ways that increase overall happiness and not just their own. At this point, Bentham draws heavily from Helvetius. Though he admits with Hartley that there are some informal "sanctions," such as public approval and religious beliefs, that attach special pleasures to actions which are good for the entire community and pains to those which are evil, he is convinced that they are frequently inadequate and that governments are thus instituted to create public sanctions through laws that reward contributions to the general happiness and punish actions which detract from it (*PML*, 70).

9

Political Economy and the Consolidation of Economic Liberalism, 1695–1775

Throughout the seventeenth century, French economic policy under the ministries of Cardinal Richelieu (1624–42), Cardinal Mazarin (1642–61), and Jean-Baptiste Colbert (1661–83) was aimed at increasing the power and prestige of France and its centralized monarchy.[1] This policy of aggrandizement, which sought to make the French monarchy the greatest in Europe, to undermine the political power of the traditional nobility, and to thwart Habsburg ambitions throughout Europe and the New World, was extremely costly. Under Louis XIV the French court spent profligately on spectacular architectural and landscaping projects and on drama, dance, opera, and other forms of spectacle and entertainment. Even more costly were the incessant anti-Habsburg wars of the late seventeenth century, including the Dutch War (1672–79) and the War of the League of Augsburg (1689–1707).

In an attempt to build French economic strength to support a system of taxes with some chance of yielding enough income to meet the huge state expenses, Colbert, in particular, followed a set of policies which have often been labeled mercantilist, though they had no systematic theoretical expression. Colbert understood international trade as a zero-sum game, a competition among nations in which the goal of each player was to create a favorable balance of trade such that there was a constant net inflow of specie. For this reason he sought to prohibit the export of silver and gold and the import of manufactured goods. He also sought to keep wages low in order to keep the price of exported manufactured goods down.

At the same time, he attempted to increase population and productivity. In order to encourage population growth he regulated food prices and prohibited the export of grain; in order to encourage productivity, he instituted a detailed regulation of all industry by the central government, prescribing in minute detail what processes of production should be used and setting standards of quality to be met. The aim of such regulations was to ensure that the most efficient methods of production might be used and quality kept high in order to guarantee the acceptability of goods in luxury markets. The result, however, was almost certainly to stultify innovation and discourage entrepreneurial activity.

Whether an intelligent application of Colbert's policies could have succeeded in improving the French economy even in the absence of increasing court and military expenditures is questionable, but they were really never given a chance. The need for ever more cash to meet current expenditures led to a series of emergency fiscal measures that drove France into a cycle of increasingly deep depressions. By the first decade of the eighteenth century, it was estimated that real national income had been reduced to about half of what it had been in 1660. Moreover, the failure of even the most stringent attempts to impose and collect taxes had led the monarchy into extensive borrowing. By 1707, debt service alone accounted for 50 percent of expenditures, and ordinary tax revenues were meeting less than 50 percent of annual expenditures.[2]

Most taxes were extremely retrogressive, and the property of the nobility and the church was exempted from many. In addition, grain prices were kept at artificially low levels. As a consequence, the heavy tax burdens imposed upon non-noble agricultural producers could not be passed on to consumers, so farmers were often left with too little money at the end of one agricultural cycle to purchase seed or materials to initiate the next. Farmers went bankrupt, and in some regions they plowed their vines under in order to avoid paying taxes on resources that were not producing income. Underproduction then sent prices up. But the consequent prosperity was always short-lived as new taxes were imposed on the increased income, pushing farmers into a new cycle of impoverishment.

"*La misere*" spread throughout rural France, but the situation was almost as bad in urban areas. In Auvergne, for example, paper making declined during the last three decades of the seventeenth century to half its earlier output. In Touraine the 8,000 looms for weaving silk cloth which had been operating in 1640 were reduced to 1,000 at the beginning of the eighteenth century, in part because of the reduced demand for silk resulting from the cheaper fine cottons and linens being produced elsewhere. At Rouen, one of the wealthier regions in France, the consequence of the general economic downturn was that by 1700, only 50,000 out of a population of 700,000 were getting enough to eat (*Boisguilbert*, 8).

It was largely in response to the French economic crisis of the late seventeenth century that the center of innovative and important writing on political economy moved from England to France, where the most significant early author was a lawyer, farmer, minor noble, and local civil servant in the city of Rouen, Pierre le Pesant de Boisguilbert.

Pierre Boisguilbert and the New French Political Economy

Boisguilbert wrote four major works, *La detail de la France: la cause de la diminution des ses biens, et la facultie du remede* (The ruin of France: the cause of the diminution of its well-being, and the ways to remedy it) (1695), *Traité des grains* (A treatise on grains) (1700), *Factum de la France, ou Moyens tres-faciles de faire recevoir au Roy quartre vingts millions* (A brief for France, or an easy way for the king to receive eighty million [Livres]) (1702), and *Dissertation sur la nature des richesses, de l'argent et des tributs* (Dissertation on the nature of wealth, money, and taxes) (1704). All of these works were notable for their complex and obscure style, which turned away all but the most dedicated readers. But in them and in an almost endless series of letters written to the chief financial officers of France between 1690 and his death in 1714, Boisguilbert set French political economy on a path which changed only slowly and incrementally throughout the century.

Boisguilbert's approach to economic issues pulled together several strands of earlier social-scientific thought. For its foundation, he adopted Becher's emphasis on consumption, his absolutist and paternalist political assumptions, his insistence that the wealth of the king depended most fundamentally on that of his subjects, and his concern for the interdependence of the welfare of different groups within the economic community. But on this foundation he built a structure that looked very different. First, he added a historical dimension drawn from the French school of historical jurisprudence. Second, he incorporated a number of important notions from William Petty, especially his emphasis on the role of circulation in moderating the need for money.

From the Petty school he also adopted Charles Davenant's analysis of how a free international market in grain would establish a natural price. This was particularly important because Boisguilbert offered a new emphasis on the uniquely important role of agriculture in the economy which modified the cameralist focus on commerce. Finally, in order to account for the role of the market as an economic regulator, he adopted an understanding of the relationship between private economic motives and public interests drawn from the Jansenist moralist Pierre Nicole and the legal scholar Jean Domat. Comparing himself to Copernicus, Galileo, and Columbus (*Boisguilbert*, 28), Boisguilbert combined all of these elements to develop a systematic explanation of the workings of the economy that offered a compelling account of the causes of the disastrous state of the French economy at the beginning of the eighteenth century.

Like the cameralists, Boisguilbert ultimately addresses all of his economic discussions to the problem of supporting an absolutist state and argues that the wealth of the state rests on the wealth of its subjects. The monarch, according to Boisguilbert, has a right to extract as much from his subjects as he can get away with, subject only to the constraint that his taxes "give no blow to those two mammae of every republic, agriculture and commerce" (*Boisguilbert*, 160).

But in order to understand how to keep taxes from destroying agriculture and commerce, one must have an understanding of the working of the economy; especially the complex interdependence of different elements and the dependence of all on consumption. Like Becher, Boisguilbert sometimes appeals to the notion of a body politic to justify his emphasis on interdependence. But unlike his predecessors, he follows this image specifically to suggest that some elements of the economy are more sensitive than others and might need to be more protected. Thus he argues:

> . . . the body of the State is like a human body, of which all
> the parts and all the members must act together to maintain
> life, in view of the fact that the affliction of one part quickly
> affects the rest of it, and causes the death of the individual.
> The parts not being of equal strength and vigor, it is this
> interdependence of the whole which causes the most robust
> to expose themselves, and even to present themselves to
> receive the blows that would be carried to the weakest and
> most delicate parts, which cannot stand the least attack.

In particular, Boisguilbert attempts to show that since the ordinary
workers and laborers constitute the weakest element in the state, the
wealthy should be more willing to support the economic demands of
the state in order to protect the economic health of the whole
(*Boisguilbert*, 177–78).

Following William Petty, Boisguilbert argues that where money is
used as a medium of exchange, it must do more to increase
prosperity where its circulation is more rapid. This fact had extremely important policy implications; for it is generally true that
money moves much more rapidly through the hands of the poor
than through those of the rich:

> An ecu with a poor man, or a very small merchant, has a
> hundred times more effect in creating revenue than it does
> with a rich man, on account of the continual and daily
> turnover which this modest sum undergoes with the former,
> which does not happen with respect to the rich, in whose
> coffers great sums remain idle for months and whole years,
> useless. . . . from this custody the king and the body of the
> state draw no benefit, and it constitutes so much theft from
> both. (*Boisguilbert*, 171)

Given this fact, taxes ought to be progressive rather than regres-
sive with the rich taxed at higher rates than the poor; for money
taken from the rich will have little impact on consumption, while
money taken from the poor must inevitably have a major depressing
effect. If the rich could simply be taught this fundamental principle
they would welcome a shift in tax burdens, for they would realize
that they would soon be indemnified several times over. Unfortunately, blinded by narrow self-interest, the wealthy have compelled
the monarchy to establish taxes which fall almost exclusively on the

relatively poor, creating the general economic depression of France, and leading to a precipitous drop in state revenues.

Boisguilbert realized that it would be impossible to establish any kind of progressive tax structure in France in the short run, because any attempt to do so would be blocked by powerful special interests (*Boisguilbert*, 119–21). He proposed instead an initial series of more modest reforms on the grounds that "in a very great illness doctors do not at first give strong medicine for fear the indisposed person could not endure their violence" (*Boisguilbert*, 156). At the least, taxes should be certain rather than arbitrary, proportioned to the ability to pay, convenient to collect, payable directly to the government from the people, with no exclusions for the nobility or the clergy.

For all these reasons, Bosguilbert recommended that the complex network of hundreds of different kinds of taxes (mostly levied on property and certain commodities, and mostly contracted out to tax "farmers") be replaced by a single 10 percent "capitation" or income tax to be paid by every citizen (*Boisguilbert*, 157). Even if such a tax did not lead to an immediate increase in personal incomes, Boisguilbert calculated, it would increase state revenues by nearly 20 percent (*Boisguilbert*, 158). Within a few years, by stimulating spending among the ordinary people it would become large enough to pay off the state debts and allow for a reduction of rates.

Turning from tax policy to broader economic considerations, Boisguilbert argued that any sustainable productive activity must at least generate enough income to cover costs of production. In the case of some goods, the loss of producers might cause minimal problems, for workers could just shift their activities. But agriculture was a special case both because everyone has to eat and because the great majority of all Frenchmen were employed in agriculture, so a depression in agriculture automatically spread through the entire economy (*Boisguilbert*, 135). In addition, while most tax-induced problems were largely a result of a mere lack of concern for the public welfare, the special problems of farmers were also a consequence of well-intentioned but fundamentally misguided government policies (*Boisguilbert*, 133).

Before Colbert forbade grain exports, grain sales abroad had been a source of French national income and of national prosperity. But because of Colbert's export restrictions and price controls that tended to set ceilings on grain prices in bad years without providing price supports in good ones, grain prices fluctuated wildly, and in such a way that over the long run farmers could not cover their costs of production. Consequently, not only could farmers not purchase the products of others, driving consumption down, but famine was virtually assured.

To correct this situation Boisguilbert insisted on the institution of a free market in grains, for a free market would guarantee adequate profits to farmers. Boisguilbert explains how this principle works in his *Brief for France*:

> There is not a single worker who does not try with all his power to sell his merchandise for three times what it is worth, and to buy that of his neighbor for three times less than it costs to produce it. It is only at the point of a sword that justice is maintained in these encounters. It is the function of nature, of Providence, nevertheless to bring this about; . . . *in the commerce of life she has established such an order that, provided she is left alone, it is not at all in the power of the most powerful in buying the product of the most wretched, to prevent the sale from providing the subsistence of the latter.* It is that which maintains the prosperity, to which both are equally indebted for the subsistence proportioned to their estate. . . . I said providing that nature is left alone, that is, that she is given her liberty, and that one mix in this commerce only in order to provide protection to all and to prevent violence. (*Boisguilbert*, 250–51. Emphasis mine.)

As long as the state or some other agent does not force one party to an exchange to accept an unnatural bargain or prohibit one party from seeking its own benefit in the market, all exchanges will occur only if both parties benefit from them and (assuming that only parties to an exchange are affected by it) every commercial transaction will increase the overall well-being. The trouble with all attempts to constrict the rights of sellers to find the best bargain or to limit the prices they can ask, is that such attempts can so easily force a bargain in which the seller does not benefit, disrupting the providential mechanism which guarantees that all exchanges produce an overall benefit to society.

Boisguilbert did recognize certain limits on the principle of laissez-faire based on an awareness that the free market could work its magic only if both parties in an exchange are equally free in their bargaining. In connection with grain, for example, he argued that because there are fluctuations in supply that cannot be controlled and because grain is a perishable commodity which cannot be withheld from the market for long, in years of surplus farmers are not truly free, and might have to accept prices so low that they could not survive. For this reason he argued in favor of price *supports* (*Boisguilbert*, 270). The farmer in Boisguilbert did not see that the hungry poor are equally unfree in their bargaining for food.

Richard Cantillon and Economic Modelling

Though general overviews of an economy are sketched in the works of Becher, Petty, and Boisguilbert, their works were always openly addressed to particular policy issues. The first major modern work to present itself as aimed primarily at providing a non-polemical general theory of economic life was Richard Cantillon's *Essai sur la nature du commerce en general* (*An Essay on the Nature of Trade in General*), which was composed between 1728 and 1730 and widely circulated in manuscript versions among French economic thinkers before it was finally published in 1755. Though Cantillon constantly sought to assume a disinterested stance with regard to all economic issues, he was an extremely successful banker and stock market speculator, whose sophisticated knowledge of international banking and money markets both allowed him to produce a more comprehensive investigation of monetary economics than anyone before him and inclined him to treat financial institutions in a much more favorable light than most previous authors.

Cantillon's *Essay* was divided into three parts, reflecting increasing levels of analytic complexity. In the first part he defines wealth ("the maintenance, conveniences, and superfluities of life"[3]); identifies its sources (land and labor); identifies the difference between what he calls intrinsic value (cost of production) and market value, which is determined by the relationship between the "quantity of produce or merchandise offered for sale in proportion to the demand" (*ENTG*, 119); and explains that market prices in a well-regulated economy will fluctuate around a price that is equal to or greater than the intrinsic value (*ENTG*, 31). In general, Cantillon identifies and discusses the roles of three groups of economic actors associated with production: landowners, whose income is in the form of rents; laborers, whose income is in the form of wages; and undertakers (*entrepreneures*) whose income is in the form of profits (*ENTG*, 43). Moreover, he discusses the role of entrepreneurship much more extensively than any of his predecessors. Finally, he concludes part 1 with an analysis of the causes of increase and decrease of population, which was a central concern of early political economy (*ENTG*, 65–85), and with a brief discussion of how precious metals, as commodities with their own intrinsic value, became common measures of economic value (*ENTG*, 97–113).

Part 2 of the *Essay* is dedicated to analyzing the workings of a money-based market economy. It gives a general account of the functioning of markets in setting prices, and then turns to an analysis of the circulation of money among the different classes that expands greatly on the brief discussions of Petty and Boisguilbert (*ENTG*, 121–49). In fact, Cantillon's verbal-quantitative model of circulation unquestionably stimulated the graphical representation of circulation in the *Tableau Economique* produced and refined by François Quesnay and Victor Riquetti, marquis de Mirabeau, in late 1758 and first published in Mirabeau's *Ami du peuple* (Friend of the People) (1759).

Cantillon concludes part 2 of the *Essay* with a discussion of the importance of capital advances and the loaning of money at interest in an entrepreneurial economy. In this section he insists that it is absolutely futile for a government to try to keep interest rates artificially low, for lenders must charge enough to compensate for their risks and their lost-opportunity costs. If a government tries to limit interest rates below the free-market rate, it must inevitably fail. Speaking out of his own banking experience, he writes, "the contracting parties, obedient to the force of competition or the current price settled by the proportion of lenders to borrowers, will make secret bargains, and this legal constraint will only embarrass trade and raise the rate of interest instead of settling it" (*ENTG*, 221).

Part 3 of the *Essay* is devoted to increasingly complex issues created by international trade, fluctuating foreign exchange rates, and the creation of national and international banks. With respect to international trade, Cantillon begins from the traditional mercantilist view that, all other things being equal, it is desirable to trade so as to have a net inflow of specie. As in many other cases, however, Cantillon turns quickly to challenge the all-other-things-being-equal assumption. He argues, for example, that in the absence of transfers of gold, silver, or cash a nation which sells manufactured goods and imports raw materials gains an economic advantage by providing greater resources to feed and employ a larger population (*ENTG*, 233). More importantly, Cantillon argues that as long as money has intrinsic value, when a nation does succeed in increasing its money supply, wages and prices will increase, making the nation's products less competitive internationally until the specie's flow is reversed. So in the long run traditional mercantilist policies must be ineffectual (*ENTG*, 235–37).

Cantillon's work was no less a response to French economic crisis than Boisguilbert's. It too had a variety of policy recommendations to offer and grew out of the particular experiences of the small but identifiable class of international bankers and financiers. But the scientific form of Cantillon's *Essai* offered rhetorical advantages which have led almost all twentieth-century historians of economics to see it as the single greatest and most comprehensive treatise in economics prior to Adam Smith's *Wealth of Nations*. There is also no doubt that the comprehensiveness of Cantillon's system gave it substantial contemporary appeal. It was able to account for an unprecedented range of economic phenomena with the use of a very small number of assumptions, all of which were already widely accepted among political economists in England and France. Among the most important of these were the assumptions shared with Davenant, Boisguilbert, and Mandeville that every economic actor seeks his or her rationally calculated self-interest and that there is a *natural* mechanism, the market, which guarantees that both parties to any freely negotiated transaction will benefit from it. Any government interference with private free-market exchanges thus became dangerous because it voided the only natural assurance of equity in exchanges. Through the writings of the Physiocrats and Adam Smith, these assumptions became cornerstones of a powerful new political ideology which came to be called *liberalism*.

The Economically Based Politics of Physiocracy

During a brief period, from 1756 to 1774, Paris became the locus of an unprecedented political movement centered on the person of François Quesnay and grounded in the development of the economic theories of Boisguilbert and Cantillon. Quesnay, the dictatorial leader of the movement, came very late to an interest in economics and politics, publishing his first article on economics for Diderot and D'Alembert's *Encyclopaedie* in 1756 when he was 62 years of age. He had been born into a modest farm family near Paris in 1694 and he never lost interest in agriculture. But because financial prospects for farmers were so bleak, his family sent him to Paris as an apprentice engraver when he was 17 years old. His career interests soon turned to surgery and then to medicine. He became an extremely successful doctor, becoming physician to Mme. du Pompadour and then, in 1749, first physician to the king. He had also become a member of the Parisian Academie des Chirugens and had begun to publish on animal physiology. This work earned him an invitation to membership in the Academie des Sciences and led to a friendship with Jean D'Alembert. Impressed with Quesnay's abilities, and aware of his long-standing interest in agriculture, D'Alembert invited him to write the *Encyclopaedie* articles on farmers, grain (corn), men, and taxation, and Quesnay was launched on a new career.

In preparing his articles, Quesnay borrowed heavily from Boisguilbert's analysis of the condition of French agriculture. He also investigated the recent agricultural improvement movement in England and his knowledge of English developments led him to impart a new twist to Boisguilbert's arguments. The productivity of English agriculture had improved dramatically during the late seventeenth and early eighteenth century, largely as the consequence of a move to larger-scale and more capital intensive farming. Investment in new tools, livestock, rolling stock, fences, and the like, had nearly trebled per-acre productivity while only doubling costs of production. The results were huge net gains from increased farm profits and a simultaneous lowering of commodity prices.[4]

Quesnay argued that French agriculture could also be made vastly more efficient through capital investment. But this could happen only if the farmers' *"net produit"* (net profit after deduction for costs of production) was sufficiently large to provide the necessary capital to invest and the disincentives to investment produced by traditional property taxes were eliminated. To provide for an adequate net profit and to encourage reinvestment Quesnay urged a slight modification of those policies which had been recommended by Boisguilbert. First, farmers had to be allowed to raise their prices through free-market exchanges and access to export markets. Short-run increases in bread prices would soon lead to higher productivity and to a subsequent lowering of prices without any lowering of profits if farmers reinvested in agriculture. And they would automatically do so if they knew that their improvements would not be taxed.

In developing his ideas about taxation, Quesnay depended heavily on Cantillon's discussions of circulation, which he had learned about from his first convert, Mirabeau. Together, Quesnay and Mirabeau developed their ideas on circulation into the *Tableau Économique* (see figure 1), a development Mirabeau considered as important as the invention of printing. Though the *Tableau* really adds little to Cantillon's analysis, its visual form makes it easy to see certain implications. It is clear, for example, that any tax on consumption will have a negative effect that is multiplied with the frequency of exchanges; so taxes on consumption are highly undesirable. In fact there is only one transfer in the entire scheme which occurs only once in the annual cycle, and that is the transfer from the farmer to the landowner for the rent of the land. Thus Quesnay argued for a single tax on the *revenue* of landed proprietors because it would discourage neither investment nor consumption (*EP*, 107).

During the late 1750s Quesnay began to collect around himself a group of men dedicated to implementing his policy recommendations. Members of the group met weekly at Mirabeau's apartment in Paris and included Mirabeau, Merciere de la Rivière, Pierre Samuel Du Pont de Nemours, Louis-Paul Abeille, Pierre Roubaud, Guillaume-François Le Trosne, the Abbé Nicolas Baudeau and, on occasion, Vincent Gournay, Henri Leonard, Jean Baptiste Bertin, and Anna Robert Jacques Turgot. Under Du Pont de Nemours' editorship they published the *Journal de l'Agriculture, du Commerce, et des Finances* (The journal of agriculture, commerce, and finance) from 1765 through 1766 and the *Ephemeridies du Citoyen* (Citizen's almanach) from 1768 through 1772. Du Pont, who was the chief polemicist and popularizer of the movement, coined the name *physiocracy*, in order to highlight its ambitious character. In the past, political theorists had discussed monarchy, aristocracy, and democracy. But Quesnay and his followers had now come to lead France into physiocracy, or the rule of *nature*. What they sought was nothing less than to establish and implement "the science of natural law applied, as it should be, to all civilized societies."[5]

Though physiocracy clearly extended its interests beyond those of economics and into politics more broadly understood, it reversed the traditional sense of priorities and grounded its politics in its economics rather than vice-versa. It started from the premises that *subsistence* is the primary object of all societies and that subsistence depends primarily on agriculture in modern societies. All other considerations became subordinate to questions of economic policy and to policies affecting agriculture in particular. Thus, for reasons that had been thoroughly explained by Boisguilbert, Cantillon, and Tucker, citizens should be given economic liberty, the freedom to

TABLEAU ÉCONOMIQUE[1]

Objects to be considered: (1) three kinds of expenditure; (2) their source; (3) their advances; (4) their distribution; (5) their effects; (6) their reproduction; (7) their relations with one another; (8) their relations with the population; (9) with agriculture; (10) with industry; (11) with trade; (12) with the total wealth of a nation.

PRODUCTIVE EXPENDITURE relative to agriculture, etc.	EXPENDITURE OF THE REVENUE after deduction of taxes, is divided between productive expenditure and sterile expenditure	*STERILE EXPENDITURE* relative to industry, etc.
Annual advances required to produce a revenue of 600^l are 600^l	Annual revenue	Annual advances for the works of sterile expenditure are

600^l produce net ....600^l 300^l

Products *one-half goes here* .... *one-half goes here* Works, etc.

300^l reproduce net ....300^l *one-half goes here* ....300^l
    one-half goes here

150 reproduce net 150   *one-half, etc.* 150
    one-half, etc.

75 reproduce net 75   75

37..10^d reproduce net ....37..10   37..10

18..15 reproduce net ....18..15   18..15

9... 7... 6^d reproduce net ......9...7...6^d 9...7...6^d

4..13... 9 reproduce net ......4..13...9   4..13...9

2... 6..10 reproduce net ......2...6..10   2...6..10

1... 3... 5 reproduce net ......1...3...5   1...3...5

0..11... 8 reproduce net ......0..11...8   0..11...8

0... 5..10 reproduce net ......0...5..10   0...5..10

0...2..11 reproduce net ......0...2..11   0...2..11

0...1...5 reproduce net ......0...1...5   0...1...5

etc.

TOTAL REPRODUCED ...... 600^l of revenue; in addition, the annual costs of 600^l and the interest on the original advances of the husbandman amounting to 300^l, which the land restores. Thus the reproduction is 1500^l, including the revenue of 600^l which forms the base of the calculation, abstraction being made of the taxes deducted and of the advances which their annual reproduction entails, etc. See the Explanation on the following page.

Reprinted from *Quesnay's Tableau Économique.* **Edited and translated by Marguerite Kuczynski and Ronald L. Meek. London: Macmillan and New York: Augustus M. Kelley Publishers, 1972.**

dispose of their labor or property with one another at will, but they have no need for political liberty. Indeed, to allow citizens a direct role in their own governance could cause nothing but confusion. By the same token, claims that there should be any kind of balance of forces or separation of powers in a government made no sense since "such a division would play havoc with the order of govern-ment . . . which ought to reconcile all interests for one main purpose—that of securing the prosperity of agriculture, which is the source of all wealth of the state and that of all its citizens" (*EP*, 231). For this reason, the Physiocrats generally advocated what they called "legal despotism," rule by a single individual, knowledgeable about the laws of nature, and committed to governing so as not to interfere with their operation.[6]

In spite of their instrumental support for absolute monarchy, the constant and often strident emphasis of the Physiocrats (more widely known as the *economistes* in Paris) was on economic liberty as a universal natural law. Their dogmatism and disrespect for any authority other than their own generated much hostility, especially among relatively conservative intellectuals. Thus the able Italian political economist, Ferdinando Galiani, labeled them economic dogs and argued that their incessant preaching of the doctrine of liberty was responsible for a major public riot which occurred in Paris on 30 May 1770 when a crowd leaving a public spectacle held at the Place de Concorde refused to follow police directives about departing in a particular order. Writing about the riot to Mme. d'Epinay a few weeks later Galiani argued, "Madame, I accuse the *economistes*. They have preached property and liberty with such insistence, they have worked so hard at undermining the police, order, the regulations; they have said so often that nature left to itself was so beautiful, functioned so well, put itself in equilibrium, etc., that finally, sure of their ownership of the street and of their liberty to walk, everyone wanted to profit from this."[7] Even the usually mild mannered David Hume was moved to attack the group with uncharacteristic bitterness. They are, he argued "the most chimerical and most arrogant set of men that now exists," and he urged their enemies to "crush them, and pound them, and reduce them to ashes" (*BAS*, 294).

Perhaps one of the reasons for the near paranoia of Galiani and Hume was the fact that the Physiocrats, with whom they disagreed on fundamental theoretical issues, actually managed to have a substantial impact on French financial policies between 1762 (when

Bertin was made *controleur general des finances*) and 1776 (when Turgot, who had hired Du Pont de Nemours as his deputy, was asked to resign). Under Bertin, barriers to the free movement of grain within France were abolished in 1663 and prohibitions against the export of grain to foreign countries were abolished in 1764. Moreover, in 1774 Turgot, Bertin's successor, finally convinced the new king, Louis XVI, to allow him to abolish price controls over grain. But harvests were unusually low during these years and the newly unregulated bread prices rose so rapidly that bread riots broke out throughout France. As a consequence, reactionary groups led by the mercantilist financier Jacques Necker forced an end to physiocratic influence in the government. The long-term impact of physiocracy on economic theory ended up being greater than its immediate impact on practice.

The fundamental disagreements between the Physiocrats and such conservative economists as Galiani and Hume were directly related to the same kind of methodological split that we saw in connection with Helvetius's rejection of Montesquieu's historical relativism. Quesnay and his disciples (though not Turgot and not Mirabeau before his association with Quesnay) argued, like Helvetius, against using historical investigation in discovering economic laws. Thus Quesnay wrote; "Let us not seek into the history of nations or the mistakes of men, for that only presents an abyss of confusion . . . [these] do not serve to throw a light which can illuminate the darkness" (*BAS*, 284). Merciere de la Rivière exposed the physiocratic dependence on what was already an old-fashioned Cartesian focus on rationality and self-evidence in his *L'ordre naturel et essentiel des sociétés politiques* (*The Natural and Essential Order of Political Societies*) of 1767. "I do not cast my eye on any particular nation or sect, I seek to describe things as they must *essentially* be, without considering what they have been, or in what country they may have been. As the truth exists by, or of, itself, it is the truth in all places and at all times . . . by examining and reasoning we arrive at knowing the truth self-evidently, and with all the practical consequences which result from it; examples which appear to contrast with these consequences prove nothing" (*BAS*, 293).

It can hardly be surprising that an empiricist like Hume, especially one committed to the anti-essentialist tradition following from Locke, should have found such arguments unconvincing. Nor is it surprising that Galiani, whose perspectives were deeply influenced by the historical tradition of Vico and Montesquieu, should have seen them as appallingly shallow. To Hume and Galiani, and to many epistemologically sophisticated readers, the Physiocrats seemed to be intellectual charlatans at least in part because of their outmoded methods of argumentation.

In spite of their old-fashioned methods and their dogmatic insistence that all non-agricultural production was "sterile," however, the Physiocrats did have a substantial impact on the development of economics. First, and perhaps most importantly, their works served to generate increasing interest in economic topics and to popularize the notion of circulation and the idea of free-market exchanges. Though discussed by others before them, these same ideas had little impact on policy before the Physiocrats.

Second, they were among the first political economists to focus on the contribution of capital investment to *increases* in productivity and to economic growth. In connection with this emphasis on the relation between investment and productivity, the Physiocrats explicitly turned away from the notion that increases in population were in themselves desirable. Instead, they argued that the net product, or the surplus of income over costs of production that we call capital accumulation, was the most important measure of economic well-being. But the surplus had to be put to work and not merely hoarded by the wealthy. Its reinvestment, they urged, would lead to "the greatest possible reduction in expense [and] the greatest possible reduction in disagreeable labor with the greatest possible enjoyment" (*EP*, 212).

During the late eighteenth century, after the fall of Turgot, leadership in liberal economic theorizing moved away from France to Italy and Scotland. In Italy, especially at Milan, physiocratic doctrines were modified primarily by contact with associationist psychology. There, both Cesare Beccaria and Pietro Verri, who were among the first expositors of Helvetian philosophy and co-editors of a reform-oriented journal, *Il Caffe*, also became interested in political economy and published major works in the field. In Scotland, associationist psychology also influenced the development of political economy. But even more important was the philosophical-historical tradition derived from Montesquieu. Its impact was so great that we will defer discussing Scottish political economy until after our discussion of Montesquieu in the next chapter.

The Cameralist Alternative to Liberal Economics in the Eighteenth Century

While physiocracy probably played the major role in popularizing political economy and moving economic topics to the center of all non-academic social-scientific discourse on the Continent during the late eighteenth century, it was the cameralist tradition deriving from Becher, von Schröder, and von Horningk that played the major role in making political economy an important and autonomous part of university education.

Between 1727, when the first professorships of cameral science were established at Frankfurt and Halle, and the end of the century, 36 German and Austrian universities came to have professors of cameral and economic sciences. During a difficult period for German universities, some would almost certainly have closed had it not been for the enrollments in cameral studies, which had become a preferred alternative to family influence for entrance into administrative bureaucracies.[8]

Given the academic orientation of eighteenth-century cameralism, almost all cameralist writing appeared in the form of textbooks intended for student use. Keith Tribe had identified over sixty such texts produced between 1760 and 1790 (*GE*, 91). Though these texts vary considerably in pedagogical approach and in the relative weights they assign to various topics, they show remarkable continuity with regard to basic assumptions and doctrines. All seem modeled on a single paradigmatic text, Johann Heinrich Gottlob von Justi's *Staatswirthschaft, oder systematische Abhandlung aller Oekonomischen und Cameral-Wissenschaften, die zur Reqierung eines Landes erfodert werden* (Political economy, or a systematic treatise on all economic and administrative sciences which are requisite for the government of a country), which first appeared in 1758. I will therefore follow both Albion Small and Keith Tribe in letting von Justi's works represent the entire cameralist tradition.

Unlike English political economy and that of Cantillon, which sought to isolate economic topics from broader moral and political concerns for analytic simplicity, and unlike physiocracy, which tended to subordinate political considerations to economic ones, eighteenth-century cameralism continued the seventeenth-century pattern of embedding what we call economic discussions within broader political policy considerations. It was aimed at producing administrators or bureaucrats whose concern with the well-being of the state-incorporated interests not just in wealth in the narrow sense, but in the security of the state and the moral and physical health of the population as well. So when the student of cameralism considered the grain trade he was concerned with balancing the need of farmers to get prices adequate to stay in business with the need to have sufficient food supplies for the army, the need for able-bodied workers to be able to afford their food, the need to maintain full employment of agricultural workers, and even the need to keep grains uncontaminated to protect health.

It was simply unimaginable that the self-interests of producers and consumers, which the cameralists acknowledged to be the guides for unregulated economic behavior, could optimize public well-being. Thus, with respect to virtually every aspect of the economy von Justi insisted upon the necessity for state intervention and direction. In connection with agriculture, for example, he insists that "a wise ruler will not leave the food supply and employment of subjects to care for themselves, but will see that they are systematically made abundant."[9] Similarly, in connection with domestic trade he argues, "The fundamental principles of merchants must be distinguished from the measures and purposes of the government. While the merchant aims only at gain, and is not always concerned whether his gain corresponds with the chief advantage of the state, a wise government, on the contrary, must give the chief attention to this latter consideration" (*Cameralists*, 348). As a consequence of the difference between the interests of merchants and those of the state, the state may need to regulate trade in ways that merchants find repugnant. In the long run, von Justi admits, the prosperity of the merchants is necessary for the prosperity of the whole; but the state must act to proportion the well-being of the merchants to that of all other groups. Precisely the same principle is applied to questions of foreign trade. "A wise ordering of the tariff and excise system is the principle means by which a wise government can guide foreign commerce according to its purpose. Instead of being detrimental to trade, since traders always have their own interest in view more than that of the state, and it would be ruinous to leave the ways and means of commerce to their enterprise, no trade can be carried on in a way which is not in this way guided, controlled, and to a certain extent, promoted" (*Cameralists*, 355).

The last sentence of this passage raises a critically important concern for von Justi and the eighteenth-century cameralists. They were not only interested in regulation and control, but also in promotion and encouragement, which had been the chief focus of Becher's generation. In connection with manufacturing, for example, von Justi insisted that it was often desirable for the government to stimulate production by offering prizes and rewards for innovations, by granting direct support of relevant scientific research, and by offering cash payments to entice knowledgeable foreigners to relocate (*Cameralists*, 352). And in connection with mining, which von Justi saw as a major potential economic resource in the Germanies, he even argued that it would be appropriate for the government to subsidize mines during relatively extended and unprofitable start-up periods, because many people would be profitably engaged in the processes of fabricating the raw metals into valuable commodities (*Cameralists*, 360–62).

Finally, von Justi and his cameralist colleagues placed heavy emphasis on and played a major role in establishing government support for technical education to provide competent labor and management in all major industries, especially in agriculture and mining. This emphasis clearly had a major long-term impact. The educational infrastructure in the form of agricultural colleges, schools of mines, and scientific research institutes that was established in late-eighteenth-century Germany at state expense formed one of the key foundations for Germany's nineteenth-century pre-eminence in heavy industry and pharmaceuticals.[10]

Von Justi and his cameralist colleagues were widely read in English and French political economy. In many cases they adopted specific arguments from Petty, Tucker, and the physiocratic school in connection with specific policy issues. But they generally redirected foreign arguments to suit their own general statist and managerial orientation. Thus, for example, von Justi adopts the principle, stated by almost all liberal economic writers, that "a wise government must take care to remove all obstacles which may embarrass commerce." Where Tucker and Quesnay thought primarily of government interventions, such as discriminatory tax structures, price controls, and export restrictions, as the obstacles to be removed, von Justi identified scarcity of materials and lack of capital. And he argued that government interventionist policies to encourage extractive industries and improve the balance of trade were needed to remove the obstacles he identified (*Cameralists*, 358).

Cameralist doctrines had almost no impact on political economy in Western Europe during the eighteenth century. None of the major cameralist texts were translated into French, English, or Italian. The Scottish Jacobite exile, James Steuart, who wrote much of his monumental *An Inquiry into the Principles of Political Economy* (1767) while living in Tübingen, was the only major political economist writing in English to adopt cameralist claims. He agreed with the cameralists that the state is fundamentally a large household, of which the monarch is "both lord and steward" and that it was up to the monarch, aided by his advisors, "to judge of the expediency of different schemes of economy, and by degrees to model the minds of his subjects so as to induce them, from the allurement of private interest, to concur in the execution of his plan" (*GE*, 138).

Outside of the German states it was only in the Russia of Catherine the Great that cameralist policies were seriously implemented; and there they provided the blueprint for rapid movements toward modernization between 1762 and 1796.[11]

10

Philosophical History (Sociology) and the Emergence of Conservative Ideology, 1725–67

In the last two chapters we saw that associationist psychologists such as Helvetius and physiocratic political economists such as Quesnay self-consciously developed approaches to social-scientific issues in opposition to the historical methods which they attributed to Montesquieu. In turn, the most outspoken critic of physiocracy, Ferdinando Galiani, grounded many of his criticisms in the historical approach of Giambattista Vico. For both Helvetius and Galiani, methodological antagonisms were openly linked to political commitments. Helvetius was particularly concerned that Montesquieu's historical investigation of laws and institutions provided de facto support for what he considered to be the corrupt social and legal structure of Ancien Régime France. Galiani, on the other hand, was particularly concerned that the physiocratic disrespect for the authority of tradition encouraged a dangerous antagonism to legitimately constituted political authority and thereby threatened the security and stability of society.

In this chapter we will explore the eighteenth-century tradition of philosophical history in which Vico and Montesquieu played central roles, paying special attention to the way in which the cultural relativist tendencies of the tradition seemed to emerge as a foundation for conservative attacks on the radical implications of associationist psychology and the liberal tendencies of the dominant tradition of political economy.

Natural Law and Pufendorf's *The Duties of Man and Citizen*: Setting the Stage for Eighteenth-Century Philosophical History

One of the most important historical strands in the emergence of philosophical history in the late sixteenth century was the tradition of scientific jurisprudence which was embodied in Jean Bodin's *Six Books of a Commonweale* (see chapter 6). This tradition was subsequently developed by Hugo Grotius in *De jure belli ac pacis* (*On the Law of War and Peace*) (1623) and by Samuel Pufendorf in *On the Law of Nature and of Man* (1672), and its shortened textbook version *De officio hominis et civis iuxta legem naturalem* (*On the Duty of Man and Citizen According to Natural Law*) (1673).

For present purposes, Pufendorf's *On the Duty of Man and Citizen* is particularly important because it was widely adopted in France, Holland, England, and Scotland for the teaching of moral philosophy, dramatically restructuring the core of undergraduate university education throughout Western Europe. Gershom Carmichael, who introduced Pufendorf into Scottish education as professor of moral philosophy at the University of Glasgow in 1727, wrote that moral philosophy was now transformed into "nothing but the study of natural jurisprudence or the demonstration of the duties of man and the citizen from knowledge of the nature of things and the circumstances of human life."[1]

Two features of Pufendorf's work had a special bearing on the development of social science. The first of these was the range of new issues that the use of his work as a model text brought within the scope of moral philosophy. The second was the special way in which his approach to natural law highlighted the divergences between the norms which he espoused and the reality of existing customs and laws.

By extending the concerns of moral philosophy to all of the issues addressed by Roman law, Pufendorf supplemented the traditional "public" emphasis of scholastic moral philosophy with a much greater emphasis on the private productive and reproductive realms.

But when moral philosophers tried to understand virtually all human institutions and behaviors within a context dominated by Pufendorf's claims that human action is guided by universal natural law, they were struck by the local particularity of human customs. As William Paley wrote in his *Principles of Moral Philosophy* (1785), one of the greatest problems for moral philosophy was to discover "why, since the maxims of natural justice are few and evident . . . and the principles of the law of nature . . . simple and sufficiently obvious, should there exist nevertheless in every system of municiple laws . . . numerous uncertainties and acknowledged difficulties."[2]

Associationist psychology, as we have seen, sought to answer this question by retaining universalist claims about human nature and natural law and interpreting the failure of known societies to live up to their standards as a consequence of human ignorance or malice. Philosophical history, or sociology, on the other hand, challenged the universal claims of Pufendorf and the associationists. Its practitioners either denied that there are any rationally grounded universal laws at the level of generality assumed by Pufendorf or argued that a whole range of special conditions, including climate, modes of subsistence, religious traditions, and governmental forms, placed such constraints on how such universal laws could be manifested in particular circumstances that only a complex analysis could allow one to discover the common foundations for apparently conflicting customs.

Though its scope expanded to incorporate many extra-legal considerations—including even variations in literary taste— philosophical history was dominated by men with legal training until the end of the eighteenth century. Giambattista Vico was trained in law at Naples, and though he held the professorship of rhetoric there for 42 years (from 1699 to 1741), he always hoped to become professor of civil law. Moreover, the subtitle of the first edition of his major work, *Principi di una scienza nuova d'intorno alla natura delle natzioni (Principles of a New Science Concerning the Nature of the Nations)* (1725), was *par li quali si trovano altri principi del dritto naturale delle genti* (By which are found the principles of another system of the natural law of the gentiles). Montesquieu was also trained in law, and his major work of philosophical history was *The Spirit of the Laws* (1749). Most of the major Scottish contributors to philosophical history, including Lord Kames, Lord Monboddo, and John Millar, were either judges or professors of law. Those few who were not, including Adam Smith and Adam Ferguson, were moral philosophers who consciously organized their moral philosophy courses around the topics covered by Pufendorf.

Vico's *New Science* and the Attack on Traditional Notions of Natural Law

Though Vico's *New Science* remained virtually unknown outside Italy throughout the eighteenth century, it did have a major impact on several Italian authors, and through them at least some of its ideas were disseminated in France, Germany, and Scotland. For present purposes, Vico is interesting because he offered one of the most original and sophisticated scientific approaches to human society to appear in the eighteenth century, and because that approach incorporated a number of features that were common to virtually all philosophical historians.[3] Vico's *New Science* was intended to provide a more certain grounding for natural-law jurisprudence than it had been given by Grotius and Pufendorf. But it altered the very notion of natural law so much that it completely transformed the older theory into one which justified a thoroughgoing cultural relativism.

Vico began with an idea of science derived principally from Hobbes and Spinoza, rather than from the more recent Lockean tradition. He insisted that if knowledge was to be called scientific, it should be necessary rather than merely probable. Unfortunately, he argued, "if we weigh the principles of Grotius [and Pufendorf] on the scales of criticism, they all turn out to be probable and verisimilar, rather than necessary and irrefutable."[4] Traditional natural-law jurisprudence went wrong because its authors accepted Descartes's notion that we can trust our intuition to guarantee the truth of propositions regarding any domain of knowledge. Hobbes, Vico thought, had demonstrated that we can only be certain about the truth of claims made about those things which humans have created themselves. Like Hobbes, then, Vico argued that we can have a true science of civil society only because it has been created by men.[5]

In explaining how men create society, however, Vico diverges radically from Hobbes. Hobbes had argued that civil society is created by men through some kind of contract, consciously intended and rationally devised to ensure their security. Vico, on the other hand, does not believe that men were *rational* in the Hobbesian sense until well after the origin of civil society, so they could not have been responding to dictates of reason in creating it. Since, as the subtitle of the *New Science* suggests, Vico did believe both that there are natural laws governing society and that we can have a true science of them, he had to address three key questions. First, what are natural laws if they are not simply truths accessible to reason? Second, how are these laws manifested in various societies? Third, how can we come to know them and use them in creating a new science of society?

At one level, Vico argues, natural laws are a matter of divine providence; they are manifested in the divine imposition of institutions and customs, and we can learn them only through the empirical study of past and present societies (*NS*, 338: 100 and 342: 102). But if the story of human society were *only* the story of direct divinely willed arrangements, we could no more have scientific knowledge of it than we have of nature. In order to explain how a true science of society can exist, Vico insists that God operates in the social domain as he does in the natural, both through his special providence, which is reflected in his direct revelation to the Hebrews and Christians, and through his ordinary providence, which is expressed in the gentile tradition through the *human* creation of civil societies. Science can thus have nothing to say about the unique aspects of the Judeo-Christian tradition, for those are the direct creation of God, but it can deal with the common elements of all societies, which are human creations even though they express God's will (*NS*, 313: 92).

Though human institutions are created by human beings, they are often created "without human discernment and counsel, and often against the designs of men." How can this be? According to Vico, providence often operates so that while humans intend one thing, they actually act to produce something else (*NS*, 38: 24).

If there is a single principle which is central to all of the philosophical historians, it is this "law of unintended consequences."[6] Montesquieu used it to emphasize the way in which human vanity led to the creation of "fashion" which, in turn, "by encouraging a trifling turn of mind, continually increases the branches of . . . commerce" and increases the public welfare by providing jobs for many.[7] Adam Smith appealed to it in numerous contexts, none more important than in his discussion of the division of labor. And Adam Ferguson used it much more generally, like Vico, to argue that almost all human institutions are essentially unintended. "The forms of society are derived from an obscure and distant origin; they arise, long before the date of philosophy, from the instincts, not from the speculations of men . . . and nations stumble upon establishments, which are indeed the result of human action, but not the execution of any human design."[8]

At the hands of the political economists this providentialist argument, shorn of its religious connotations, had been put to predominantly liberal uses. It had been used to justify the claim that long-standing traditions of government involvement in economic affairs should be abandoned because the wisdom of governments could not be as great as the wisdom of the market. At the hands of the philosophical historians, on the other hand, it was put to conservative uses, even though, ironically, they might not have intended it that way.

One can make a strong case that both Vico and Montesquieu had reformist goals in mind as they developed their social science. Vico, for example, clearly supported a movement toward democratic forms of government (*NS*, 29: 18–19). And Montesquieu almost certainly viewed his own advocacy of constitutional monarchy with authority divided among legislative, executive, and judicial branches of government as supporting progressive reform rather than a reactionary return to the semi-feudal past.[9] Yet, as we have already seen, men like Helvetius and Condorcet viewed the philosophical historians' works as justifications of the status quo, and men like Edmund Burke and Joseph de Maistre found in them a powerful source of ammunition against philosophical reformers. If providence had, in the course of time, used human agents to express the divine wisdom in social institutions, surely we should not trust in the merely human wisdom of those philosophers who urge us to transform those institutions because they purport to know how better to accommodate human needs and desires.

Vico certainly comes close to expressing this point of view when he says of the providentially guided process through which men act: "Since it has for its end its own immeasurable goodness, whatever it institutes must be directed to a good always superior to that which men have proposed to themselves" (*NS*, 343: 102). Similarly, he insists that the process has produced a civil world "so wisely ordered that it could only be the effect of superhuman wisdom" (*NS*, 362: 109). Ferguson is even more explicit about the disproportion between human understanding and the complexity of human institutions. Institutions which arose through human action, but not through human intention, "bring human affairs to a state of complication, which the greatest reach of capacity with which human nature was ever adorned, could not have projected; nor even when the whole is carried into execution, can it be comprehended in its full extent" (*HCS*, 182). From their different perspectives both Vico and Ferguson thought that what humans can know about their institutions they can know adequately, thus there can be a *science* of society; but their knowledge does not extend far enough to encompass a prescription for future development. Edmund Burke takes precisely this point of view when he argues in his *Reflections on the Revolution in France* (1790) that governments "admit of [such] infinite modifications, they cannot be settled upon by any abstract rule; and nothing is so foolish as to discuss them upon that principle."[10]

All of the philosophical historians from Vico on admitted, indeed, they insisted, that human institutions have changed over time. But they also insisted that social changes were slow and driven by natural processes rather than rapid and driven by the rational and abstract speculations of philosophers. No example makes this point more clearly than Adam Smith's discussion of the gradual extension of the division of labor, with its consequent impact on the growth of productivity and wealth. Smith writes, "This division of labor, from which so many advantages are derived, is not originally the effect of any human wisdom, which foresees and intends that general opulence to which it gives occasion. It is the necessary, though very slow and gradual consequence of a certain propensity in human nature which has no view to such extensive utility; the propensity to truck, barter, and exchange one thing for another."[11]

For Vico, those philosophers who purported to be able to derive human institutions from some universal definition of human nature, especially from the assumption that humans are essentially *rational* animals or that they are essentially *political* animals, were misguided. Evidence regarding the early history of humankind and the development of the most fundamental and universal human customs and institutions showed that humans were neither rational nor political in the critical early stages of their history.

Vico argues that every nation (we would now say culture) goes through a natural development in a series of stages, or ages, which he identifies with the ancient Egyptian division of history into the age of the gods, the age of the heroes, and the age of humanity. The basic model for this common developmental pattern that he calls "the ideal eternal history" (*NS*, 393: 124) is the development of the human individual from childhood, through young adulthood, to maturity. And just as individual humans are not understood to reach their full rationality until maturity, peoples, collectively, are understood to reach their full rationality and humanity only in the late stages of their development (*NS*, 218: 75).

Vico is particularly interested in the "childhood" of humanity because this early age is the most creative. It produces "all the arts of the necessary, the useful, the convenient, and even in large part, those of human pleasure" (*NS*, 217: 75). Furthermore, it produces the three most important and lasting human institutions, religion, marriage, and burial (*NS*, 333: 97). Since, at every stage, institutions are created or transformed in accordance with the specific ideas which humans are capable of having at that stage, an understanding of any society must begin with an understanding of the mentality of the people; and this mentality is most obviously expressed in a society's language and literature, the myths and fables of its early stages, the heroic poetry of its middle stages, and the law codes and philosophy of its later stages.

Because each culture passes through the same series of stages, we can get evidence of how things were in the ancient world by consulting contemporary nations at early stages of their development. So Vico argues that his theory that the early Greeks and Egyptians created their gods by anthropomorphising the things of nature is confirmed by the practices of American Indian cultures that assign divine status to natural objects which transcend their understanding (*NS*, 375: 116–17).

Even what later come to be law and justice have their origins in the poetic imaginings of the earliest peoples, who project their desires for vengeance and retribution against those who violate community customs onto their more powerful divinities. So the earliest notions of justice are expressed in terms of divine punishments for wrongs done to members of the community. And in the absence of any abstract rules, humans first exercise judgments through the interpretation of divine oracles (*NS*, 398: 125–26).

At each stage in the development of each particular nation, the way in which human agency can be exercised depends on both where in the developmental sequence the nation stands and what the particular local physical and linquistic conditions are. As a consequence, no fact or piece of evidence can be said to be understandable outside of the particular time and place in which it was produced. There are no overarching universal and abstract features of human nature, for example, that provide invariable standards against which to measure the institutional creations of a particular culture.

It is, however, the case that all of the institutions of a given culture at a particular time, including its literature, religious practices, and laws, will have a kind of coherence or correspondence with one another. They will all reflect the stage of development at which the culture stands and the environment in which it has grown. One way of expressing all of these ideas in modern language is to say that in spite of the fact that Vico seems to have believed that the historical process expressed a providential wisdom, he was a complete cultural relativist, insisting that acts are both explicable and legitimately judged only in terms of standards appropriate to a particular time and place.

Montesquieu and the Factors Influencing Laws and Customs

If Vico's *New Science* appears to some late-twentieth-century scholars as among the most original and insightful of Enlightenment contributions to the social sciences, there is little doubt that to most philosophical historians living in the second half of the eighteenth century first place would have gone to *The Spirit of the Laws* by Charles-Louis de Secondat, baron de la Brede et de Montesquieu. Montesquieu had been born into the French landed nobility at la Brede, near Bordeaux, in 1689. He was sent to the College de Juilly, a progressive Oratorian college when he was 11 years old. There he became familiar with mathematics and Cartesian philosophy as well as with the Latin classics and French history. After legal study at Bordeaux, he moved to Paris, where he probably worked as a lawyer between 1709 and 1713. His major intellectual interests, indicated by the contents of his personal notebooks from this period, were in natural history, especially geography and meteorology. Late in 1713, after his father's death, he returned home and became a member of the Bordeaux *parlement*. Then, in 1716, he inherited his uncle's position as president and chief justice of *parlement* as well as his title, baron de Montesquieu. At the same time, he continued his scientific interests, joining the Academy of Bordeaux and publishing papers in acoustics, mechanics, and the physiological reactions of sheep's tongues to heat and cold.

As president of the local *parlement*, Montesquieu became increasingly involved in defending local prerogatives against extensions of central monarchical power. Meanwhile, in connection with his geographical studies, Montesquieu had been reading the almost endless stream of travelers' accounts mentioned in chapter 6. Several of these, especially Lahontan's, had used dialogues with non-Europeans as vehicles for criticizing current European society; so Montesquieu decided to create a fictional set of letters, ostensibly sent home by two Persian ambassadors in Paris during the final years of Louis XIV's reign, in order to criticize French society and the French monarchy.

The *Lettres Persienne* (*Persian Letters*), which appeared in 1721, were witty, irreverent, filled with slightly risqué stories, pointedly critical of religious intolerance and of the monarchy's fiscal policies and centralizing tendencies, and immensely popular. Montesquieu became the new literary lion of the Marquise de Lambert's salon in Paris. In 1725 he published a semi-pornographic novel, *Le Temple de Gnide*, then, in 1726 he sold his parliamentary office to clear his debts and set out to become a full-time savant. By this time he clearly had in mind the topics for his next two works. One was to be a history of Rome that would focus on the *causes* of Rome's greatness and decline, rather than on the details of events. The second projected work was a general and comparative history of law and customs which would, like Vico's *New Science*, emend and extend the treatment of Pufendorf.

Unlike Vico, however, Montesquieu did believe both in the existence of universal laws and in the constancy of human nature over time. For him, laws are "necessary relations arising from the nature of things" and they are "fixed and invariable" because they are created by God. Thus Montesquieu argues that Hobbes's notion that men create their own justice is absurd. To think that something became just or unjust only after men prescribed or prohibited it is the same as saying "that before the describing of the circle, all the radii were not equal" (*SL*, 1–2). For Montesquieu, as for Descartes, Grotius, and Pufendorf, these laws are intuitively recognized; they are articulated; and then particular institutions and events are derived from them (*SL*, lxvii).

How then do different nations come to have such different positive laws and customs? In order to begin answering this question Montesquieu makes two critical sets of distinctions. First, he accepts the Cartesian distinction between men as physical beings, subject to physical laws, and men as intelligent beings subject to moral laws.

Then he claims that moral and physical laws, though both are equally constant, operate in slightly different ways, the result being that moral laws are not as deterministic (*SL*, 2).

Much more important for most purposes than the distinction between physical and moral law is Montesquieu's second distinction between the paticular circumstances which occasion an action and the cause of that action. The first of these factors is what we today call *contingent*. It depends upon a whole host of considerations which create the context for an action, such as climate, the principal occupations of the citizens, religious traditions, laws, the form of government, and local customs, all of which Montesquieu includes in what he calls "the general spirit" of a nation (*SL*, 6: 293). The second factor is *necessary*. It is the general physical or moral law which produces the action and it is universal rather than particular.

In physics we say that the solution to any problem depends both on the laws of physics and on the initial conditions of the problem. Radically different solutions emerge when the initial conditions are changed. In much the same way, Montesquieu argued that people behave very differently in different circumstances in spite of the fact that their behaviors are produced by universal physical and moral laws. This he attributed to variations in the specific preexisting conditions, or the "general spirits" of the nations in which they live. The explanation for why human customs and institutions differ from one society to another, then, must depend upon understanding how particular conditions influence the ways in which universal physical and moral laws take specific forms.

For Montesquieu the form of government is one of the most important factors in shaping the general spirit of a people, and almost one-third of *The Spirit of the Laws* is devoted to a discussion of "the relations which laws bear to the nature and principle of each government" (*SL*, 7). Following the classical tradition as it had been developed by Machiavelli, Bodin, and Harrington, Montesquieu argued that there are three fundamental types of government. But he labeled these republican, monarchical, and despotic, rather than democratic, aristocratic, and monarchical. This difference in taxonomy reflected a particular political agenda that Montesquieu had in mind in composing his work, a particular understanding of the historical conditions out of which republican governments grow, and a particular fondness for the English form of constitutional monarchy that he had studied while in England.

Politically, Montesquieu was concerned to demonstrate that under

Louis XIV and Louis XV a long-standing French monarchical tradition was being transformed into a much less desirable despotic one. But contrary to the fears and perceptions of some of his enemies, he was certainly not arguing for a revival of the power of the traditional nobility. Indeed, in speaking of that nobility he emphasized their "natural ignorance," their "indolence," and their "contempt for civil government" (*SL*, 17). What he sought was the perpetuation of an independent "depository of the laws" that would protect the customs and institutions of the nation from being changed to satisfy "the momentary will of the prince." Not surprisingly, for someone who had led innumerable battles against the crown from his position of chief justice of a powerful *parlement*, Montesquieu argued that "this depository can only be the judges of the supreme courts of justice, who promulgate new laws and revive the obsolete" (*SL*, 17).

Historically, Montesquieu wanted to argue that both democratic and aristocratic governments have the same form and that they merge insensibly into one another, so that they are variants on the same pattern (*SL*, 14–15). Finally, he was particularly impressed by the English monarchy as it was understood by the group of Tory intellectuals with which he had associated most closely during his English visit. That monarchy, with its divided sovereignty and separation of governmental powers, seemed to him to offer both the brightest long-term prospects for governmental stability and the maximum liberty for all classes of citizens to express their own particular virtues.

Montesquieu claims that republics, both democratic and aristocratic, depend upon the principle of virtue, defined as the love of the people for the state, and upon their honesty. Monarchies depend upon the principle of honor, especially upon competition among the nobility to achieve a reputation through military and other service to the crown. And depotisms depend upon the principle of fear. To be most effective in each kind of state, laws should be formulated in such a way as to both reinforce and conform to the dominant principles. That is, in republics, laws should both encourage honesty and love of country and take advantage of those sentiments. Similarly, in monarchies, laws should always be sensitive to the need to provide recognition for service and to provide for ways for the nobility to retain their sense of honor. Finally, in despotisms laws must sustain the sense of fear which keeps the people under control.

The great failure of the French government was that it had acted in such a way as to undermine the positive principles associated with both republics and monarchies without establishing the negative principle that would support despotism. Through its retrogressive tax policies and through the high-handed manipulation of fiscal policies it had created a disaffected citizenry that not only did not love its country, but which felt that its self-preservation depended upon being dishonest. Moreover, by simply selling titles of nobility for cash, the crown had removed honor from the very notion of nobility; by shrinking the real service asked of the aristocracy and replacing it with artificial and trivial role-playing at court, it had robbed the nobility of its sense of dignity and self-worth. Moreover, it had done both without creating the kind of discipline and reputation for severity that could create obedience through terror. It had thus become something which could not sustain itself in the long run, a government without principle.

Seen through Montesquieu's rose-colored glasses, the constitutional monarchy in England had managed to do precisely the opposite. It had managed to foster both a love of country and a sense of honesty among its citizens as well as a sense of honor within its aristocracy. It offered the best features of both desirable forms of government within a system of tremendous stability. By vesting legislative power in a parliament that incorporated both a house for commons and one for nobles, it simultaneously provided the feeling that every citizen had a stake in his own governance and a sense within the nobility that it played its own special and superior role (*SL*, 154–55). At the same time, by vesting executive power in the crown it allowed for the efficient execution of the law (*SL*, 156). By separating the judicial powers from both the legislative and executive in common-law courts, the English established a system which provided a depository of national law and custom independent of both crown and parliament and capable of making certain that laws were enforced neither oppressively nor arbitrarily (*SL*, 152–53).

Montesquieu's discussions of the nature and principles of government and his subsequent advocacy of the separation of legislative, executive, and judicial functions within governments took on a life of its own and played a major role in American constitutional debates.[12] But this aspect of *The Spirit of the Laws* played a distinctly secondary role for intellectuals who viewed Montesquieu as the chief source of the tradition of Enlightenment philosophical history. These readers tended to focus on his analyses of environmental factors and even more on his discussion of how the "principle occupations" of the people shape their laws. We shall focus the remainder of our attention on these two topics.

Chapters 14 through 18 of *The Spirit of the Laws* all deal with the relationship between the physical environment of a nation and its laws. Montesquieu fairly clearly derived his interest in this topic, at least in part, from conversations with the English Tory natural philosopher, John Arbuthnot, whose 1733 *An Essay Concerning the Effects of Air on Human Bodies* discussed the contraction of tissue under the influence of cold and also speculated about the effects of climate on temperament. Montesquieu's experiments on the impact of cold on sheep's tongues came some time after his conversations with Arbuthnot and used his general explanatory devices. But Montesquieu's discussion of the relationship between climate and social development also seems to owe much to Bodin and many of the specific identifications made by Bodin are retained by Montesquieu. Thus, like Bodin, Montesquieu argues that inhabitants of warm regions are physically weaker, lazier, more sensuous, generally more passionate, and more clever than their counterparts from colder regions. Moreover, he identifies the cold climates with both physical vigor and a lack of sensitivity. But Montesquieu goes further. He replaces the older humoral theory as a foundation for such arguments and substitutes his own experimentally developed theory of the contraction of muscle fibers by cold (*SL*, 221–23). He then presents an attitude completely different from that of his French predecessor on the relationship between law and climate. Bodin had argued that laws should work *with* climatic factors to exploit the virtues associated with the local climate. Montesquieu breaks not only with Bodin but also with his own general principle that the laws should "follow the spirit of the nation" (*SL*, 294) in arguing that laws and customs should be formulated in relation to climate largely in order to combat its negative effects. Thus the title of the fifth section of chapter 14 is "That those are bad Legislators who favor the Vices of the Climate, and good Legislators who oppose those Vices" (*SL*, 225).

Of all the topics which Montesquieu relates to climate, civil and domestic servitude are among the most interesting. Though Montesquieu generally disapproves of slavery on the grounds that "as all men are born equal, slavery must be accounted unnatural," and though he expresses his relief that it has been abandoned in Europe, he claims that in some countries slavery may be founded on natural reason because of climatic factors. In particular, he writes, "There are countries where the excess of heat enervates the body, and renders men so slothful and dispirited that nothing but the fear of chastisement can oblige them to perform any laborious duty: Slavery is there more reconcilable to reason" (*SL*, 240). This is one of the most dramatic cases in which Montesquieu's climate theory justifies the most radically different laws and customs in different places.

Almost equally disconcerting is Montesquieu's treatment of marriage, which he understands as a form of domestic servitude for women in some countries. In hot climates, Montesquieu argues, women reach sexual maturity much earlier than in temperate or cold ones and they also lose their sexual attractiveness much sooner. Consequently, they are married and bearing children before they reach the age of reason and it is appropriate that they be subordinate to their husbands. By the same token, once they have reached their age of reason, they have lost their sexual appeal; so it is appropriate that their husbands take up new wives, and polygamy is appropriate (*SL*, 251).

Once again, as in the case of civil slavery, Montesquieu seems to have some idea of a normal state of affairs which would exist in the absence of climatic influences. In connection with polygamy, for example, he argues that "independent of the [climatic] circumstances which render it tolerable, it is not of the least service to mankind, nor to either of the two sexes, whether it be that which abuses or that which is abused" (*SL*, 254). In using terms like abuse and in denying the utility of polygamy, Montesquieu makes it clear that for him the more *natural* condition is monogamy; yet he acknowledges that the influence of climate may be so great that it can override such considerations. Similarly, in connection with the relative independence and equality of both partners in a marriage, though Montesquieu does believe that men naturally have greater strength and somewhat greater reason than women, he argues that the natural state involves a "kind of equality." Thus laws which place women in a state of dependency are not appropriate except where special climatic conditions justify them.

In the cases of civil and domestic slavery, it is clear that of all those factors influencing the laws of a place, climate may have a particularly powerful role to play. It is important to recognize, however, that Montesquieu does not argue that any one factor is always predominant. In fact, he insists that in different circumstances different factors may have greater impact, although he does believe that "nature and climate rule almost alone over the savages" (*SL*,

293–94). For future reference, it is also important to note that, in practice, all of Montesquieu's reflections regarding the relationships between law and climate were justificatory rather than prescriptive. They all involved rationalizing traditional practices rather than criticizing them to recommend alternatives. In this sense, even where Montesquieu proffered a theoretical justification for reform, he simultaneously offered a practical justification of the status quo ante.

A second feature of Montesquieu's work that was almost unanimously viewed as important and innovative was his emphasis on the relationship between laws and principle occupations, or modes of subsistence. Montesquieu's analysis of these issues begins in chapter 18 of *The Spirit of the Laws*, where he establishes a four-fold typology of nations based on modes of subsistence and argues that the extent of the codes of laws will vary from one type of nation to another:

> The laws have a very great relation to the manner in which the several nations procure their subsistence. There should be a code of laws of a much larger extent for a nation attached to trade and navigation [i.e., commercial nations] than for people who are content with cultivating the earth [i.e., agricultural nations]. There should be a much greater for the latter than for those who subsist by their flocks and herds [i.e., pastoral or barbarian nations]. There must be a still greater for these than for such as live by hunting [i.e., savage nations]. (*SL*, 275)

The series of savage, barbarian, agricultural, and commercial societies was not necessarily a developmental series for Montesquieu. That is, the members of the series were not necessarily understood as stages in a process of maturation in the way that Vico understood the age of gods, the age of heroes, and the age of humanity. Instead, they were simply treated as different kinds of societies to be compared with one another in terms of the laws and customs they promoted. Yet, in spite of the fact that he nowhere explicitly stated that nations naturally progress from hunting to herding to agriculture to commerce, virtually all of those who saw themselves as his followers read into Montesquieu a theory of progressive stages.

All four kinds of society were surveyed in chapters of *The Spirit of the Laws* relating to the general effects of the nature of the soil (chapter 18) and the influence of the number of inhabitants in a nation on its laws (chapter 23); but three separate chapters (chapters

20–22) were directed specifically at different aspects of the laws and customs of commercial societies. No other form of society was separately treated. In part this weighting toward commercial society made sense because, according to his theory, the laws and customs of commercial society are simply more complex than those of any other form. But it was also the case that Montesquieu had a special interest in contemporary France, which he, unlike the Physiocrats, identified as a commercial rather than an agrarian society.

Montesquieu is certainly ambivalent about the spirit of commercial nations, as were most of the philosophical historians who came after him. On the one hand, he and his followers are virtually unanimous in insisting that commerce necessarily promotes peace and cooperation among nations. In Montesquieu's words, "Peace is the natural effect of trade. Two nations that trade with one another become reciprocally dependent; for if one has an interest in buying, the other has an interest in selling; and thus their union is founded on their mutual necessities" (*SL*, 316). Since Montesquieu values peace because peace was emphasized in the natural-law tradition and because the prosecution of wars under Louis XIV had contributed greatly to the financial ills of France, there is no question that he sees the promotion of peace through commerce as a positive feature of commercial societies.

Similarly, he argues that commerce, by bringing together people from different places and backgrounds within a context in which they have to learn to get along and cooperate with one another, provides "a cure for the most destructive prejudices" (*SL*, 316). The breakdown of prejudice is one of the reasons that trade promotes peace between nations; but it also becomes a factor in promoting toleration, and hence peace in a more general sense. Finally, commerce leads to "civility" and to the refinement of manners and tastes, for it diffuses "a knowledge of the manners of all nations: these are compared with one another, and from this arise the greatest advantages" (*SL*, 316).

Against the benefits Montesquieu sets the negative features of the commercial spirit, all associated with its tendency to sacrifice traditional moral virtues to an exclusive concern with private economic interests. "The spirit of trade produces in the mind of a man a certain exact sense of justice, opposite . . . to those moral virtues which forbid our always adhering rigidly to the rules of private interest and suffer us to neglect this for the advantage of others" (*SL*, 317).

At a time when political economists were increasingly insisting that self-interest is the sole and universal motive for economic behavior, Montesquieu and followers such as Adam Ferguson were insisting that the acceptance of self-interest as a dominating consideration in human behavior was confined to one of the four types of society. And they were identifying this tendency of commercial societies as clearly undesirable.

Of the specific factors influencing the laws and customs of nations, Montesquieu's discussions of the forms and principles of government, of the environment, and of the modes of subsistence undoubtedly had the greatest impact. But perhaps more important than any one of these was his detailed support for the claim that the laws appropriate to any given place, time, and people depend in complex ways on a wide range of factors. Thus the claim of such associationists as Condorcet and Catherine Macaulay that because human nature was everywhere the same, justice and the law must be everywhere the same, seemed outrageously simplistic to those philosophical historians who developed Montesquieu's arguments. This feature of the tradition of philosophical history was widely appropriated to justify late-eighteenth-century conservative reactions to the French Revolution. Joseph de Maistre, for example, wrote, "Is not a constitution a solution to the following problem: Given the population, customs, religion, geographical situation, political relations, wealth, good and bad qualities of a particular nation, to find the laws which suit it? Yet this problem is not even approached in the 1795 constitution which was aimed solely at *man*. . . . A constitution that is made for all nations is made for none."[13]

Adam Ferguson's Natural History of Society

One of the shrewdest self-styled followers of Montesquieu was Adam Ferguson. Born in 1723 into the family of a minister to the village of Logerait, on the edge of the Scottish Highlands, Ferguson attended the University of St. Andrews and then studied divinity at the University of Edinburgh before he joined the First Highland Regiment of Foot for a nine-year stint as their chaplain. His time in the military with an Erse-speaking group of highlanders was a critical part of Ferguson's background; it gave him a much more positive attitude toward war than most of his intellectual friends and predecessors and it left him with a special appreciation for the values of a precommercial culture.

Ferguson seems to have been an outstanding soldier and chaplain, but his deepest interests were scholarly. He left his military position, returned to Edinburgh, and succeeded his friend, David Hume, as librarian of the Advocates Library. In 1759, he became professor of natural philosophy at Edinburgh and advanced to the more prestigious and lucrative chair of moral philosophy in 1764.

Like Montesquieu, Ferguson wrote a massive history of Rome (*History of the Progress and Termination of the Roman Republic*, 1783), and a more general work on the history of society (*An Essay on the History of Civil Society*, 1767). Ferguson's *Essay* was, by contemporary standards, a very brief work; yet it was generally acknowledged to be his most important. It was translated rapidly into French and German and came to have a major impact on the development of nineteenth-century German social theories of the right and the left through the writings of Schiller and Marx.[14] In Scotland it was admired by virtually all major intellectuals except David Hume, who criticized its literary style, but who, I suspect, was more disturbed by Ferguson's openly religious orientation than by the character of his prose.

Partly because of his earlier teaching of Newtonian natural philosophy and partly because of his admiration for Hume's empiricist approach to all philosophical subjects, Ferguson began his *Essay* with a methodological discussion which was most directly aimed at Hobbes but which also departed substantially from Montesquieu's Cartesian orientation. Attacking both the Hobbesian notion of a presocietal state of nature, and Montesquieu's a priori notion of human nature, Ferguson takes the position that the claims we make about human nature should be grounded empirically and since we have no experience of human beings except "as assembled in troops and companies," we should stop speculating about what men might have been like before they became socialized, "a time of which we have no record, and in relation to which our opinions can serve no purpose, and are supported by no evidence" (*HCS*, 6).

Complaining equally of those who, like Vico, "represent mankind in their first condition, as possessed of mere animal sensibility, without any faculties that render them superior to the brutes, without any political union, without any means of explaining their sentiments, and even without possessing any of the apprehensions and passions which the voice and gestures are so well fitted to express," and those like Hobbes, "who have made the state of nature to consist in perpetual wars," Ferguson argues that students of humanity should adopt the approach of natural historians:

> In every other instance . . . the natural historian thinks himself obliged to collect facts, not to offer conjectures. When he treats of any particular species of animals, he supposes that their present dispositions and instincts are the same as they originally had, and that their present life is a continuance of their first destination. He admits that his knowledge of the material system of the world consists of a collection of facts, or at most, in general tenets derived from particular observations and experiments. It is only as relates to himself, and in matters the most important, and the most easily known, that he substitutes hypotheses instead of reality, and confounds the provinces of imagination and reason, of poetry and science. (*HCS*, 2)

Thus Ferguson adopts the same anti-hypothetical form of Newtonian empiricism that Hume does in his works. Moreover, in doing so he explicitly rejects the Lockean strategy of developing hypotheses through the use of analogies. Because the human being is ineluctibly different from other animals, he insists, "we can learn nothing of its nature from the analogy of other animals" (*HCS*, 6).

What most distinguishes humans from the other animals is the fact that they express a drive "to invent and contrive" (*HCS*, 6) and the fact that they use language, which allows them to preserve past inventions so that they can build upon them and progress as a species. "In other classes of animals, the individual advances from infancy to age or maturity and he attains in the compass of a single life, to all the perfection his nature can reach: but in the human kind, the species has a progress as well as the individual; they build in every subsequent age on foundations formerly laid; and in a succession of years, tend to a perfection in the application of their faculties, to which the aid of long experience is required, and to which many generations must have combined their endeavours" (*HCS*, 4–5). It is in this sense that we can truly say that humans are the artificers or creators of themselves and their societies. And it is for this reason that Ferguson insists that opposition between natural and artificial has no legitimacy in connection with humans. Humans are natural artisans, and they act just as naturally in urban commercial settings as they do in the primitive conditions at the Cape of

Good Hope or the Straits of Magellan (*HCS*, 8). It is also for this reason that a natural history of mankind, unlike that of any other species, must include an historical analysis of the dynamical processes by which men move from their earliest, savage and barbarian societies to the most recent, commercial ones.

When Ferguson approaches the problem of relating their ancient ancestors to the contemporary civil societies of Europe, however, he sees another critical methodological problem. All of the accounts we have of the most ancient and primitive nations are deeply flawed because they have all reflected the cultural biases of the reporters (*HCS*, 76). How then are we to gain access to the customs and institutions of the ancient Britons, Gauls, and Germans? Ferguson takes a tack much like that of Vico. We learn about European ancestors by studying contemporary cultures at the same stage of development (*HCS*, 80–81).

Drawing heavily from the presumably objective observations of recent scientifically trained travelers in America (especially P. F. X. Charlevoix's *Histoire et description generale de la Nouvelle-France* [History and description of New France] [1744], J. F. Lafitau's *Moers des sauvages américains* [Customs of the American Indians] [1724], and Cadwallader Colden's *History of the Five Indian Nations* [1727] Ferguson continued to explore the major topics that had interested Montesquieu and added investigations of new issues, including kinship patterns and the sexual division of labor.

We have already seen that Ferguson shared and even made more explicit the claims of Vico and Montesquieu that changes in human societies were most often the result of unintended consequences. But he also focused on two particular mechanisms through which unintended consequences were produced, giving them a new and important significance. First, Ferguson was among the first philosophical historians to clearly argue that conflict among factional interests may be a major source of social benefit and progress, rather than something to be avoided or controlled.

With rare exceptions, earlier social scientists had considered partial interests or special interest groups impediments to all attempts to serve the general good of society. Within cameralist thought, for example, one of the major justifications for governmental regulation of economic life was that in the absence of regulation, the class of merchants and the class of artisans would each seek to serve its own interests to the detriment of the common good. Within associationist psychology, especially in its Helvetian form, the existence of powerful group interests was seen as invariably opposed to the general welfare. Even in the philosophical-historical tradition as represented in the works of Harrington and Montesquieu, while it was acknowledged that different class interests existed, the major goal was to control and balance them and to constrain individuals to act in the common interest rather than in the interests of their particular class or faction.

Ferguson admits that "amidst the contentions of party, the interests of the public, even the maxims of justice and candor are *sometimes* forgotten." But, he insists, "those fatal consequences which such a measure of corruption seems to portend, do not invariably follow. . . . Liberty is maintained by the continued differences and oppositions of numbers, not by their concurring in zeal in behalf of equitable government. In Free states, therefore, the wisest laws are never, perhaps, dictated by the interest and spirit of any order of men: they are moved, they are opposed, or amended, by different hands; and come at last to express that medium and composition which contending parties have forced one another to adopt" (*HCS*, 128). The improvement of laws thus emerges out of a process of competition among party or class interests, and though this process is often slow, it leads to perpetual change. Indeed, Ferguson argues, "we mistake human nature, if we wish for a termination of labor, or a scene of repose" (*HCS*, 7).

The notion that progress in legislation emerges frequently, if not always, out of conflict rather than as an automatic result of greater enlightenment is just one example illustrating Ferguson's generally positive evaluation of human conflict. That evaluation differentiated him radically from virtually all of the natural-law theorists and psychological theorists who preceded him and who saw the desire for peace as the most fundamental foundation of civil societies (*HCS*, 24).

When the human proclivity for conflict is aimed at individuals within the community, Ferguson sees it as detestable; but when it is harnessed to serve community interests rather than private ones, it becomes admirable. In another marvelous case of providential action, comparable to that by which the private vice of avarice comes to serve the common interests in economic life, the private vice of animosity comes to serve the national interest through war or the threat of war. It is not simply the case that the practice of violence is necessary for immediate purposes of national defense. More importantly, the very creation of community solidarity depends upon the perception of hostile outsiders (*HCS*, 22, 25).

Ferguson's tendency to admit the excercise of force and violence for public purposes to a prominent role among "the greatest and most improving exertions" of humankind (*HCS*, 119) has clear resonances with classical political theory in which participation in military activity is a key feature of public life. But Ferguson's argument is vastly different from that of the classical theorists in that it is grounded in a descriptive social science rather than a normative social theory.

If Ferguson's analysis of the positive and progressive roles of both intranational and international conflict is unique among eighteenth-century philosophical historians, his discussions of the centrality of the division of labor as a driving force in social development and his deep ambivalence toward the long-term consequences of its increasing are typical.

Ferguson clearly articulated the belief, probably derived from Hume and Hutcheson, that though humans act both out of private self-interest and social passions, the social passions offer by far the greater scope for human happiness. "It should seem . . . to be the happiness of man to make his social disposition the ruling spring of his occupations; to state himself as a member of a community, for whose general good his heart may glow with an ardent zeal, to the suppression of those personal cares which are the foundation of painful anxieties, fear, jealousy, and envy" (*HCS*, 54). Until the emergence of private property there is a very limited domain in which private interests can grow to challenge and interfere with the social passions. But when, in savage societies, the division of labor first begins and humans begin to develop specialized skills and "lucrative arts," such as flint working and bow making, they hoard their own products in order to exchange them for other things that they need, and these hoards constitute the first appearance of private wealth (*HCS*, 97). In this way, the division of labor initiates a process by which economic issues (the domain of self-interest) begin to expand relative to public issues (the domain of social passions) in motivating human behavior.

At each successive stage in society, private economic consider-ations become more dominant, until in advanced commercial soci-ety, which offers tremendous economic benefits, there is virtually no room left for the social bonds which enrich community life. "It is here indeed, if ever, that man is sometimes found a detached and solitary being: he has found an object which sets him in competition with his fellow creatures, and he deals with them as he does with his cattle and his soil, for the sake of the profits they bring. The mighty engine which we suppose to have formed [commercial] society, only tends to set its members at variance, or to continue their intercourse after the bonds of affection are broken" (*HCS*, 19).

Where the division of labor has proceeded the furthest—in manufacturing—this process of desocialization or dehumanization is most complete. Mechanic arts, in particular, "succeed best under a total suppression of sentiment and reason; and . . . prosper most where the mind is least consulted, and where the workshop may, without any great effort of imagination, be considered as an engine, the parts of which are men" (*HCS*, 182–83). As we shall see, Adam Smith, too, was concerned with the unfortunate human implications of the division of labor; but his vision was much more ambivalent than Ferguson's.

Once again, the enterprise of philosophical history offered an analysis which became central to conservative attitudes at the end of the century. For conservatives such as Burke saw in the calculated self-interest celebrated by the economists an attack on those social passions of love, veneration, admiration, and attachment which, they argued, more rightfully guided human actions (*RRF*, 91).

11

Fused Sciences and Mixed Ideological Messages: The Glasgow School of Hutcheson, Smith, and Millar

Although the psychological, political-economic, and philosophical-historical strategies of social-scientific analysis interpenetrated one another increasingly throughout the eighteenth century, the perspectives of most self-styled scientific students of human society prior to the French Revolution were dominated by one of the three. This generalization does not, however, hold true for one important and continuous tradition of social science that began with Francis Hutcheson, professor of moral philosophy at Glasgow from 1730 to 1746, and continued with his student Adam Smith, professor of moral philosophy at Glasgow from 1751 to 1766, and Smith's student, John Millar, professor of civil law at Glasgow from 1761 to his death in 1801.

Hutcheson sought to fuse a psychologically based system of ethics with political economy and to transform the study of jurisprudence patterned on Pufendorf and Harrington into a comprehensive scheme of moral philosophy. This project was taken over by Smith, who departed from Hutcheson's treatment and undertook a historically based approach to jurisprudence grounded in Montesquieu's four-fold division of societies into hunting, herding, agricultural, and commercial. Finally, Millar refined Smith's approach to moral-philosophical issues and extended it to produce one of the earliest comparative psychological, economic, and sociological analyses of sexuality and gender in a wide range of cultures.

Arguably, the psychological, political-economic, and philosophical-historical schools of early social science began by incorporating mutually incompatible assumptions and grew up initially in competition with one another. Moreover, by the mid eighteenth century each of these traditions can be described as having its own characteristic ideological implications. If both propositions are true, then attempts to fuse the three traditions into a single approach should have involved special methodological and conceptual problems and tensions. Such attempts should also have had ambiguous ideological implications. In what follows, I will try to show that both expectations are borne out.

Hutcheson and Smith on the Distinction Between Virtues and Duties

Though all of the members of the Glasgow School sought to develop a comprehensive moral philosophy, they began by admitting a fundamental distinction between ethics on the one hand and economics and politics on the other which resulted in a tension that, for all of their efforts, was never completely resolved. Though this tradition sought comprehensiveness, it never really achieved unity or coherence.

Hutcheson laid out this distinction at the beginning of his *A Short Introduction to Moral Philosophy* (1747). Initially, Hutcheson distinguishes between the domain of ethics involving the notion of virtue and the analysis of motives for actions, and the domain of natural law including an analysis of individual rights in society, economics, and politics.[1] This first distinction focuses on the different sources of ethical judgments which lie in internal sentiments and instincts, and of legal, political, and economic decisions which lie in reason and law. A few pages later, Hutcheson returns to look at this same distinction from a slightly different point of view in discussing the Stoics' moral doctrines and Cicero's *De officiis*:

> 'Tis well known that the Stoicks made such difference between *virtue*, which they counted the sole good, and the *officia*, or external duties of life, that they counted these duties among the *things indifferent*, neither morally good nor

evil. The design of these books, [Cicero's] *de officiis* is this; to show how persons in higher stations, already well in-structed in the fundamentals of moral philosophy, should so conduct themselves in life, that in perfect consistence with virtue they may obtain great interest, power, popularity, high offices, and glory. (*SIMP*, iii)

In several ways, Hutcheson's perspective differed from those of Cicero and the Stoics. First, he addressed himself to persons of modest situation as well as those of high station. Second, in line with the jurisprudential perspective inherited from Pufendorf through Gershom Carmichael, he placed greater emphasis on practical eco-nomic activity and interests than on political activity and glory as the realm in which humans pursue the vast majority of their life's goals. Indeed, for Hutcheson as well as for Smith and Millar, political activity was to be understood almost exclusively as aimed at providing a stable and protective structure and set of rules within which to carry out productive and procreative activities, rather than as the highest form of human activity in its own right. Smith stated this position most clearly in his lectures on jurisprudence when he insisted that "all the arts, the sciences, law and government, wisdom, and even virtue itself tend all to this one thing, the providing of meat, drink, raiment, and lodging for men, which are commonly reckoned the meanest of employments."[2]

In spite of their reinterpretation of activities traditionally under-stood to be superior to mere economic ones as now subordinate to them, Hutcheson and his followers retained the Stoic distinction between ethics and virtues on the one hand and economic and political rights and duties on the other. Furthermore, they all struggled with the problem of how humans could conduct them-selves in seeking their various interests with no express intention of being virtuous but in ways that were nonetheless consistent with the exercise of virtue.

In their analysis of ethics and virtue, which was prior to their analysis of economics, law, and government in all of their didactic works, the members of the Glasgow School drew primarily from the psychological tradition. Beginning from the claim that moral notions of good and evil are derived from our pleasures and pains, Hutcheson sought to understand how we come to experience pleasures that are not directly associated with our external senses and which seem to depend ultimately on the pleasures that others experience. It is a matter confirmed by many experiences, he insisted, that we feel a joy in the happiness of others and we admire and approve actions that give pleasure to others. It is even true, in violation of Hobbesian notions, that many people willingly sacrifice their goods, and even at times their lives, in order to protect their spouses, children, and members of their community. How are such actions to be understood?

Hutcheson claims that in addition to our external senses, we have an internal moral sense, which we sometimes call our conscience, "by which we discern what is graceful, becoming, beautiful and honorable in the affections of the soul, in our conduct of life, our words, and in our actions." Furthermore, "what is approved by this sense we count *right* and *beautiful*, and we call it *virtue*; what is condemned, we count *base* and *deformed*, and *vicious*" (*SIMP*, 17). One of the most important features of this claim is that judgments of virtue have nothing to do with reasonings about the consequences of acts. They are immediate emotional responses to the acts; so they lead to no claims about truth, only to admiration or revulsion.

When Smith took over the teaching of moral philosophy at the University of Glasgow, he followed Hutcheson's order of proceeding and began his course with a similar discussion of ethics, or virtue, publishing his reflections on this topic in *The Theory of Moral Sentiments* (1759). Moreover, though he incorporated several new insights derived from his reading of Hume's *Treatise on Human Nature*, he continued to accept Hutcheson's insistence that we have internal senses which respond immmediately and emotionally to virtuous and vicious actions. There is no way to establish moral rules in advance through any kind of rational analysis, we must simply discover them empirically (*TMS*, 159).

According to Hutcheson, when we explore what kinds of things our moral sense moves us to approve and admire, we discover that they are first and foremost what are often called the social passions (passions directed at the well-being of others) characterized by the terms beneficence or benevolence (*SIMP*, 17).

Very closely related to the moral sense is a second internal sense, that of honor and shame. This sense "makes the approbations, the gratitude, and the esteem of others who approve our conduct, [a] matter of high pleasure; and their censures, and condemnation, and infamy, [a] matter of severe uneasiness" (*SIMP*, 26). That is, humans want to be liked, just for the pleasure that the approval of others gives and regardless of whether that approval leads to any other rewards.

Smith recognizes a serious problem with Hutcheson's formulation of the consequences of the human desire to be admired. It is obvious to him that it could easily lead, in Machiavellian terms, more to a wish to *appear* virtuous than to *be* virtuous, which could indeed be narrowly selfish. Thus, when Smith deals with this issue, he offers an important modification to Hutcheson's argument. He insists that we not only want to be admired, we also want to *deserve* to be admired. "Nature, accordingly, has endowed [man], not only with a desire of being approved of, but with a desire of being what ought to be approved of; of being what he himself approves of in other men. The first desire could only have made him wish to appear to be fit for society. The second was necessary in order to render him anxious to be really fit."[3] Indeed, Smith goes on to argue very shrewdly that it is even more important for humans to approve of themselves than to have others approve of them.

Hutcheson and Smith on the Compatability Between Economic Activity and Virtue

When Hutcheson turned to analyze economic activities, he attempted to link them to the social passions, focusing on the notion that men do not only aim at their own private well-being but that they are motivated as well by their desire to seek the welfare of family and friends.[4] Even when he comes to his discussion of the division of labor, Hutcheson emphasizes the argument that specialization is consciously done for *mutual* benefit and that it furnishes "more joyful excercise of our social disposition" (*SMP*, 228).

Smith diverged radically from Hutcheson on the general nature of economic motives, arguing both in *The Theory of Moral Sentiments* and in the *Wealth of Nations*, that human actions in the economic domain are universally motivated out of self-love and not out of any social passions. Nonetheless, he insisted that such actions, properly constrained, might be virtuous or at least morally neutral.

In order to understand how this could be so, we need to understand how Smith extended the notion of virtue beyond Hutcheson's focus on benevolence by incorporating and developing David Hume's doctrine of *sympathy*. We have seen that for Smith, as for

Hutcheson, saying that an act or passion is virtuous is identical to saying that it deserves the general approval of those who do not directly benefit from the act. A person is said to be virtuous when he or she acts in such a way as to command approval. But Smith diverges from Hutcheson in understanding the mechanism by which approval is granted and consequently in understanding what range of passions and behaviors can be approved.

Smith begins, not by positing a distinct moral sense, but by arguing that all humans have a general ability to sympathize with the feelings of others by imagining themselves in the other's place (*TMS*, 12). Hume had already used this notion in an economic context to explain why wealth and power are approved and admired. "Riches give satisfaction to their possessor; and this satisfaction is conveyed to the beholder by the imagination, which produces an idea resembling the original impression in force and vivacity."[5]

Smith accepts Hume's analysis, but he turns it on its head by asking why people seek to become wealthy and powerful in the first place. "To what purpose is all the toil and bustle of this world? What is the end of avarice and ambition, of the pursuit of wealth, of power, of preeminence? . . . . What are the advantages which we propose by that great purpose of human life which we call bettering our condition?" (*TMS*, 50). His answer to this question is that all humans have a need "to be observed, to be attended to, to be taken notice of with *sympathy*, complacency, and approbation." It is not the goods which a rich person possesses so much as the admiration and compliance that they occasion that constitute the ultimate source of satisfaction produced by wealth. In Smith's extremely illuminating phrase "it is the *vanity*, not the ease, or the pleasure, which interests us" (*TMS*, 50–51).

Smith carries his discussion of the sympathetic grounds for approving actions or passions and our reciprocal desire to be objects of sympathy in important directions that Hume had left unexplored. These directions were probably suggested by Aristotle's doctrine of imitation which Smith had explored in preparation for his 1750 lectures on rhetoric and belles lettres at Edinburgh. For Aristotle, there is a special pleasure which derives from the artistic imitation of reality. This is why we get pleasure from looking at the painting of an unpleasant scene. The pleasure given by our awareness of the successful imitation prevails over the unhappy associations of the subject matter. Analogously, for Smith, we get a special pleasure from our sympathetic entrance into another's situation when that person acts or expresses emotion in just the way and to the degree that we would imagine ourselves to act or feel in the same situation. Thus, we get a special pleasure from and unreservedly approve an expression of sorrow we imagine we would feel in like circumstances (*TMS*, 46, note b). In this case we say that the person feels or acts appropriately or with *propriety* and we may judge the act or feeling to be *virtuous*.

Many, indeed most, completely appropriate acts are not normally thought of as virtuous. For example, says Smith, it is completely appropriate to eat when we are hungry; but such an act does not call forth special approval from others. Only behaviors and passions which are simultaneously appropriate and out of the ordinary, or, as Smith says, "uncommonly great and beautiful," deserve the term virtuous (*TMS*, 25). For this reason, though acting out of self-interest in economic matters may be completely appropriate, it is not ordinarily virtuous. On the other hand, self-interested acts are not automatically excluded from being virtuous. In the sixth edition of *The Theory of Moral Sentiments*, published in 1790, Smith emphasized the *virtue* of the prudent man, who is the very epitome of the purely self-interested economic actor and the very opposite of Hutcheson's benevolent man who always directs his actions toward the good of others. "The prudent man is not willing to subject himself to any responsibility which duty does not impose upon him. . . . He confines himself, as much as his duty will permit, to his own affairs. . . . In the bottom of his heart he would prefer the undisturbed enjoyment of secure tranquility not only to all the splendor of successful ambition, but to the real and solid glory of performing the greatest and most magnanimous actions" (*TMS*, 216).

Such a man may not command the greatest love and esteem, but he is nonetheless deserving of approval. "In the steadiness of his industry and frugality, in his steadily sacrificing the ease and enjoyment of the present moment for the probable expectation of the still greater ease and enjoyment of a more distant but more lasting period of time, the prudent man is always both supported and rewarded by the entire approbation of the impartial spectator" (*TMS*, 215). Thus, the pursuit of economic self-interest, when it exhibits unusual prudence, may itself be virtuous.

Both in *The Theory of Moral Sentiments* and in the *Wealth of Nations*, Smith recognizes that in many cases economic motives are unfortunately neither virtuous nor morally neutral. Yet, they may still lead to outcomes which benefit society as a whole and for that reason deserve approval. In order to account for this situation Smith abandons the psychological strategies that ground most of his arguments regarding the consistency of economic activity with virtue and adopts the unintended consequences or providentialist arguments of the philosophical historians and political economists, calling forth his famous invisible hand.

In *The Theory of Moral Sentiments*, for example, when Smith seeks to understand how the acquisition of land and wealth by a very few can be consistent with the general welfare of all, he calls on providence:

> When Providence divided the earth among a few Lordly masters, it neither forgot nor abandoned those who seemed to have been left out of the partition. The rich . . . in spite of their natural selfishness and rapacity, though they mean only their own coveniency, though the sole end which they propose from the labors of the thousands whom they employ, be the gratification of their own vain and insatiable desires, they divide with the poor the produce of all their improvements. *They are led as by an invisible hand* to make nearly the same distribution of the necessaries of life, which would have been made, had the earth been divided into equal portions among all its inhabitants. (*TMS*, 184–85)

In this case the general economic benefit derives from actions characterized explicitly as not simply amoral but as immoral.

In the *Wealth of Nations* Smith returns to an almost identical use of the vanity of wealthy landowners, this time to account for the historical and progressive transformation of agricultural society into commercial society. "A revolution of the greatest importance to the publick happiness, was in this manner brought about by two different orders of people, who had not the least intention to serve the public. To gratify the most childish vanity was the sole motive of the great proprietors. The merchants and artificers, much less ridiculous, acted merely from a view to their own interest, and in pursuit of their own pedlar principle of turning a penny wherever a penny was to be got. Neither of them had either knowledge or foresight of that great revolution which the folly of the one and the industry of the other, was gradually bringing about."[6]

It is true that Smith was consistent throughout his career in his analyses of the motives for economic activity. It is also true that his analyses were *comprehensive* in arguing that socially beneficial economic actions could emerge out of virtuous, morally neutral, and vicious motives alike. But it is hard to see coherence in a system that accounts for the legitimacy of economic activities through an analysis of human psychology only so long as their motives are morally acceptable and then switches to a sociological account when they are not.

The Glasgow School on the Relationships Among Justice, Law, and Government

Francis Hutcheson distinguished between virtue, grounded in benevolence and judged by the moral sense, and duty grounded in reason and judged by conformity to law. Stated in a slightly different way, he followed Pufendorf in distinguishing between *imperfect rights*, which relate to actions that we might expect others to do on our behalf but which we cannot compel them to do, and *perfect rights*, which relate to actions that others ought to do for us and which we may compel them to do if they do not do them voluntarily. Virtue is about imperfect rights, and justice is about perfect rights.

In *The Theory of Moral Sentiments*, Smith contended that justice is itself a virtue, grounded in the sympathy that humans have for those injured through violence, fraud, and theft. Furthermore, he insisted that our acceptance of the general rules of justice, or laws, does not arise out of a rational consideration of the necessity of law for the preservation of society, but out of our sympathy for particular victims of injury (*TMS*, 89). Smith did, however, accept the Hutcheson-Pufendorf distinction between perfect and imperfect rights in relation to the notion of compulsion.[7] Perfect rights form, for Smith, the subject matter of *commutative justice* or jurisprudence, whereas imperfect rights form the subject matter of *distributive justice* or morality. Commutative justice then becomes the subject of a special section of Smith's moral philosophy on the grounds that it is the one virtue that humans can be compelled to exhibit through the creation and enforcement of laws by governments, or civil societies.

Strictly speaking, for Smith, as for the jurisprudential tradition from the time of Rome, injury can be done to a person in connection with property only if the person has a prior exclusive interest in the property. Laws, then, are properly rules to redress injury. Thus it is appropriate to compel persons to respect my right to what I already own, but it is inappropriate to try to compel persons to share part of what they own with me. This is why, according to Smith, jurisprudence, or law—and therefore, governments—cannot legitimately intervene in people's lives to redistribute property and income.

This association of compulsion with commutative justice and voluntarism with distributive justice is the consequence of the acceptance of a particular legal tradition; and Smith offers only an assertion of the legitimacy of the distinction, not a justification. However, Smith's student, John Millar, does offer a fascinating justification for why compulsion is appropriate in connection with commutative but not distributive justice. He does not use Smith's terminology but instead uses the term justice to stand exclusively for commutative justice. Millar also implies that this justification was shared by Smith.

Millar argues that the greatest difference between justice and all other virtues is that the rules of justice are capable of accuracy and precision whereas the other virtues are more uncertain and open to interpretation.[8] The reason then that we are justified in compelling adherence to justice is that we are capable of creating consensus regarding the precise character of its applications while we cannot do the same with respect to other virtues, that is, we can produce a genuine *science* of law (*Millar*, 344). Compulsion is justified only where precise agreement is attainable. That Millar thought this view was consistent with Smith's is suggested by the fact that in giving an account of Smith's lectures on moral philosophy Millar wrote that after the doctrines of ethics, which were subsequently published in *The Theory of Moral Sentiments*, Smith "treated at more length that branch of morality which relates to *justice*, and which, being susceptible of precise and accurate rules, is for that reason capable of a full and particular explanation" (*LJ*, Introduction, 3).

When he treated the topic of justice and its relationships to law and government in his lectures on jurisprudence, Smith openly abandoned the approach of Pufendorf and Hutcheson because it had begun with lengthy discussions of "natural law," that is, laws as they relate to humans in a state of nature, or outside of civil society. Like his friend Ferguson, Smith found such discussions vacuous. "It in reality serves no purpose to treat the laws which would take place in a state of nature," Smith argued, "as there is no such state existing" (*LJ*, 398). Unlike Pufendorf and Hutcheson, Montesquieu had dealt with laws as they emerged as a matter of historical fact in various societies. Smith thought that we had to study the virtues empirically and insisted that we use the same approach with justice. He thus adopted the historical approach of Montesquieu. When he did so, he began to view governments in a new light:

> [When] some have great wealth and others nothing, it is necessary that the arm of authority should be continually stretched forth, and permanent laws, or regulations made which may ascertain the property of the rich from the inroads of the poor, who would otherwise continually make encroachments upon it. . . . *Laws and government may be considered in this, and indeed, in every case, as a combination of the rich to oppress the poor,* and preserve themselves in the inequality of goods which would otherwise soon be destroyed by the attacks of the poor, who, if not hindered by the government would soon reduce the others to an equality with themselves by open violence. (*LJ*, 208)

The use of the notion of oppression here to indicate the relationship of the rich to the poor suggests a serious tension between Smith's sociological account of the nature of commutative justice and the Utilitarian ideals implicitly accepted from his reading of Hutcheson's and Hume's psychological theories. In spite of his belief in both the inevitability of distinctions of wealth and their moral legitimacy, he was constantly bothered by the fact that "the labor and time of the poor, are in civilized countries, sacrificed to the maintaining of the rich in ease and luxury" (*SMA*, 11). Even in the *Wealth of Nations* he continued to argue that there was a principle of equity that was not supported by laws and which suggested "that they who feed, clothe, and lodge the whole body of the people, should have such a share of the produce of their own labor as to be themselves, tolerably well fed, clothed, and lodged." And he further argued that "no society can surely be flourishing and happy, of which the greater part of the members are poor and miserable" (*WN*, 96).

Since governments are in no position to ensure or even encourage the well-being of the poor vis-à-vis the rich, Smith had increasingly to appeal to a providential invisible hand to ensure that the poor did not simply become increasingly impoverished. Most importantly, the division of labor, which increased apace with the movement of society from hunting to commercial forms, increased productivity so spectacularly that even in the face of increasing differentials of wealth, the situation of the poor improved. Thus, writes Smith, "among civilized and thriving nations . . . though a great many people do not labor at all, many of whom consume the produce of ten times, frequently of a hundred times more labor than the greater part of those who work; yet the produce of the whole labor of the society is so great, that all are often abundantly supplied, and a workman, even of the lowest and poorest order, if he is frugal and industrious, may enjoy a greater share of the necessities and conveniences of life than it is possible for any savage to acquire" (*WN*, 10).

Fortunately for Smith's peace of mind, it seemed that even within commercial society the division of labor continued to increase productivity. An investigation of the relationship between wages paid to common laborers and the price of necessities—especially that of grain—over the 40 year period before the publication of the *Wealth of Nations* assured him that the standard of living of the laboring poor was still on the rise (*WN*, 95–96). But given his argument in *The Theory of Moral Sentiments* that the relative wealth or poverty of people is much more important than their absolute material standard of living (*TMS*, 50), it is surprising that Smith has nothing to say about this potentially embarrassing issue in the *Wealth of Nations*.

Smith's Ambivalence Toward the Consequences of the Extreme Division of Labor

Among the many topics which Smith investigated from both a relatively narrow economic perspective and from a more inclusive sociological perspective none was more important, and none demonstrates the divergent implications of the two perspectives more clearly, than the division of labor. This topic is especially important because the division of labor stands as the central guiding principle of Smith's *Wealth of Nations* in much the same way that the principle of sympathy stands as the guiding principle of *The Theory of Moral Sentiments*.

Although Smith insists that the division of labor emerges as an unintended consequence of the human tendency to "truck, barter, and exchange" rather than out of some wisdom that "foresees and intends the general opulence to which it gives occasion" (*WN*, 25), he also insists that once it has been initiated, the division of labor is responsible for the vast increases in productivity that lead to ever greater wealth. Though the invention of and investment in machinery and other technological innovations is granted some role, even innovation is seen to be largely a product of the division of labor. For on the one hand, the division creates a special category of "philosophers" who have special responsibility for innovation (*WN*, 21–22), while on the other, when men focus all of their attention on a single task, they are more likely to find ways of doing it more efficiently and with less effort (*WN*, 20).

Considered from a purely economic standpoint, which is the perspective taken by Smith in book 1 of the *Wealth of Nations*, the division of labor is an unmixed blessing. It is capable of increasing the productivity of a single laborer between 240- and 4,800-fold (*WN*, 14–15) and, as such, it is the great engine which drives economic progress. Moreover, because the division of labor can be carried further where markets are greater, it is the principle that drives a wide range of economic policies. Not only does it drive the demand to increase population densities, it also leads to the desirability of foreign trade, to the search for ever-expanding export markets, and to the need for the state to take responsibility for improving transportation networks in order to expand local markets.

But when the division of labor is considered from the broader perspectives of philosophical history or of individual psychology, as in Smith's lectures on jurisprudence and in book 5 of the *Wealth of Nations*, it is seen to have serious negative consequences. It is, for example, responsible for producing a kind of intellectual and moral degeneracy. In rude societies where there is little division of labor and where everyone must be virtually self-sufficient, "every man has a considerable degree of knowledge, ingenuity, and invention" (*WN*, 783). But in advanced societies, where the division of labor has become extensive, the range of activities engaged in by any laboring man is so narrowly confined that his intellect and ingenuity is stultified:

> The man whose whole life is spent in performing a few simple operations, of which the effects too are, perhaps, always the same, or very nearly the same, has no occasion to exert his understanding, or to excercise his invention in finding out expedients for removing difficulties which never occur. He naturally loses, therefore, the habit of such exertion, and generally becomes as stupid and ignorant as it is possible for a human creature to become. The torpor of his

mind renders him, not only incapable of relishing or bearing a part in any rational conversation, but of conceiving any generous, noble, or tender sentiment, and consequently of forming any just judgment concerning many even of the ordinary duties of private life. (*WN*, 782)

In this passage and in his economic analyses of the division of labor Smith exhibits one of his few open inconsistencies. When he wants to focus on the economic value of the division of labor, he argues that innovation is the logical consequence of concentrating on a single task; whereas when he wants to discuss the broader psychological impact of the division of labor he insists that the ability to innovate is "obliterated and extinguished" (*WN*, 783–84) in a person who narrows his attention excessively.

Where manufacturing has proceeded the furthest all of the problems associated with the division of labor are intensified; for as Smith argues, if narrow experience produces stupidity and ignorance," this must be much more the case when a person's whole attention is bestowed on the 17th part of a pin or the 80th part of a button" (*LJ*, 539).

In principle, the extreme ignorance of the laboring poor might be obviated by the provision of universal education; but the division of labor puts increasing barriers in the way of this proposed solution by making tasks so simple that children can be employed at increasingly young ages. Thus, in Scotland, where the division of labor was not yet extensive, Smith argued, education was relatively cheap because there was no cost in lost opportunity until a child was 8 or 9 years old. For this reason, most children received at least a rudimentary education. In the English Midlands, however, the situation was completely different. There, where the division of labor had been pushed much further in manufacturing establishments, "a boy of 6 or 7 years of age in Birmingham can gain his 3 pence or sixpence a day, and parents find it to be their interest to set them soon to work. Thus their education is neglected" (*LJ*, 540).

Ultimately, Smith ended up in a position much like that of his colleague Adam Ferguson, arguing that in spite of the great material advantages produced by the division of labor, unless governments took some active role in combating its negative impact, its price would be the creation of an underclass that was "mutilated and deformed" in the most essential parts of its human character (*WN*, 788).

The Success of the *Wealth of Nations*

When Adam Smith's *Wealth of Nations* finally appeared in 1776, after a decade of preparation, it was both an immediate and a long-term success. In the short run its appeal in Britain was at least partly dependent on the fact that it addressed a great many contemporary policy issues and, despite some of its odd qualifications, it largely told people what they wanted to hear.

In an era of spectacular economic growth led by increasing agricultural productivity brought about by investment in farm equipment, manuring, and the like, Smith demonstrated that investment in agriculture was the first priority for economic growth (*WN*, 363). In an era of rising standards of living for almost all and of immense concern for individual liberties, Smith affirmed the widespread perception that life was good and getting better and he assured people that the pattern of economic growth and increases in real income would continue without the need for government meddling in the private lives of people. The "system of natural liberty" promoted by Hutcheson was now shown to be one which maximized the economic well-being of both individual economic actors and the group. The government did not, for example, have to worry about directing capital flows into industries that would benefit the nation because the investor's natural desire for risk-free, high-yield investments would automatically lead him to do the correct thing for the entire nation (*WN*, 456). And the laborer is under no less compulsion to maximize the national well-being when he seeks to improve his own wages by moving into areas with high labor demands (*WN*, 454).

In the rousing conclusion to book 4 of the *Wealth of Nations*, Smith surveys the mercantile (cameralist) system with its emphases on commerce and governmental regulation, the agricultural (physiocratic) system with its preferential treatment of agriculture, and his own system of natural liberty. After he has shown that the alternative systems must all fail in achieving their goals, he writes:

> All systems either of preference or restraint, therefore, being thus completely taken away, the obvious and simple system of natural liberty establishes itself of its own accord. Every man, as long as he does not violate the laws of justice, is left perfectly free to pursue his own interest in his own way, and to bring both his industry and capital into competition with

those of any other man, or order of men. The sovereign is completely discharged from a duty, in the attempting to perform which he must always be exposed to innumerable delusions, and for the proper performance of which no human wisdom or knowledge could ever be sufficient: the duty of superintending the industry of private people, and of directing it toward the employments most suitable to the interest of the society. (*WN*, 687)

Liberal economic ideas had been on the ascendant in Britain throughout the eighteenth century, and Smith's work systematized and synthesized these liberal trends in a stirring way.

Smith accomplished his task in a way that seemed to offer both material and psychic rewards to every person and class. To the laboring and minor artisanal classes he offered the prospect of upward economic mobility through the excercise of industry and prudence. To the wealthy landowning class he offered assurance that the established hierarchy of wealth and power that gave them their status was both appropriate and secure. And to the class of wealthy entrepreneurs and merchants he offered both the freedom of unregulated economic maneuvering and the assurance that their role was absolutely central to the process of economic growth, in spite of the fact that their interests in particular cases might not always coincide with those of the laboring and landowning classes (*WN*, 266).

Finally, Smith managed to offer his recommendations in a remarkably non-threatening way. If he proposed colonial policies that were opposed to the mercantilist dominated ones of the government, or if he opposed the preferential governmental treatment of industries that exercised well-established interest-group pressures on Parliament, he was much too shrewd to exhibit the doctrinaire "enthusiasm" of some of the Utilitarians who shared many of his basic economic attitudes. Though he was an unflagging advocate of free trade, for example, he was sufficiently aware of the tenacious hold of tradition and of power politics so that he neither expected nor advocated a massive immediate abandonment of all economic regulations. "To expect, indeed, that the freedom of trade should ever be entirely restored in Great Britain, is as absurd as to expect that an Oceana or Utopia should ever be established in it. Not only the prejudices of the public, but what is more unconquerable, the private interests of many individuals, irresistibly oppose it" (*WN*, 471). The deep pragmatic streak in Smith illustrated in this passage

certainly helped to cushion the shock that many of his recommendations might have given to certain special interests. It was thus
possible to accept his general arguments without giving in on any of
his specific discomforting policy advice.

The *Wealth of Nations* was more than a brilliantly conceived and
executed tract for the times, however. As late as 1954, Joseph
Schumpeter, whose major interest in the history of economics was in
technical methods of analysis, wrote that the *Wealth of Nations* was
"the most successful, not only of all books on economics, but, with
the possible exception of Darwin's *Origin of Species*, of all scientific
books that have appeared to this day."[9] While strong cases might be
made for Newton's *Principia* or Euclid's *Elements of Geometry*, there is
no doubt that in terms of its combined general cultural impact and
more narrowly construed impact on the development of a professional discipline, Smith's work stands in a very select group.

Smith's thorough scavenging of prior and contemporary economic
literature, coupled with his summary of his opponent's systems in
book 4, made the *Wealth of Nations* into such a comprehensive and
encyclopedic treatment that its readers had little need to look
elsewhere for information on any topic treated by political economy.
In creating an eminently readable work that offered clear illustrative
examples for every point it sought to make and that incorporated
such a huge fraction of the widely accepted results from its predecessors, Smith produced a text which, like Euclid's *Elements of
Geometry*, came to form a barrier between his predecessors and his
successors. Economists, from the early-nineteenth to the late-
twentieth centuries, have viewed Smith as the initiator and codifier
of political economy.

John Millar and the Beginnings of a Sociology of Gender

Though its long-term pattern of reception was very different from
that accorded to the *Wealth of Nations, The Origin of the Distinction of
Ranks: or an Enquiry into the Circumstances Which Give Rise to Influence
and Authority in the Different Members of Society*, first published in
1771 and written by Smith's former student John Millar, is an equally
fascinating product of the Glasgow School's fusion of social-scientific
approaches. The *Origin of Ranks* had a substantial initial success,
going through at least six English-language editions as well as
translations into German, French, and Italian by 1798. But it virtually

disappeared in the English-speaking world between 1810 and 1960. Since its reissue in 1960, historians of sociology and anthropology have begun to see Millar's work as among the most important and insightful foundational works in both fields.[10]

One feature of the *Origin of Ranks* which distinguishes it from any other eighteenth-century analysis of society that purports to be general and scientific is the priority and centrality which it gives to the roles and status of women. The first and by far the longest chapter in the work, comprising some 36 percent of the text, is descriptively titled "Of the Rank and Condition of Women in Different Ages." While one might not have been surprised at seeing the emphasis on what we now call gender in a French work of the period, it is unexpected in a work on the sources of societal power and influence written for an exclusively male audience and within one of the most rigidly patriarchal cultures in Europe.

Some discussion of the role of women in society was a traditional part of jusrisprudentially based moral philosophy from Pufendorf on, and both Hume and Hutcheson had focused on the centrality of sexual attraction in promoting the development of the social passions in general. Moreover, Hutcheson had been particularly emphatic in insisting that men and women have equal and identical biological and moral interests in their unions. That Millar would have to say something about women as part of a discussion of marriage and family was thus a natural consequence of his writing within the Glasgow tradition of moral philosophy. In addition, his decision to emphasize the relative equality of male and female within discussions of sexuality and family followed naturally from his Hutchesonian leanings. But even Hutcheson had only devoted about 3 percent of his *Short Introduction to Moral Philosophy* to these issues. We therefore need to look elsewhere to understand the extent of Millar's consideration of male/female relations and the status of women.

When Millar left Glasgow as a 17 year old, he moved to Edinburgh to study law. Adam Smith, who had become closely attached to his enthusiastic student, arranged for Millar to live with his old friend, Henry Home, lord Kames, as tutor to Kames's son. Kames was, at the time, chief justice of the Court of Sessions in Edinburgh, and he was deeply involved in attempts to reform Scots law to bring it more closely into alignment with the Roman law foundations of continental jurisprudence. For two years Millar lived with Kames, serving not only as his son's tutor, but as his chief intellectual foil while Kames struggled with issues of law reform. Kames and Millar came to realize that there was no subject on which Justinian's version of Roman law differed from both English and Scots common law more than in its treatment of women.

Many feminist scholars have emphasized that English common law treated women very poorly; and Scots law tended to be even more discriminatory. In English and Scots common law, for example, women were not treated as competent to enter into contracts except in connection with household management; and in Scots law a husband could even repudiate his wife's right to purchase groceries. But under Roman law as it had been codified under Justinian, adult women had precisely the same rights with regard to owning property and entering into contracts that males who were under the authority of a paterfamilias had, that is, they were treated as independent Roman citizens. Similarly, whereas intestate inheritance was completely in the male line under English and Scots law, under Justinian's code all children, male and female alike, shared the inheritance equally. Moreover, this inheritance pattern was explicitly justified in terms of sex equity. Thus Justinian's *Institutes* argues, "No difference should be made between males and females in this connection . . . each sex plays its own part in the procreation of mankind, and from early times the Twelve Tables gave them equal rights of intestate succession."[11]

Though there were some major differences in Roman law treatment of males and females produced by the patriarchal structure of the late-Roman family, for most private purposes Roman law under Justinian treated males and females under the authority of a paterfamilias identically, whereas English and Scots common law certainly did not.

Here lies one of the central reasons that both Millar and Kames became so concerned with investigating the changing conditions of women in society. Both men believed, following Montesquieu, that formal laws reflect deeply rooted cultural patterns. Thus, if law codes vary widely with regard to a particular issue, that issue is one in which large variations in cultural practices should be anticipated and it is one which should provide a particularly sensitive probe for the investigation of differences among cultures. For this reason, Millar begins the very first sentence of the first chapter of the *Origin of Ranks* with the claim that "of all our passions, it would seem that those which unite the sexes are most easily affected by the particular circumstances in which we are placed, and most liable to be influenced by the power of habit and education. Upon this account they exhibit the most wonderful variety of appearances, and, in different ages and different countries, have produced the greatest diversity of manners and customs" (*Millar*, 183).

When Pufendorf, Hutcheson, Smith, and even Adam Ferguson took up the discussion of sexual passions it had always been in the context of the notion of family as it had been used within the Roman juridical tradition. The family was understood to be a stable social grouping created by an act of marriage and built upon a dominant male, a subordinate female, and their offspring. Moreover, all of these men continued to argue as if such a family unit was somehow both natural and universal. Pushing the cultural relativism of the philosophical-historical school much further than his colleagues, Millar recognized that this kind of family unit was itself a particular cultural artifact that did not exist in all early societies, and may not have existed in any of them.

Millar argues rather that "there is good reason to believe, that in the state of simplicity which precedes all cultivation and improvement, the intercourse of the sexes is chiefly regulated by the primary intention of nature; and that it is of consequence, totally interrupted by the periods of pregnancy" (*Millar*, 184). In a few hunting societies, especially where the function of paternity may not have been well understood when social arrangements were being established, permanent male-female couples may not even be the norm. Polyandry may be common, and the typical "family" of later cultures may be preceded by matrilineal and sometimes even by matriarchal social organizations such as those described in Lafitau's accounts of the Iroquois nations.

Millar did not have the terms matrilineal and matriarchal available. He therefore had to speak about cultures in which "if any person was desired to give an account of the family to which he belonged, he was naturally led to recount his maternal genealogy in the female line" (*Millar*, 199). Likewise, he had to speak of cultures in which the habit of deference to women extended to allowing them roles in public deliberative bodies and even to giving them "the priviledge of being the first called to give their opinion on every subject of deliberation" (*Millar*, 200). Thus Millar turned away from terms like family and marriage to initiate his discussion of the relations between the sexes in favor of what seemed to him the more general phrase "the condition of women."

When we turn to understand the status which women have in

different cultures according to Millar, we need to recognize the extent to which he adopted the broad utilitarian psychology of his friend David Hume. For Millar two major themes determine the status of women in every society. First, women are more highly valued when circumstances focus attention on and intensify sexual passion, or in Millar's terms, "when love becomes a passion, instead of being a mere sensual appetite" (*Millar*, 204). Second, women are more highly valued where there is an increase in "the value of those occupations that are suited to the female character" [leaving open for the moment whether that character is biologically given or socially constructed] (*Millar*, 203).

In general, Millar argued that sexual passion is intensified where there is both adequate leisure from productive activities to allow for the allocation of sufficient time, energy, and imagination to sexual activities and where there are some kinds of barriers established against the casual satisfaction of sexual appetites. Neither of these conditions apply in hunting and gathering societies. In the first place, there is nothing that would serve to inhibit casual sexual activity (*Millar*, 190). In the second place, although males in hunting and gathering societies may have substantial leisure, women certainly do not: "They are forced to labor without intermission in digging roots, in drawing water, in carrying wood . . . in dressing the victuals, in rearing the children, and in those other kinds of work *which their situation has taught them to perform*. The husband, when his is not engaged in some warlike excercise, indulges himself in idleness, and devolves upon his wife the whole burden of his domestic affairs" (*Millar*, 193).

Millar does not argue that women are suited by some special biological character to be particularly good at doing the kind of work that they do in hunting societies. Rather, he insists that they are taught to do such work by their situation. Elsewhere he formally admits that he is unable to establish whether the differences between women's characters and those of men are generally "derived from original constitution or from her way of life" (*Millar*, 219).

The fact that women are assigned what Millar takes to be the least desirable tasks and forced to work much longer than males in hunting societies is related to the second aspect of the utilitarian analysis of women's status in society. For Millar, the second aspect is the relevance of their special abilities to activities highly valued in the society, and here physiological differences clearly play a role. In hunting societies, neighboring groups are almost constantly warring over territory because it takes large tracts of land to provide game for small numbers of people. Thus brute strength and military valor will be particularly highly prized (*Millar*, 192). Lacking status either by virtue of their socially relevant skills or by virtue of any special regard for sexuality, women in hunting societies are treated as inferior persons and as the virtual slaves of men. In such societies, Montesquieu's understanding of marriage as a form of domestic slavery for women is completely appropriate.

Within pastoral societies two things begin to happen to raise the utility of sexual activity and therefore to raise the status of women. First, neither males nor females have to work as hard in herding cultures to provide for the bare necessities of life. As a consequence, they can pay more attention to "the enjoyments derived from the intercourse of the sexes" (*Millar*, 204). Second, a new mechanism suggested by Smith's idea that wealth brings its own special form of admiration and status comes into play in pastoral societies.

When people become wealthy, as Smith had pointed out, they come to have greater notions of their own dignity and worth. As a consequence, "they disdain to contract an alliance with their own dependents, or with people of inferior condition" (*Millar*, 205). At the same time, within the wealthy ranks, families compete with one another for superiority and their rivalries lead them to oppose intermarriage. So within wealthy societies, barriers are raised against both intra-class and inter-class intercourse between the sexes; and chastity begins to take on importance in terms of family honor (*Millar*, 205). The net result of these trends is that the relatively mild natural sex drives are "smothered by opposition." They become intensified because of delays in gratification. As a consequence, the status of women is raised in men's eyes because their importance as sexual partners increases.

With the rise of agriculture, although leisure is diminished, general standards of living and differentials of wealth increase. Consequently, the status of women as objects of (delayed) sexual gratification may continue to increase. One consequence of this trend that fascinates Millar is the emergence of chivalric codes such as those expressed in the literature of the High Middle Ages. Within the society reflected in the chivalric ideology the barriers to sexual gratification have become so high that the heightened emotional states associated with anticipation replace sexual gratification itself as the chief source of pleasure, and the status of the chaste noble woman is raised so high that it becomes the major aim of the knight to become the virtual servant of his lady (*Millar*, 214).

Millar's analysis of how the status of women changes in commercial society as it moves from its relatively modest beginnings to conditions of extreme wealth is particularly interesting. Millar draws heavily from Montesquieu and Smith in contending that the rise of commerce and industry breaks down old animosities between people from different communities and among different families in the same community. One of the first consequences of increased cooperation is the lowering of barriers to contact between the sexes. One might expect this increased contact to lower the intensity of sexual passion and thus to lead to a lowering of the status of women; and in very wealthy societies it does, especially where religious customs allow for easy divorce (*Millar*, 225–27). But in commercial societies, those personal attributes of physical strength and aggressiveness that were most highly valued in hunting societies become less important than attributes such as sociability and dexterity. Thus, as commercial societies begin to replace agrarian ones, "while the fair sex become less frequently the object of those romantic and extravagant passions [associated with feudalism and chivalry] . . . they are more universally regarded upon account of their useful and agreeable talents" (*Millar*, 219), and they achieve their highest over-all social status (*Millar*, 225).

Unhappily, where commercial society leads to extreme opulence in the upper classes a curious reversion of women's status takes place. As we have seen, commerce has broken down the barriers to intra-class social intercourse, producing a potential decline in the intensity of sexual passion. At the same time the great leisure and freedom from economic concerns which characterizes the extremely opulent simultaneously reduces the importance of women's non-sexual talents and allows for a virtual glut of sensuality, further reducing the intensity of sexual passions and the status of women derived from their sexuality. The wealthy become "too much dissipated by pleasure to feel any violent passion for an individual" (*Millar*, 227), prostitution becomes rampant, polygamy becomes common where it is allowed by the religion, marriage becomes "slight and transient," and the status of women reverts almost to that which it had been in the earliest hunting and gathering societies. Sexual activity has once again become nothing but animal enjoyment and women once again have no alternative economic source of status available.

Millar's Disappearance and the Curious Fate of the Early Social Sciences

At the beginning of the last section I pointed out that Millar's *Origin of Ranks* virtually disappeared for most of the nineteenth century and well into the middle of the twentieth, only to be reconstituted very recently as a major document in the history of sociology and anthropology. Some of the reasons for this disappearance and recovery are a consequence of the peculiar amalgamation of psychological and sociological perspectives specific to Millar's work; but others illustrate general considerations which served to make most work in the social sciences done before the early nineteenth century invisible to later social scientists and to historians until the second half of this century.

Considering those factors specific to the *Origin of Ranks*, I want to focus on the complete silence with regard to Millar's work on the part of the philosophically radical feminists of late-eighteenth-century England. Millar's well-known support for the American Revolution, his sympathy for the early stages of the French Revolution, his outspoken attacks on slavery, the fact that he was deeply admired by James Mill, who was a central figure in radical circles in London, and the fact that, like Catherine Macaulay, he published an extremely liberal history of England,[12] combined with his extensive interest in the historical changes of the condition of women, make it virtually impossible to believe that his works were unknown to Macaulay. Yet we find no mention of him either in Macaulay's *Letters on Education* (1790) or in Mary Wollstonecraft's *Vindication of the Rights of Woman* (1791). This silence is especially odd because Macaulay took great care to call attention to her intellectual indebtedness to such associationists as Claude Adrienne Helvetius and David Hartley as well as her opposition to such ideological enemies as Montesquieu and Edmund Burke.

This last fact may help to explain the silence on Millar, for the *Origin of Ranks* involved what seemed in the late eighteenth century to be an anomalous fusion between radical politics and historical relativism. Macaulay and Wollstonecraft had built their arguments around a methodological opposition to the philosophical-historical approach of Montesquieu and Burke. They appealed instead to Helvetius's and Condorcet's claims that human nature was everywhere and always the same and that there were therefore universal standards of justice which were only perverted by local customs and habits.

Millar's clear insistence on the appropriateness of situational variations in morality and law made his position completely unacceptable to radical feminists. At the same time, because his work also used both associationist and historical arguments to problematize current patriarchal claims about the natural inferiority of women, Millar could not be identified with Montesquieu and Burke as among the opposition. Millar simply did not fit within a discourse characterized by the identification of historical relativism with conservative political stances and associationist universalism with radical political stances. Since no one knew quite how to use him or what to do with him, Millar was basically ignored and forgotten.

The disappearance of the *Origin of Ranks* from nineteenth-century anthropological discourse seems to have had less to do with its uniqueness than with a general tendency among nineteenth-century scholars to discount the kind of philosophical history done by Montesquieu and all of his Scottish followers, including Adam Ferguson, Lord Kames, William Robertson, and Lord Monboddo, as well as Millar. Once again the silence regarding Millar's work is peculiarly noteworthy in view of the fact that the question of whether matriarchal societies may have preceded patriarchy in the early development of human communities was a central topic of debate among mid-nineteenth-century anthropological and sociological writers.

Between 1861 and 1871, a great debate over matriarchy and matrilinearity took place. J. J. Bachofen's *Das Mutterecht* (Mother right) (1861) argued in favor of early matriarchy; Sir Henry Maine's *Ancient Law* (1861) insisted that all early societies were patriarchal; John McLennan's *Primitive Marriage* (1865) supported a modified version of Bachofen's work; and Lewis Henry Morgan's *Systems of Consanguinity and Affinity of the Human Family* (1870) also argued for the existence of some very early matriarchal societies. Each of the major parties to this debate had been trained in Roman law. In fact, both Bachofen and Maine were professors of Roman and civil law, and McLennan had been a student of Millar's student, David Hume, nephew of the philosopher and himself an outstanding legal scholar. Moreover, there is clear evidence that each of them was well read in the Scottish school of philosophical history. Yet only one member of the group, McLennan, ever acknowledged Millar's discussions of early matrilinearity and matriarchy, and McLennan's incidental acknowledgment came long after the nineteenth-century debate had concluded (*Millar*, 153).

How could it be that this entire group of nineteenth-century anthropologists and sociologists, focusing on the roles and status of women in early societies and knowledgeable about the scholarly tradition to which Millar's *Origin of Ranks* was arguably the most sophisticated and certainly the most directly relevant contribution, were either unaware of, unwilling, or unable to admit the significance of Millar's work? The answer, I am quite certain, is related to changing styles of doing social-scientific research that emerged in the early nineteenth century in connection with growing specialization and early professionalizing trends. Millar's work stands as a paradigmatic example of all that nineteenth-century social scientists found wanting in the works of their predecessors.

Specifically, it represented that Newtonianizing "spirit of system" which led so many eighteenth-century social theorists to try to explain everything in terms of hypothetical structures grounded in a few simple principles. Just as psychological thinkers such as Condillac, Hume, Helvetius, and Hartley tried to build complete accounts of human nature, society, and the state on the principles of associationist psychology, Millar and his colleagues tried to explain many if not most social customs and institutions in terms of responses to the transformation of modes of production from hunting and gathering to animal tending to agriculture to commerce. In every case, nineteenth-century social scientists viewed these as superficial and speculative attempts unsupported or inadequately supported by factual evidence.

Millar's *Origin of Ranks* purported to be a natural history of society. But to nineteenth-century anthropologists and sociologists it seemed typical of armchair natural history built on the most insignificant amounts and insubstantial kinds of evidence. One recent historian of social anthropology has argued that philosophical history became, for these more rigorous scholars, the "original sin" of anthropology which expressed a new "guilt ridden conscientiousness about data and its high standards of documentation."[13] According to Maine, for example, only the nineteenth-century fieldwork of archaeologists and philologists had established the evidentiary groundwork on which any legitimate interpretations of ancient Roman law could rest. Bachofen did extensive detailed studies of early-Roman gravesites before he wrote his theoretical discussion of matriarchy. And Morgan spent years in fieldwork among American Indian tribes before he published on kinship patterns. It was simply unthinkable to such meticulous scholars that the amateur speculations of men such as Millar could have offered valuable insights. Consequently, they tended either to ignore them entirely or to be blind to what was potentially important in them. In either case they did not recommend them to their students; so knowledge of such works rapidly faded.

Very much the same kind of professionalizing amnesia about the early development of the discipline occurred in psychology as it became institutionalized in the German university. The reconstruction of nineteenth-century psychology as a branch of experimental physiology by Wilhelm Wundt and his students and by Charles Bell in Scotland shifted the emphasis of psychological specialists to detailed laboratory studies, leaving the works of speculative theorists such as Hartley, Hume, Helvetius, and others to be studied seriously, if at all, in undergraduate moral philosophy classes. Among *real* psychologists, they were presented as curious anachronisms illustrating the primitive state of their discipline before the rise of experimental psychology.

As we have already suggested, seventeenth- and eighteenth-century political economy received a slightly different response from its nineteenth-century inheritors for several reasons. From its inception, political economy incorporated a dual emphasis on the accumulation of statistical data and on the mathematical treatment of that data. Within the nascent discipline, intellectual styles in the nineteenth century thus departed less from those of the earlier generation of thinkers. Economics as a discipline tended to forget pre-seventeenth-century moral economy and to retain figures such as Petty, Graunt, and Quesnay within its hagiography. Even here, however, the hugely successful *Wealth of Nations* produced a barrier behind which most previous work was hidden from new recruits to the field.

At least three major factors have led recently to a renewed interest in seventeenth- and eighteenth-century social-scientific thought. First, the late twentieth century is seeing a new major change in intellectual styles and methods within some of the social sciences. Confidence in concepts like objectivity is on the wane, and there is a new interest and enthusiasm—especially in anthropology, sociology, and the clinical branches of psychology—for interpretive theorizing and "system" building. As a consequence, a number of social scientists, reflecting on the history of their own disciplines, have become interested in reinstating the reputations of past synthetic thinkers.

Second, since the 1950s, the discipline of the history of science has changed in such a way as to encourage interest in the early social sciences. On the one hand, it has become more clearly differentiated from the disciplines which it studies and is thus less closely bound to the current assumptions and values of those disciplines. This has occurred largely because younger historians of science come to their interests from training in history, whereas older generations had graduate training and professional experiences as scientists. For much the same reason, as it has seen an influx of new recruits whose backgrounds are not in the physical, biological, and mathematical sciences, its traditional focus on natural science has been increasingly extended into the social sciences.

Finally, new trends in cultural history have begun to explore both the ways in which cultural contexts shape the character of formal theorizing and the ways in which formal theorizing plays a role in the construction of broad ideological and cultural configurations. As I hope to have shown, the early history of the social sciences offers a rich field for exploring both of these issues.

12

Conclusion

Prior to the middle of the seventeenth century virtually all European discussions of society were guided by a twofold and very powerful set of assumptions. Those assumptions discouraged the use of explanatory strategies that were applied to understanding nature in any attempts to understand and account for human interactions. First, the dominant classical tradition, exemplified in Aristotelian philosophy, insisted that human actions and institutions were of a fundamentally different kind than those of the rest of nature. *Prudential* knowledge, or indeterminate practical sciences, governed the first because of the human ability to make conscious choices; theoretical knowledge, or deterministic sciences, governed the second because natural entities lack *will*. Second, the Judeo-Christian tradition reinforced this human/nature division by insisting that humanity alone was created in the image of God. Humans were not so much a part of the natural world as the beneficiaries of its bounties. A few classical thinkers, including the atomic materialist Epicurus and his Roman follower Lucretius, sought to understand humanity as a part of the natural cosmos; and a few Renaissance thinkers, including Niccolo Machiavelli and Jean Bodin, sought naturalistic accounts of some human institutions. But they remained in a very small minority.

The late sixteenth and early seventeenth centuries saw a radical change in this situation. On the one hand, a series of political, economic, and religious crises seemed to show that earlier attempts to understand and direct human society were inadequate to their task. On the other hand, a series of new approaches to natural knowledge—several closely linked to a revival of ancient atomist philosophical ideas—were displacing the Aristotelian natural sciences because they seemed to offer greater hope in allowing humans to use their knowledge for the betterment of human life. As a consequence, the middle decades of the seventeenth century saw numerous attempts to appropriate the methods and concepts of the new natural sciences for application to human society. Just as there were several interrelated but mutually incompatible scientific approaches vying for the attention and support of seventeenth-century seekers after *natural* knowledge, however, there were several parallel alternatives for those seeking scientific knowledge of society.

In Central and Eastern Europe, where alchemy and the alchemically based medicine associated with Paracelsus were particularly strong, court advisors such as Johann Becher applied both the experiential methods and the theories of alchemy to the problems of princes whose realms faced fiscal crises. They created *Kameralwissenschaft*, or the cameral sciences. Alchemy was grounded in the assumption that the alchemist must intervene in natural processes in order to direct nature into paths beneficial to humans, that is, into the production of precious metals to increase wealth or medicines to improve health. Thus it should be no surprise that the cameral sciences emphasized the need for princes to intervene in social and economic processes in order to improve the health and wealth of their subjects and to add to their own power and prestige. The simultaneous promotion and regulation of many aspects of society, but especially of commercial life, became the hallmark of cameralism, which dominated German social discourse well into the nineteenth century.

In most of Western Europe at least three self-consciously competing and programmatic approaches to the social sciences were initiated, beginning in the 1640s. In 1644, Thomas Hobbes claimed to be the founder of a new scientific approach to political life. Hobbes wrote: "Galileus in our time was the first that opened the gate of natural philosophy universal, which is the knowledge of the nature of motion. . . . The science of man's body, the most profitable part of natural science, was first discovered by our countryman, Doctor Harvey. Natural philosophy is but young; but civil philosophy is yet much younger, as being no older . . . than my own *De Cive* (EW, 1: vii–ix).

In *De Cive* (1643) and in his much more widely influential *Leviathan* of 1651, Hobbes drew heavily upon the methods of Euclidean geometry, the basic materialist assumptions of ancient atomism, and the medical discoveries of Harvey in order to create a science of the state. His strategy was to begin with an analysis of human sensations, ideas, and passions and to view both society and the state as responses to the needs of individual human beings. Thus, I have argued that he initiated a *psychological* approach to social science. Hobbes intended his arguments to head off civil war in England by supporting the undivided sovereignty associated with absolute monarchy. But the egalitarian individualism implicit in his initial assumptions showed itself almost immediately as the psychological approach was adopted by radical sectarians in England and developed by Spinoza in Holland. In spite of Hobbes's aims, his approach ultimately provided the intellectual foundation for increasingly democratic and radical social movements during the eighteenth century. Through the writings of Claude Adrienne Helvetius, it even became a major source of the stream of socialist thought in the early nineteenth century.

James Harrington, who opposed both Hobbes's monarchist politics and his mathematical-mechanist methodology, initiated a second approach to social science. Hobbes, he argued, was much too simplistic in his assumptions and too geometrical in his arguments. What was needed was an historical, empirically based political anatomy that took into account the tremendous complexity of human customs, interests, and institutions and their interrelationships with one another. In *Oceana* (1655) Harrington followed the connections between economically based class interests and the exercise of political power through classical, medieval, and early modern Europe, initiating what I have variously called the *sociological* tradition, or that of philosophical history. As in Hobbes's case, Harrington clearly intended his scientific discussion for political purposes. He wanted to support the republican tendencies of the English Civil Wars. In order to convince his readers that republican government was inevitable in England, he coupled his conclusion that political power must reflect the distribution of economic power in society with the information that by the early seventeenth century land (and hence wealth) in England was widely distributed. But once again the intentions of a founder were thwarted; for the implicit tendency of the sociological tradition to invest whatever has been generated by historical forces with special value became increasingly explicit as time went on. Thus philosophical history ended up the eighteenth century in the hands of men like Edmund Burke, Joseph De Maistre, and the Abbé Ferdinando Galiani as the intellectual foundation for modern conservative political movements.

Finally, in 1678, another Englishman closely linked to Hobbes, William Petty, laid claim to initiating the third approach under the name of "political arithmetic." Writing to his cousin, Lord South-well, Petty bragged: "Archimedes had algebra 1,900 years ago, but concealed it. Diopantus had it in great perfection 1,400 years since. Vieta, Descartes, Roberval, Harriot, Pell, Oughtred, van Schoeten and Dr. Wallis have done much in this last age. It came out of Arabia by the Moors into Spain, and from thence hither, and W[illiam] P[etty] hath applied it to other than purely mathematical matters, viz: to *policy* by the name of *Political Arithmetic*, by reducing many terms of matter to number, weight, and measure, in order to be handled mathematically."[1] Eschewing both human psychology and any interest in the historical development of human institutions, Petty and those who followed him in the tradition that came to be known as political economy, or *economics*, sought to provide a quantitatively based science that might guide any government in improving the material well-being of its subjects. "God send me," Petty wrote, "the use of things and notions, whose foundations are sense and the superstructures mathematical reasoning; for want of which props so many governments do reel and stagger, and crush the honest subjects that live under them" (*PP*, 1: 111). For the third time in three tries the initial aims of a social science were skewed by practices imported from the natural sciences. Intended to increase the abilities of central governments to manage resources for the general welfare, the statistical techniques of the early social sciences focused attention on averages and made it very difficult to deal with key issues like distributive justice. In addition, the homeostatic medical model, which informed almost all Anglo-French political economy, led to the conclusion that governmental intervention in economic life is almost certain to be ineffectual and thence to the establishment of *laissez-faire* economics. By the end of the eighteenth century, political economy had become one of the most important sources of *liberal* ideology. According to classical liberal doctrine, the central planning and management of economies is counterproduc-tive and governments should function only to provide a context in which economic freedoms are protected.

At the end of the seventeenth century the writings of Isaac Newton and John Locke increased the general level of sophistication regarding the epistemological and methodological foundations of the natural sciences. New practices modeled on the works of Newton and Locke soon entered the social sciences through the methodologically oriented works of men like David Hartley and David Hume in Britain and Etienne Condillac in France. For the most part, however, the traditions initiated in the seventeenth century retained their coherence and their late-seventeenth-century ideological thrusts even though their epistemic assumptions were gradually transformed.

During the 1730s the cameral sciences entered the curriculum of the German universities, where they virtually monopolized academic discussions of social issues. More importantly, the continued existence and development of the traditions of psychologically grounded political science, philosophical history, and political economy are attested by the division of fields of study laid out by Marie-Jean-Antoine-Nicolas Caritat de Condorcet in the *Rapport et projet de décret de l'organization générale de l'instruction publique* (*Report on the General Organization of Public Instruction*), submitted to the French National Assembly in April of 1792. At the *Instituts*, corresponding roughly to American undergraduate colleges, Condorcet proposed three instructors in the moral or social sciences. Each of these instructors was to deal with social issues from a particular methodological perspective. The first would begin with the analysis of sensations and ideas, particularly the generation of moral ideas, and then move to an analysis of the implication of these ideas for the creation of political structures, that is, he would explore the psychological tradition. The second would discuss the elements of commerce and political economy and their implication for legislation in the new republic, that is, he would cover the economic tradition. Finally, the third would deal with geography and "the philosophical history of peoples," that is, with the way in which different communities develop special customs and patterns of organization in response to the particular environments in which they are placed.[2]

Such a division of topics, Condorcet argued, reflects the organization "which has spontaneously developed in the last half-century during which all branches of human knowledge have made rapid progress."[3] As we have seen, Condorcet accurately reflected the existence of three methodologically distinctive social-science traditions in the eighteenth century, but he could and should have pushed their origins back at least a hundred years.

When Condorcet wrote he also argued that in the future, much of the progress in the moral and political (social) sciences would depend upon the interaction among and integration of the three historical traditions which he had identified (*RPI*, 358). On this score, Condorcet's judgments were less sound. Although there had already been major attempts at integrating the three traditions, especially among Scottish moral writers such as John Millar and Adam Smith, most of those attempts at integration had little long-term impact. In the case of Adam Smith, whose *Wealth of Nations* certainly shaped subsequent economic thought, later economists, following J. B. Say, tended to emphasize only those elements most closely linked to the political economy thread of Smith's work. They tended to jettison those features of Smith's work that drew more extensively from philosophical history and the psychological tradition. As they became professionalized and the subjects of academic specialization during the early nineteenth century, the social sciences, with the exception of economics, tended to turn their backs on their eighteenth-century progenitors and to rebuild themselves anew. Modern psychology, for example, reshaped itself along lines initiated by Wilhelm Wundt, drawing from the techniques of experimental physiology. Modern anthropology, which might have built upon eighteenth-century philosophical history, turned instead to physical anthropometry and the study of race.[4] Even sociology, under the guidance of Auguste Comte and his followers, turned away from any concern with historical developments until evolutionary thinkers reinstituted a concern with temporal development during the late nineteenth century.

If the social sciences in the course of their development through the nineteenth century were virtually unaware of the influence of their seventeenth- and eighteenth-century predecessors, why should we be concerned with them? First, and in a sense, least importantly, as I suggested at the end of chapter 11, the social sciences, like any other intellectual endeavors, are subject to fads. And in a number of cases, the twentieth century has seen the revival of perspectives which emerged before the nineteenth century. Just to consider one extreme example, Vico's work was not widely influential even during the eighteenth century, in large part because its methods were incompatible with the empiricist thrust of the dominant trends. But since 1911 when the Italian philosopher Benedetto Croce published his *La filosofia di Giambattista Vico* (translated in 1913 by Robin Collingwood as *The Philosophy of Giambattista Vico*), Vichian elements seem to be appearing in virtually all of the social sciences from the developmental child psychology of Jean Piaget's *The Child's Conception of the World* (1969) to the structuralism of Claude Lévi Strauss's *La pensée sauvage* (*The Savage Mind*) (1962).[5] Thus a review of the early history of the social sciences can often illuminate the subsequent history of the academic tradition.

Second, and more importantly, the study of the early social sciences provides empirical evidence for a series of important insights about the nature of the sciences in general. Most simply stated, there is no single and value-free scientific method whose procedures guarantee the truth of knowledge claims. There have been, in the social sciences, as in the natural sciences, *many* different competing and at times mutually contradictory sciences and scientific methods. None of them are value free, and none have a monopoly on truth. Every science imports assumptions and goals from the culture which produces it, even though the scientist may do his or her best to avoid them and/or to seek disinterested knowledge. Furthermore, there may be features of the procedures used within any science which bias the conclusions of scientists even in ways that the scientists do not want or anticipate. This is not to discount or deny the importance of science. In fact, I continue to believe that the sciences offer us the most reliable and useful knowledge we have on most topics. It is, however, to challenge any claim that a particular finding is true *simply because it is scientific.*

Finally, and most importantly, we in the modern Western world live in a culture in which three families of *ideology,* usually identified with the terms liberal, socialist, and conservative, play a major role in directing our beliefs and our actions. They tell us what is the *right* thing to do in most of the situations that we face. We can be the active architects of our own destinies rather than their passive victims only to the extent that we understand the sources of these ideologies and become able to pick and choose among their directives. And if I am correct in what I have argued throughout this book, we cannot understand the underpinnings of any of the dominant ideological families without understanding how they were shaped at their inception by the early social sciences.

Chronology

1618–1648   The Thirty Years War leaves much of Central Europe decimated and the Holy Roman Empire broken into about 300 princedoms.

1637   René Descartes, *Discours sur la méthode*.

1642–1660   English Civil War. Concludes with the restoration of Charles II, but with power shared with Parliament.

1642   Thomas Hobbes, *De Cive*.

1648–1652   The Fronde. Attempt of French nobility in Paris to limit monarchical authority ends abortively, making the French king the most powerful in Europe.

1651   Thomas Hobbes, *Leviathan*.

1655   James Harrington, *The Commonwealth of Oceana*.

1657   Matthew Wren, *Considerations Upon Mr. Harrington's Commonwealth of Oceana*.

1662   René Descartes, *Traité de l'homme*. John Graunt, *Natural and Political Observations Made Upon the Bills of Mortality*.

1664   William Petty writes *Verbum Sapienti and the Value of People*.

1668   Johann Joachim Becher, *Politischer Discurs von den eigentlichen Ursachen des Auf und Abnehmens der Städt Länder und Republicken.*

1670   Benedict de Spinoza, *Tractatus Theologico-Politicus.*

1673   Samuel Pufendorf, *De officio hominis et civis pro ut ipsi praescribuntur lege naturali.* François Poullain de la Barre, *De l'égalité des deux sexes.*

1684   Phillip von Hornigk, *Oesterreich Über alles, Wann es nur will.*

1685   The Revocation of the Edict of Nantes (1598) by Louis XIV reinstitutes persecution of Protestants in France, leading to the flight of economically important Huguenots and to a bitter anti-clerical mood among intellectuals.

1687   Isaac Newton, *Philosophiae Naturalis Principia Mathematica.*

1688   The Glorious Revolution in England replaces James II with William and Mary, ensuring Protestant succession and increasing the power of Parliament.

1690   John Locke, *Essay Concerning Human Understanding.* Dudley North, *Discourses Upon Trade.* William Petty, *Political Arithmetic.*

1691   John Locke, *Some Considerations of the Consequences of the Lowering of Interest and Raising the Value of Money.*

1704   Pierre Boisguilbert , *Dissertation de la nature des richesses, de l'argent, et des tributes.*

1707   Union of Scotland and England.

1714   Bernard Mandeville, *The Fable of the Bees, or Private Vices, Public Benefits.*

1722   Ernst Ludwig Carl, *Traité de la Richesse des Princes et de leurs états.*

1724   R. P. Joseph-François Lafitau, *Moeurs des sauvages américains comparées aux moeurs des premiers temps.*

1725   Giambattista Vico, *Principi di Scienza Nuova.*

1738   Voltaire and Mme. du Chatelet, *Eléments de la philosophie Neuton.*

1739   David Hume, *A Treatise of Human Nature.*

1742   David Hume, *The Essays, Moral, Political, and Philosophical of David Hume.*

1746   Francis Hutcheson, *A Short Introduction to Moral Philosophy.*

1748   Montesquieu, *L'esprit des lois.*

1749   Louis Leclerc, comte du Buffon, *Histoire naturelle de l'homme.* David Hartley, *Observations on Man, His Frame, His Duty, and His Expectations.*

1754   Etienne Condillac, *Traité des sensations.*

1755   Richard Cantillon, *An Essay on the Nature of Trade in General.*

1757   Panicked by an assassination attempt, Louis XV of France tightens repression of potentially subversive books, polarizing the intellectual community. Victor Riqueti, marquis de Mirabeau, *L'ami des homes, ou traité de la population.*

1758   Claude Adrienne Helvetius, *De l'esprit.* Johann Heinrich Gottlob von Justi, *Staatwirthschaft, oder systematische Abhandlung aller Oekonomischen und Cameral-Wissenschaften*

1763   François Quesnay, *Philosophie rurale.*

1764   Cesare Beccaria, *Dei Delitti e Delle Pene.*

1766   Anne-Marie Turgot, *Réflexions sur la formation et la distribution des richesses.*

1767   Adam Ferguson, *An Essay on the History of Civil Society.* Sir James Steuart, *An Inquiry into the Principles of Political Economy.*

1771   John Millar, *The Origin of the Distinction of Ranks.*

1774–1776   The Turgot ministry in France attempts to establish free trade in grain. Louis XVI's abandonment of Turgot and his policies drives many formerly monarchist intellectuals toward republicanism.

1774   Claude Adrienne Helvetius, *De l'homme.* Henry Home, Lord Kames, *Sketches of the History of Man.*

1776   The American Revolution begins. Adam Smith, *An*

Inquiry into the Nature and Causes of the Wealth of Nations.

1785   Jean-Antoine-Nicolas Caritat, marquis de Condorcet, *Essai Sur l'application de l'analyse a la probabilite des decisions rendues a la pluralite des voix.*

1787   Joseph von Sonnenfels, *Grundsatts der Polizey, Handlung und Finanz.*

1789   The French Revolution begins. Jeremy Bentham, *An Introduction to the Principles of Morals and Legislation.*

1790   Catherine Macaulay, *Letters on Education.*

1791   Mary Wollstonecraft, *A Vindication of the Rights of Woman.*

1792   Condorcet, *Rapport et projet de l'organisation générale de l'instruction publique.*

1793   William Godwin, *An Enquiry Concerning Political Justice.*

1794   Johann Gottfried von Herder, *Ideen zur Philosophie der Geschichte der Mencheit.*

Notes and References

CHAPTER 1

1. On the inefficiencies and bureaucratic character of the German principalities under cameralist influence, see Marc Raeff, *The Well-Ordered Police State: Social and Institutional Change Through Law in the Germanies and Russia, 1600–1800* (New Haven and London: Yale University Press, 1983).

CHAPTER 2

1. Trevor Astin, ed., *Crisis in Europe: 1560–1660* (London: Routledge and Kegan Paul, 1965) collects a series of classic papers on the "Crisis" issue. For additional materials which explore different facets of the crisis see the bibliographical essay.

2. See E. M. W. Tillyard, *The Elizabethan World Picture* (New York: Columbia University Press, 1943).

3. In *Certaine Sermons or Homilies Appointed to Be Read in Churches inn the Time of Queen Elizabeth I (1547–1571)* (Gainesville, Fla.: Scholar's Facsimiles and Reprints, 1968 reproduction of 1623 edition), vol. 1, 69.

4. See, for example, James Daly, "Cosmic Harmony and Political Thinking in Early Stuart England," *Transactions of the American Philosophical Society* 69 (1979): 3–40, for the political uses of the doctrine of correspondences.

5. On the importance of astrological notions in bridging the

elite–common gap in early modern culture, see especially Bernard Capp, *English Almanacs, 1500–1800: Astrology and the Popular Press* (Ithaca, N.Y.: Cornell University Press, 1979) and Patrick Curry, ed., *Astrology, Science and Society: Historical Essays* (Woodbridge, England: Boydell Press, 1987).

6. See Robert Westman, "The Astronomer's Role in the Sixteenth Century: A Preliminary Study," *History of Science* 17 (1980): 105–47.

7. James Harrington, *The Oceana and Other Works* (London, 1737), 516. Cited hereafter in the text as *OOW*.

8. Galileo, "Letter to the Grand Duchess Christina," in Stillman Drake, ed., *Galileo, Discoveries and Opinions* (Garden City, N.Y.; Doubleday, 1957), 169.

9. Cited in Carlo Ginsburg, "High and Low: The Theme of Forbidden Knowledge in the Sixteenth and Seventeenth Centuries," *Past and Present* 73 (1976): 37.

10. Cited in Donald R. Kelley, *The Human Measure: Social Thought in the Western Legal Tradition* (Cambridge, Mass.: Harvard University Press, 1990), 139. Between 131–45 Kelley discusses the early attempt to turn law into an Aristotelian episteme.

11. Cited in Eugenio Garin, *Italian Humanism* (Oxford: Basil Blackwell, 1965), 32–33. Emphasis mine. Cited hereafter in the text as *IH*.

12. See J. G. A. Pocock, *The Machiavellian Moment: Florentine Political Thought and the Atlantic Republican Tradition* (Princeton: Princeton University Press, 1975).

13. See Marc Raeff, *The Well-Ordered Police State: Social and Institutional Change Through Law in the Germanies and Russia, 1600–1800* (New Haven and London: Yale University Press, 1983).

14. Cited in Benjamin Farrington, *The Philosophy of Francis Bacon* (Chicago: University of Chicago Press, 1964), 93.

15. Cited by Marie Boas Hall in "Science in the Early Royal Society," in Maurice Crosland, ed., *The Emergence of Science in Western Europe* (New York: Science History Publications, 1976), 74. Emphasis mine.

16. René Descartes, *The Philosophical Works of Descartes*, ed. E. Haldane and G. R. T. Ross (New York: Dover, 1955) volume 1, 7.

17. Cited in Mary B. Hesse, *Forces and Fields* (London: Thomas Nelson, 1961), 160.

CHAPTER 3

1. For both the example of the efforts of Leibniz and Becher regarding the Polish election and for virtually everything I will be saying about Johann Becher's politcal economy I am indebted to Pamela H. Smith's unpublished doctoral dissertation, "Alchemy, Credit, and the

Commerce of Words and Things: Johann Becher at the Courts of the Holy Roman Empire, 1635–82," Johns Hopkins University, 1989. Leibniz's pamphlet is cited on p. 242. Smith's dissertation will be cited hereafter in the text as *A C & C*.

2. Von Hornigk's *Oesterreich über alles, Wann es nur will* (Austria over all if only she will) of 1684 is generally recognized as one of the major documents founding "mercantilist" economic theory.

3. Cited in Albion W. Small, *The Cameralists: The Pioneers of German Social Polity* (Chicago: University of Chicago Press, 1909), 142–43. This work will be cited hereafter in the text as *Cameralists*.

4. Joseph Schumpeter, *History of Economic Analysis* (Oxford: Oxford University Press, 1954), 283–84.

CHAPTER 4

1. Hobbes to Cavendish, 23 July 1641, cited in Steven Shapin and Simon Schaffer, *Leviathan and the Air-Pump: Hobbes, Boyle, and the Experimental Life* (Princeton: Princeton University Press, 1985), 311. Cited hereafter in the text as *LAP*.

2. See David McNallay, *Political Economy and the Rise of Capitalism* (Berkeley and Los Angeles: University of California Press, 1988), 5.

3. See Linda Schiebinger, *The Mind Has No Sex? Women in the Origins of Modern Science* (Cambridge, Mass.: Harvard University Press, 1989), 175–79, for a discussion of Poullain de la Barre.

4. Thomas Hobbes, *The English Works of Thomas Hobbes*, ed. Sir William Molesworth (London: 1839), vol. 1, 675 and 693. Cited hereafter in the text as *EW*.

5. Hobbes, *De Cive*, ed. Stering Lamprecht (N.Y.: Appleton-Century-Crofts, 1949), 161.

6. Cited in Lewis Feuer, *Spinoza and the Rise of Liberalism* (Boston: Beacon Press, 1958), 53–54. Cited hereafter in text as *SRL*.

7. Cited in Christopher Hill, *The World Turned Upside Down: Radical Ideas During the English Revolution* (Harmondsworth, England: Penguin Books, 1975), 387.

8. See Ira Wade, *The Clandestine Organization and Diffusion of Philosophical Ideas in France* (Princeton: Princeton University Press, 1938), 269–70.

9. Benedict de Spinoza, *The Political Works*, ed. A. G. Wernham (Oxford: The Clarendon Press, 1958), 263. Hereafter cited in the text as *PW*.

10. Stuart Hampshire, "Spinoza and the Idea of Freedom," in Marjorie Grene, ed., *Spinoza* (Garden City, N.Y.: Anchor Books, 1973), 304.

CHAPTER 5

1. Joyce Oldham Appleby claims in her *Economic Thought and Ideology in Seventeenth-Century England* (Princeton: Princeton University Press, 1978) to have consulted no fewer than 1,500 seventeenth-century English economic books and pamphlets. See p. 4. Hereafter cited in the text as *ETI*.

2. See William Letwin, *The Origins of Scientific Economics* (Garden City, N.Y.: Doubleday, 1964), 179. Cited hereafter in the text as *OSE*.

3. Printed in Lord Edmund Fitzmaurice, *The Life of Sir William Petty* (London: John Murray, 1895), 158.

4. Cited in Charles H. Hull, ed., *The Economic Writings of Sir William Petty* (Cambridge: Cambridge University Press, 1899), vol. 1, xiii. Cited hereafter in the text as *EWSWP*.

5. See Robert Frank, Jr., *Harvey and the Oxford Physiologists* (Berkeley and Los Angeles: University of California Press, 1980), 102.

6. See Alessandro Roncoglia, *Petty: The Origins of Political Economy* (Armonk, N.Y.: M. E. Sharpe, 1985), 3. Cited hereafter in the text as *P*.

7. See Emil Strauss, *Sir William Petty: Portrait of a Genius* (Glencoe, Ill.: The Free Press, 1954), 110.

8. William Petty, *The Petty Papers: Some Unpublished Writings of Sir William Petty*, ed. the marquis of Lansdowne (London: Constable and Co., 1927), vol. 1: 111. Cited in the text hereafter as *PP*.

9. John Graunt, *Natural and Political Observations . . . Made Upon the Bills of Mortality*, ed. Walter Wilcox (Baltimore: The Johns Hopkins Press, 1939), 78. Cited hereafter in the text as *OBM*.

10. See Karl Pearson, *The History of Statistics in the Seventeenth and Eighteenth Centuries against the Changing Background of Intellectual, Scientific, and Religious Thought* (London: Charles Griffin, 1978), 33.

11. On the opposition to a centralized census, Peter Buck's "People Who Counted: Political Arithmetic in the Eighteenth Century," *Isis* 73 (1982): 28–45, is superb.

12. Cited in Terence Hutchinson, *Before Adam Smith* (Oxford: Basil Blackwell, 1988), 231. Cited hereafter as *BAS*.

13. Cited in Elizabeth Fox-Genovese, *The Origins of Physiocracy* (Ithaca: Cornell University Press, 1976), 115.

CHAPTER 6

1. Cited in Bernard Sheehan, *Savagism and Civility* (Cambridge: Cambridge University Press, 1980), 26. Many of Las Casas's writings have been collected in George Sanderlin, ed., *Bartholemé de Las Casas: Selected Writings* (New York: Knopf, 1971).

2. Cited in Sanderlin, ed. See note 1, p. 11.

3. Buffon's physical anthropology, initiated in 1749 in his *De la nature de l'homme* and *Variétés dans l'espèce humain* and continued through his *Addition aux Variétés dans l'espèce humain* of 1777 and *Epoques de la nature* of 1778, was tremendously important in the development of the human sciences—especially of racial theories. I have largely ignored it in this work both because its emphasis was largely biological rather than social and because its social implications were not worked out until after the period covered by the current work. Any treatment of the human sciences, as conceived within the French academic tradition of the nineteenth century, could not treat Buffon so cavalierly. Anyone interested in Buffon's anthropological writings should begin with Michele Duchet, *Anthropologie et Histoire au siècle des lumières: Buffon, Voltaire, Helvetius, Diderot* (Paris: François Maspero, 1971).

4. Cited in Donald Kelley, *The Human Measure: Social Thought in the Western Legal Tradition* (Cambridge, Mass.: Harvard University Press, 1990), 203.

5. For this description of Bodin's aims, see Donald Kelley, *Foundations of Modern Historical Scholarship* (New York: Columbia University Press, 1970), 137–38.

6. Cited from the *Methodus ad facilem historiarum cognitionem* by Clarence Glacken in *Traces on the Rhodian Shore: Nature and Culture in Western Thought From Ancient Times to the End of the Eighteenth Century* (Berkeley and Los Angeles: University of California Press, 1967), 445. Glacken's work will be cited henceforth in the text as *TRS*.

7. For an excellent and very clear account of Renaissance humoral psychology, see Pincus Lockyer, *Shakespeare's World* (New York: Continuum Publishing Co., 1989), 5–15.

8. Jean Bodin, *The Six Bookes of a Commonweale*, ed. Kenneth D. McRae (Cambridge, Mass.: Harvard University Press, 1972), bk. 5, ch. 1, 563–64. Cited hereafter in the Text as *SBC*.

9. Most of what I say regarding Harrington's personal life and associations comes from J. G. Pocock's historical introduction to *The Political Writings of James Harrington* (Cambridge: Cambridge University Press, 1977). Discussion of Harrington's radical associations appears on 6–14. Cited hereafter in the text as *PWJH*.

10. Cited in William Craig Diamond, "Natural Philosophy in Harrington's Thought," *Journal of the History of Philosophy* 16 (1978): 390.

11. James Harrington, *The Oceana and Other Works*, ed. John Toland (London: A. Miller, 1737), 520. Cited in the text hereafter as *OOW*.

12. Cited in Charled Blitzer's introduction to *The Political Writings of James Harrington: Representative Selections* (New York: Library of Liberal Arts, 1955), xi.

13. See Caroline Robbins, *The Eighteenth-Century Commonwealthmen* (Cambridge, Mass.: Harvard University Press, 1959).

14. On the impact of Harrington's writings in the American colonies and on the founding of the republic, see especially H. F. Russel-Smith, *Harrington and His Oceana* (Cambridge: Cambridge University Press, 1914), 185–200.

CHAPTER 7

1. One of the best places to look for an introduction to the rapid expansion of science and scientific literacy in the early eighteenth century is Margaret C. Jacob, *The Cultural Meaning of the Scientific Revolution* (New York: Alfred A. Knopf, 1988), esp. 120–31 and 144–60.

2. See Margaret Jacob, *The Newtonians and the English Revolution, 1686–1720* (Ithaca: Cornell University Press, 1976), *passim*.

3. Sergio Moravia, "The Enlightenment and the Sciences of Man," *History of Science* 17 (1980): 247–68. On 248, Moravia identifies five new epistemological options that contended with the still-present and powerful Cartesian preferences for abstraction, systematization, and deductive structures.

4. John Locke, *An Essay Concerning Human Understanding*, ed. A. C. Fraser (Oxford: Oxford University Press, 1894), "Epistle to the Reader," 14. Cited hereafter in the text as *Essay*. Except for its introduction, citations will be given to the book, chapter, and section, so any edition of the *Essay* may be used.

5. Voltaire, letter on Locke from the *Lettres Philosophiques sur la Anglais*, in *The Portable Voltaire* (New York: Viking Press, 1949), 538–39.

6. From "A Letter of Mr. Isaac Newton, Professor of Mathematics in the University of Cambridge; Containing his New Theory about Light and Colours," *Philosophical Transactions of the Royal Society of London*, 8 (for 1672), reprinted in I. B. Cohen, ed., *Isaac Newton's Papers and Letters on Natural Philosophy* (Cambridge, Mass.: Harvard University Press, 1958), 50. Cited hereafter in the text as *NTLC*.

7. Cited in I. B. Cohen, ed., *Newton's Papers and Letters* (see note 6 above), 106.

8. See I. B. Cohen, *Franklin and Newton* (Philadelphia: American Philosophical Society, 1956), *passim*.

CHAPTER 8

1. Spinoza's *Ethics*, part II, proposition 18, states, "If the human body has at any time been simultaneously affected by two or more bodies, whenever the mind afterwards imagines one of them, it will also remember the other."

2. Cited in Basil Willey, *The Eighteenth-Century Background* (New York: Columbia University Press, 1940), 140.

3. Hume, *An Abstract of A Treatise of Human Nature*, appendix 2 in Charles Wendel, ed., David Hume, *An Inquiry Concerning Human Understanding With a Supplement: An Abstract of A Treatise of Human Nature* (Indianapolis: The Bobbs-Merrill Co., 1955), 183–84. Cited Hereafter in the text as *Abstract*.

4. David Hume, *A Treatise of Human Nature*, ed. E. C. Mossner (Harmondsworth, England: Penguin Books, 1969), pt. 1, ch. 1, 328. Cited hereafter in the text as *Treatise*. All citations will include part, chapter, and page identifications so that other editions may be used.

5. David Hartley, *Observations on Man, His Frame, His Duty, and His Expectations* (London: Thomas Tegg and Son, 1834, 6th ed.). Cited hereafter in the text as *OOM*.

6. See Isaac Kramnick, "Eighteenth-Century Science and Radical Social Theory: The case of Joseph Priestley's Scientific Liberalism," *Journal of British Studies* 25 (1986): 15.

7. See Joseph Priestley, *An Examination of Dr. Reid's Inquiry into the Human Mind on the Principles of Common Sense* (London: 1774), xv and xix.

8. David Hartley, *Various Conjectures on the Perception, Motion, and Generation of Ideas* (Los Angeles: Augustan Reprint Society, 1959; reprint of 1746 edition), 54–55.

9. Robert Owen, *A New View of Society and Other Writings* (London: J. M. Dent and Sons, 1972; from 1813 original), 16.

10. Etienne Bonnot, Abbé de Condillac, *Philosophical Writings*, trans. Franklin Phillip and Harlan Lane (Hillsdale, N.J.: Lawrence Erlbaum Associates, 1982), 464. Cited hereafter in the text as *PWC*.

11. Adam Smith, "Essays on Philosophical Subjects" (1795), in Ralph J. Lindgren, ed., *The Early Writings of Adam Smith* (New York: Augustus M. Kelley, 1967), 66.

12. See, for example, the discussion of Condillac's reputation in Ellen McNiven Hine, *A Critical Study of Condillac's Traité Des Systems* (The Hague: Martinus Nijhoff, 1979), 1–21.

13. The correspondence between Turgot and Condorcet on Helvetius's works is discussed and cited by Keith M. Baker in his *Condorcet: From Natural Philosophy to Social Mathematics* (Chicago: University of Chicago Press, 1975), 215–16.

14. Ernst Cassirer, *The Philosophy of the Enlightenment* (Princeton: Princeton University Press, 1951), 25.

15. Cited in Robert Shackleton, *Montesquieu, A Critical Biography* (Oxford: Oxford University Press, 1961), 181.

16. See, for example, G. V. Plekhanov's *Essays in the History of Materialism* (London: John Lane, 1934).

17. D. W. Smith's *Helvetius: A Study in Persecution* (Oxford: Oxford University Press, 1965) offers a detailed and beautifully crafted analysis of the intellectual politics of the *De l'esprit affair.*

18. Claude Adrienne Helvetius, *Treatise on Man,* trans. W. Hooper (New York: Burt Franklin, 1969), vol. 1, vi–vii; vol. 2, 311. Cited hereafter in the text as *TOM.*

19. Claude Adrienne Helvetius, *De l'esprit, or Essays on the Mind and Its Several Faculties* (New York: Burt Franklin, 1970; reprint of the 1809 American edition), 183. Cited hereafter in the text as *DE.*

20. Montesquieu, *The Spirit of the Laws* (New York: Hafner, 1949; from 1749 French original), 2. Cited hereafter in the text as *SL.*

21. On this issue see Frank Manuel, *The Prophets of Paris: Turgot, Condorcet, Saint-Simon, Fourier, and Comte* (Cambridge, Mass.: Harvard University Press, 1962), 114–16.

22. See especially Constance Jordan's *Renaissance Feminism: Literary Texts and Political Models* (Ithaca: Cornell University Press, 1990) on this issue.

23. See esp. ch. 6, "Competing Cosmologies: Locating Sex and Gender in the Natural Order," in Londa Scheibinger, *The Mind Has No Sex: Women in the Origins of Modern Science* (Cambridge, Mass.: Harvard University Press, 1989). Cited hereafter in the text as *TMHNS.*

24. Jean Jacques Rousseau, *Emile, or On Education,* trans. Allan Bloom (New York: Basic Books, 1979), 357–58. Cited hereafter in the text as *Emile.*

25. Catherine Macaulay, *Letters on Education* (New York: Garland Publishing, 1974, reprinted from the 1790 London edition), 201–204. Cited hereafter in the text as *LOE.*

26. Mary Wollstonecraft, *A Vindication of the Rights of Woman* (New York: W. W. Norton, 1975; from 1792 original), 36.

27. Condorcet, "On the Admission of Women to the Rights of Citizenship," in Keith Baker, ed., *Condorcet, Selected Writings* (Indianapolis: The Bobbs-Merrill Co., 1976), 98.

28. Cesare Becaria, *On Crimes and Punishments* (Indianapolis: The Bobbs-Merrill Co., 1963), 8.

29. In W. Stark, ed., *Jeremy Bentham's Economic Writings* (London: Royal Economic Society, 1952), vol. 1, 101. Cited hereafter in the text as *EWJB.*

30. Jeremy Bentham, *An Introduction to the Principles of Morals and Legislation,* ed., Laurence J. Lafleur (New York: Hafner, 1948; from the 1823 edition containing Bentham's final corrections), 29–30. Cited hereafter in the text as *PML.*

CHAPTER 9

1. See David McNally, *Political Economy and the Rise of Capitalism: A Reinterpretation.* (Berkeley and Los Angeles: University of California Press, 1988), 74.

2. Hazel Van Dyke Roberts, *Boisguilbert: Economist of the Reign of Louis XIV* (New York: Columbia University Press, 1935), 5. Cited hereafter in the text as *Boisguilbert.*

3. Richard Cantillon, *Essay on the Nature of Trade in General*, ed. Henry Higgs (London: Royal Economic Society, 1931), 3. Cited hereafter in the text as *ENTG.*

4. François Quesnay, "Corn," in Ronald Meek, ed., *The Economics of Physiocracy: Essays and Translations* (Cambridge, Mass., Harvard University Press, 1963), 81. Cited hereafter in the text as *EP.*

5. Du Pont de Nemours to Jean-Baptiste Say, 22 April 1815, cited in Elizabeth Fox-Genovese *The Origins of Physiocracy* (Ithaca: Cornell University Press, 1976), 10. Cited hereafter in the text as *OP.*

6. V. Mirabeau, *Philosophie Rurale*, cited in Keith Tribe, *Governing Economy: The Reformation of German Economic Discourse, 1750–1840* (Cambridge: Cambridge University Press, 1988), 122.

7. In Steven Laurence Kaplan, ed., *La Bagarre: Galiani's Lost Parody* (The Hague: Martinus Nijhoff, 1979), 22–23.

8. On the role of cameralism in German universities, see Keith Tribe, *Governing Economy: The Reformation of German Economic Discourse, 1750–1840*, esp. 91–119. Cited hereafter in the text as *GE.*

9. Cited in Albion Small, *The Cameralists: The Pioneers of German Social Polity* (Chicago: University of Chicago Press, 1909), 342. Cited hereafter in the text as *Cameralists.*

10. See, for example, ch. 7 in Joseph Ben-David, *The Scientists Role in Society* (Chicago: University of Chicago Press, 1971), 108–38.

11. See part 3, "The Russian Experience," in Marc Raeff, *The Well-Ordered Police State: Social and Institutional Change Through Law in the Germanies and Russia, 1600–1800* (New Haven: Yale University Press, 1983), esp. 229–30 and 249.

CHAPTER 10

1. Cited in James Moore and Michael Silverthorne, "Gershom Carmichael and the Natural Jurisprudence Tradition in Eighteenth-Century Scotland," in Istvan Hont and Michael Ignatieff, *Wealth and Virtue: The Shaping of Political Economy in the Scottish Enlightenment* (Cambridge: Cambridge University Press, 1983), 76.

2. Cited in David Lieberman, "The Legal Needs of a Commercial

Society: The Jurisprudence of Lord Kames," in Istvan Hont and Michael Ignatieff, eds., *Wealth and Virtue: The Shaping of Political Economy in the Scottish Enlightenment*, 209.

3. Giorgio Tagliacozzo has edited or co-edited three major collections of articles on Vico since 1969: *Giambattista Vico: An International Symposium* (Baltimore: The Johns Hopkins Press, 1969); *Giambattista's Science of Humanity* (Baltimore: The Johns Hopkins University Press, 1976); and *Vico, Past and Present* (Atlantic Heights, N.J.: Humanities Press, 1981). Each of these has contained a set of papers on the twentieth-century impact of Vico. Of these papers, H. Stuart Hughes's "Vico and Contemporary Social Theory and Social History" in the 1969 volume offers perhaps the best overview of his twentieth-century importance.

4. Cited from Vico's *Il Diritto Universale* (1720) in Dario Faucci, "Vico and Grotius: Jurisconsults of Mankind," in Giorgio Tagliacozzo, *Giambattista Vico*, 67.

5. Giambattista Vico, *The New Science of Giambattista Vico: Revised Translation of the Third Edition (1744)*, trans. Thomas G. Bergin and Max H. Fisch (Ithaca: Cornell University Press, 1968), 96, paragraph 331. Cited hereafter in the text as *NS*. I will follow the convention in Vico scholarship of identifying the paragraph number, so other editions may be used.

6. See, for example, Ronald Meek, *Social Science and the Ignoble Savage* (Cambridge: Cambridge University Press, 1976), 1.

7. Montesquieu, *Spirit of the Laws*, trans. Thomas Nugent (New York: Hafner Press, 1949), 317. Cited hereafter in the text as *SL*.

8. Adam Ferguson *An Essay on the History of Civil Society* (New Brunswick: Transaction Books, 1980 reprint of 1767 edition), 122. Cited hereafter in the text as *HCS*.

9. On Montesquieu's reformist orientation, see Mark Hulling, *Montequieu and the Old Regime* (Berkeley and Los Angeles: University of California Press, 1976).

10. Edmund Burke, *Reflection on the Revolution in France* (Garden City, N. Y.: Anchor Books, 1973), 73. Cited hereafter in the text as *RRF*.

11. Adam Smith, *An Inquiry into the Nature and Causes of the Wealth of Nations* (Oxford: Oxford University Press, 1976), vol. 1., book 1, ch. 2, p. 25. Cited hereafter in the text as *WN*. Book and chapter will be indicated so other editions may be used.

12. See, for example, Paul M. Spurlin, *Montesquieu in America, 1760–1801* (Baton Rouge: Louisiana State University Press, 1940).

13. Joseph de Maistre, *The Works of Joseph de Maistre*, ed. Jack Lively (New York: Schocken Books, 1971), 80. This passage is from *Considerations on France*. Cited hereafter in the text as *Works*.

14. On the influence of Ferguson in Germany see the introduction to David Kettler, *The Social and Political Thought of Adam Ferguson* (Athens, Ohio: Ohio State University, 1965).

CHAPTER 11

1. Francis Hutcheson, *A Short Introduction to Moral Philosophy* (Hildesheim: Georg Olms Verlagsbuchandlung, 1969 reprint of 1747 original), i. Cited hereafter in the text as *SIMP*.

2. Cited in Ronald Meek, *Smith, Marx and After* (London: Chapman and Hall, 1977), 178. Cited hereafter in the text as *SMA*.

3. Adam Smith, *The Theory of Moral Sentiments*, ed. D. D. Raphael and A. L. Macfie (Oxford: The Clarendon Press, 1976), 116–17. Cited hereafter in the text as *TMS*.

4. Francis Hutcheson, *A System of Moral Philosophy* (Hildesheim: Georg Olms Verlagsbuchandlung, 1969 reprint of 1755 original), vol. 1, 321. Cited hereafter in the text as *SMP*.

5. David Hume, *A Treatise of Human Nature*, ed. E. C. Mossner (Harmonsworth, England: Penguin Books, Ltd., 1969; from 1739 original), 411. Cited hereafter in the text as *THN*.

6. Adam Smith, *An Inquiry into the Nature and the Causes of the Wealth of Nations* (Oxford: The Clarendon Press, 1976), vol. 1, 422. Cited hereafter in the text as *WN*.

7. Adam Smith, *Lectures on Jurisprudence*, ed. R. L. Meek, et al. (Oxford: The Clarendon Press, 1978), 9. Cited hereafter in the text as *LJ*.

8. In William C. Lehmann, *John Millar of Glasgow: 1735–1801: His Life and Thought and His Contributions to Sociological Analysis* (Cambridge: Cambridge University Press, 1961), 340. Cited hereafter in the text as *Millar*. This text includes a full text of Millar's *Origin of Ranks* as well as other selections from his works.

9. Joseph Schumpeter, *A History of Economic Analysis* (Oxford: Oxford University Press, 1954), 181.

10. See, for example, Marvin Harris, *The Rise of Anthropological Theory* (New York: Thomas Y. Crowell Co., 1968), 31–33 and 48–52; or Sir Edward Evans-Pritchard, *A History of Anthropological Thought* (New York: Basic Books, 1981).

11. *Justinian's Institutes*, translated with an introduction by Peter Birks and Grant McLeod (Ithaca: Cornell University Press, 1987), 73. I was fascinated to discover in reading Constance Jordan's *Renaissance Feminism* (Ithaca: Cornell University Press 1990), 93, that one of the most spectacular French Renaissance feminist texts, Martin La Franc's *La Champion des Dames* (1530), also emphasizes the differences between the

Justinian Code's treatment of women and that which was common in early modern France.

12. John Millar, *An Historical View of the English Government From the Settlement of the Saxons in Britain* . . . (London: Strahan and Caddell, and J. Murray, 1787). This work went through four London editions by 1818.

13. Sir Edward Evans-Pritchard, *A History of Anthropological Thought*, xxiii.

CHAPTER 12

1. William Petty, *The Petty Papers: Some Unpublished Writings of Sir William Petty* (London: Constable and Co., 1927), vol. 2, 51. Cited hereafter in the text as *PP*.

2. On the three-fold division of the social sciences by Condorcet, see Keith M. Baker, *Condorcet: From Natural Philosophy to Social Mathematics* (Chicago: University of Chicago Press, 1975), appendix A, 388–90.

3. Condorcet, *Report on Public Instruction*, in François de la Fontainerie, ed., *French Liberalism and Education in the Eighteenth Century* (New York and London: McGraw Hill Book Co., 1932), 337. Cited hereafter in the text as *RPI*.

4. See, for example, William Stanton, *The Leopard's Spots: Scientific Attitudes Toward Race in America, 1815–1859* (Chicago and London: University of Chicago Press, 1960), *passim*.

5. See especially Howard Gardiner, *The Quest for Mind: Piaget, Levi-Strauss and the Structuralist Movement* (New York: Alfred A. Knopf, 1973).

Bibliographic Essay

The most comprehensive treatment of the social sciences prior to the French Revolution is Gorges Gusdorf's six volume *Les sciences humaines et la pensée occidentale* (Paris: Payot, 1966–73). Donald R. Kelley's *The Human Measure: Social Thought in the Western Legal Tradition* (Cambridge, Mass.: Harvard University Press, 1990) covers a much longer time span but provides critical insights into the importance of jurisprudence for the early social sciences. J. G. A. Pocock's *The Machiavellian Moment: Florentine Republican Thought and the Atlantic Republican Tradition* (Princeton: Princeton University Press, 1975) is an extremely difficult read, but it is critical to an understanding of the early social sciences in England and Scotland. Also comprehensive and gracefully written are Albert Hirschman, *The Passions and the Interests: Political Arguments for Capitalism Before Its Triumph* (Princeton: Princeton University Press, 1977) and Terence Hutchison, *Before Adam Smith: The Emergence of Political Economy* (Oxford: Basil Blackwell, 1988).

On the extent of the potential audiences for those works discussed here, the following are valuable. *Livre et société dans la France du XVIIIe siècle*, vol. 1, ed. G. Bolleme (Lattaye, Mouton, 1965), vol. 2, ed. M. T. Bouyssy (Lattaye, Mouton, 1970); David Cressey, *Literacy and the Social Order* (Cambridge: Cambridge University Press, 1980); Robert Darnton, *The Literary Underground of the Old Regime* (Cambridge, Mass.: Harvard University Press, 1982); and Margaret Jacob, *The Cultural Meaning of the Scientific Revolution* (Ithaca: Cornell University Press, 1988).

Excellent brief introductions to the various dimensions of natural philosophy during the period covered here can be found in the three relevant volumes of the Cambridge University Press History of Science Series, Allen G. Debus's *Man and Nature in the Renaissance* (1978), Richard S. Westfall's *The Construction of Modern Science* (1972), and Thomas Hankins's *Science and the Enlightenment* (1985). These should be supplemented with Paolo Rossi's *Philosophy, Technology, and the Arts in the Early Modern Era* (New York: Harper and Row, 1970) and by J. A. Bennet, "The Mechanic's Philosophy and the Mechanical Philosophy," *History of Science* 24 (1986): 1–28, both of which focus on the links between artisanal culture and scientific culture. Roy Porter and G. S. Rousseau, eds., *The Ferment of Knowledge: Studies on the Historiography of Eighteenth-Century Science* (Cambridge: Cambridge University Press, 1980) is more detailed than Hankins on Enlightenment science and is the only recent alternative survey.

On what I have called the traditional ideology of orders, see E. M. W. Tillyard, *The Elizabethan World Picture* (New York: Columbia University Press, 1943), a brief gem that is understandably still in print after half a century, and James Daly, "Cosmic Harmony and Political Thinking in Early Stuart England," *Transactions of the American Philosophical Society* 69 (1979): 3–40. Eugenio Garin's *Italian Humanism* (Oxford: Basil Blackwell, 1965) provides a very useful brief guide to the Italian Renaissance elements which were crucial in early modern social discourses.

My brief comments on the secularism of the early social scientists are certainly inadequate to deal with the complex topic of the interrelationships between the sacred and the secular in the early modern period. A good place to begin is with the essays in David Lindberg and Ronald Numbers, eds., *God and Nature: Historical Essays on the Encounter Between Christianity and Science* (Berkeley and Los Angeles: University of California Press, 1986). On the relationship between science and religion in the Hermetic tradition and in its modifications in England, see especially Frances Yates's *Giordano Bruno and the Hermetic Tradition* (Chicago: University of Chicago Press, 1964), which was the key text in raising the consciousness of historians of science regarding the relationships between Hermeticism and science. Charles Webster's *The Great Instauration: Science, Medicine, and Reform, 1626–1660* (London: Duckworth, 1975) offers a detailed investigation of the English fusion between Paracelsan and Baconian impulses.

On early cameralism, Pamela Smith's detailed dissertation on Becher, "Alchemy, Credit, and the Commerce of Words and Things: Johann Becher at the Courts of the Holy Roman Empire," Johns Hopkins University, 1989, is outstanding. Albion Small's *The Cameralists: The Pioneers of Social Polity* (Chicago: University of Chicago Press, 1909) remains a valuable introduction to Cameralist doctrines. Marc Raef, *The*

Well-Ordered Police State: Social and Institutional Change through Law in the Germanies and Russia, 1600–1800 (New Haven and London: Yale University Press, 1983), provides an extended analysis of the political context for cameralism; and Keith Tribe, *Governing Economy: The Reformation of German Economic Discourse, 1750–1840* (Cambridge: Cambridge University Press, 1988) provides a careful discussion of the institutional academic context for the later development of cameralism.

Steven Shapin and Simon Schaffer, *Leviathan and the Air Pump: Hobbes, Boyle, and the Experimental Life* (Princeton: Princeton University Press, 1985), offers a brilliant analysis of the scientific context and controversy surrounding Hobbes's work and seems to me the single most important source for understanding Hobbesian thought. Samuel Mintz, *The Hunting of Leviathan: Seventeenth-Century Reactions to the Materialism and Moral Philosophy of Thomas Hobbes* (Cambridge: Cambridge University Press, 1969) focuses on the overwhelmingly panicky response to Hobbes's works. Robert S. McShea, *The Political Philosophy of Spinoza* (New York: Columbia University Press, 1968), is a clear and unpretentious exposition. Lewis Samuel Feuer's *Spinoza and the Rise of Liberalism* (Westport, Conn.: Greenwood Press, 1958) may overemphasize Spinoza's radicalism, but offers a fascinating and, to me, compelling biographical portrait. Ira O. Wade's, *The Clandestine Organization and Diffusion of Philosophical Ideas in France* (Princeton: Princeton University Press, 1938) offers an interpretation of the Enlightenment which highlights the importance of Spinozism.

In recent years, English political economy has had a series of insightful expositors and analysts, starting with William Letwin's acerbic *The Origins of Scientific Economics* (Garden City, N.Y.: Doubleday, 1964) and continuing through Joyce Oldham Appleby's *Economic Thought and Ideology in Seventeenth-Century England* (Princeton: Princeton University Press, 1978), and David McNally's *Political Economy and the Rise of Capitalism: A Reinterpretation* (Berkeley and Los Angeles: University of California Press, 1988). Robert Frank's *Harvey and the Oxford Physiologists* (Berkeley and Los Angeles: University of California Press, 1980) offers important material on the medical context for Petty's development; and Karl Pearson's *The History of Statistics in the Seventeenth and Eighteenth Centuries against the Changing Background of Intellectual, Scientific and Religious Thought* (London: Charles Griffin, 1978) provides an excellent detailed survey of technical developments in political arithmetic.

Of the almost uncountable number of interpretations of the impact of travel accounts on European thought, I have found the following most useful: William Brandon, *New Worlds for Old: Reports from the New World and Their Effect on the Development of Social Thought in Europe, 1500–1800*

(Athens, Ohio: Ohio University Press, 1986), and Ronald Meek, *Social Science and the Ignoble Savage* (Cambridge: Cambridge University Press, 1976). Margaret Hodgen's *Early Anthropology in the Sixteenth and Seventeenth Centuries* (Philadelphia: University of Pennsylvania Press, 1964) emphasizes the continuity between medieval and early modern ideas on the diversity of human institutions.

Clarence Glacken's *Traces on the Rhodian Shore: Nature and Culture in Western Thought from Ancient Times to the End of the Eighteenth Century* (Berkeley and Los Angeles: University of California Press, 1967) offers the best introduction to the tradition of environmental determinist ideas which was so important for both Bodin and Montesquieu.

The best introduction to Harrington is J. G. A Pocock's editor's introduction to *The Political Writings of James Harrington* (Cambridge: Cambridge University Press, 1977). On Harrington's importance for American theorizing, though Pocock's *Machiavellian Moment* is now the standard interpretation, the dated and overly worshipful *Harrington and His Oceana* (Cambridge: Cambridge University Press, 1914) by H. F. Russel-Smith still has some fascination.

Sergio Moravia's "The Enlightenment and the Sciences of Man," *History of Science* 17 (1980): 247–68, suggests the importance of Lockean epistemological liberalization for the social sciences in the eighteenth century. John Youlton's *Locke and the Compass of Human Understanding: A Selective Commentary on the Essay* (New York: Cambridge University Press, 1970) is an excellent guide to Locke's epistemology; and John Youlton, ed., *John Locke: Problems and Perspectives* (London: Cambridge University Press, 1969) offers an excellent general introduction to Locke's many facets.

A very elementary but excellent treatment of Newton's mathematical physics is I. Bernard Cohen, *The Birth of a New Physics* (New York and London: W. W. Norton, 1985, 2d. ed.); Richard S. Westfall's *Never at Rest: A Biography of Isaac Newton* (Cambridge: Cambridge University Press, 1980) is now the standard biography of Newton; and John Fauvel, et al., eds., *Let Newton Be: A New Perspective on His Life and Works* (Oxford: Oxford University Press, 1988) offers elementary accounts of many themes in Newtonian scholarship by several of the best of the younger generation of Newton scholars.

The importance of eighteenth-century psychology for radical and Utilitarian political thought has been emphasized in Elie Halevey, *The Growth of Philosophical Radicalism* (New York: Macmillan, 1928), and in Kingsley Martin, *French Liberal Thought in the Eighteenth Century* (New York: Harper and Row, 3d ed., 1962; after 1929 original).

Much of the work linking associationist theorizing to political activism remains in the journal literature rather than in monographic literature at this time. Among the most interesting articles are Donald J. D'Elia, "Benjamin Rush, David Hartley, and the Revolutionary uses of Psychology," *Proceedings of the American Philosophical Society* 114, no. 2 (April, 1970); Isaac Kramnick, "Eighteenth-Century Science and Radical Social Theory: The Case of Joseph Priestly's Scientific Liberalism," *Journal of British Studies* 25 (1986): 1–30; and Robery Weygant, "Helvetius and Jefferson: Studies of Human Nature and Government," *Journal of the History of the Behavioral Sciences* 9 (1973): 29–41.

Hume's associationism is carefully analyzed in John Bricke, *Hume's Philosophy of Mind* (Princeton: Princeton University Press, 1980); Condillac is well treated by Isabel Knight in *The Geometric Spirit: The Abbé Condillac and the French Enlightenment* (New Haven: Yale University Press, 1968). In spite of its title, D. W. Smith's *Helvetius: A Study in Persecution* (New York: Oxford University Press, 1965) is excellent and relatively broad in its scope. Irving L. Horowitz, *Claude Helvetius: Philosopher of Democracy* (New York: Paine-Whitman, 1954) is an uncritical, indeed adulatory, Marxist asessment of Helvetius, but it contains much interesting material. Keith Baker's *Condorcet: From Natural Philosophy to Social Mathematics* (Chicago: University of Chicago Press, 1975) is absolutely superb but mammoth. J. Salwyn Shapiro's *Condorcet and the Rise of Liberalism* (New York: Octagon Books, 1963) is more celebratory than critical. The relationship between psychology and educational reform is covered in Robert Palmer, *The Improvement of Humanity: Education in the French Revolution* (Princeton: Princeton University Press, 1985).

On the relationships between psychological social theories and feminism, see Linda Shiebinger, *The Mind Has No Sex? Women and the Origins of Modern Science* (Cambridge, Mass.: Harvard University Press, 1989), especially chs. 6–8.

Bentham and the early Utilitarian movement are treated in David Lyons, *In the Interest of the Governed: A Study of Bentham's Philosophy of Utility and Law* (Oxford: The Clarendon Press, 1963) and in Douglas Long's *Bentham on Liberty: Jeremy Benthams Idea of Liberty in Relation to His Utilitarianism* (Toronto: Toronto University Press, 1977).

Pierre Boisguilbert is discussed within his social context by Hazel Van Dyke Roberts in *Boisguilbert: Economist of the Reign of Louis XIV* (New York: Columbia University Press, 1935). Cantillon's life and doctrines are presented in Antoine Murphy, *Richard Cantillon: Entrepreneur and Economist* (Oxford: Oxford University Press, 1986). Elizabeth Fox-Genovese's *The Origins of Physiocracy* (Ithaca: Cornell University Press, 1976) is both readable and insightful. On eighteenth-century cameralism, see the works by Tribe and Small discussed above.

Vico is best approached through the papers in a series of volumes edited by Giorgio Tagliacozzo, *Giambattista Vico: An International Symposium* (Baltimore: The Johns Hopkins University Press, 1969), *Giambattista Vico's Science of Humanity* (Baltimore: The John Hopkins University Press, 1976), and *Vico, Past and Present* (Atlanta Heights, N.J.: The Humanities Press, 1981). On Montesquieu, Robert Shackleton's *Montesquieu: A Critical Biography* (London: Oxford University Press, 1961) is fascinating reading, at once graceful and scholarly. Henry J. Merry, *Montesquieu's System of Natural Government* (West Lafeyette, Ind.: Purdue University Press, 1970) shares my emphasis on the middle third of the *Spirit of the Laws.*

Gladys Bryson's *Man and Society: The Scottish Inquiry of the Eighteenth Century* (Princeton: Princeton University Press, 1945) is still a valuable introduction to the philosophical historians of the Scottish Enlightenment; but she should now be supplemented with Istvan Hont and Michael Ignatieff, eds., *Wealth and Virtue: The Shaping of Political Economy in the Scottish Enlightenment* (Cambridge: Cambridge University Press, 1983), which explores the recent discussions over the relative importance of a natural jurisprudential and a classical republican tradition in orienting their writings. On Ferguson in particular, see David Kettler, *The Social and Political Philosophy of Adam Ferguson* (Athens, Ohio: Ohio State University Press, 1965) and William C. Lehman, *Adam Ferguson and the Beginnings of Modern Sociology* (New York: Cambridge University Press, 1930).

For my money, J. Ralph Lindgren, *The Social Philosophy of Adam Smith* (The Hague: Martinus Nijhoff, 1973) is the best single introduction to Smith because it emphasizes his epistemological and historical relativism. Richard Teichgraeber II's *'Free Trade' and Moral Philosophy: Rethinking the Sources of Adam Smith's Wealth of Nations* (Durham, N.C.: Duke University Press, 1986) is excellent on the Hutchesonian and Humian background to Smith's works.

On John Millar, the only reliable full-length study is William C. Lehman, *John Millar of Glasgow, 1735–1801: His Life and Thought and His Contributions to Sociological Analysis* (Cambridge: Cambridge University Press, 1961).

Index

abstraction, Condillac on, 105
Academie des Sciences, 63, 111; Quesnay and, 128
Academy of Bordeaux, 146
Adams, John, 82
agricultural societies, defined, 153; status of women in, 183
agriculture, Boisguilbert's emphasis on, 121–25; Quesnay's emphasis on, 128–32
alchemy 34, 191; and cameralism, 32–34
analysis, 53; Condillac on, 105; method of, 61; promoted by Helvetius, 109
analysis and synthesis, 24–26
analytic simplicity, of English political economy, 134
analytic strategy, and insensitivity to context, 65
Andreae, Johann, 59
Anglican Church, 35, 38
anima mundi; see also world soul, 22
anti-clericalism, of Helvetius, 108, 111; Hobbes's, 35–40
approval, defines virtue, 167; Hutcheson on human need for, 165; Smith on human need for, 165
Arbuthnot, John, 151
Aristotle, 20, 42, 76; Harrington's use of, 81; poetry as guide to action, 13; taxonomy of knowledge, 15–17;
association of ideas, Hume on, 98–99; Locke on, 96–97; Spinoza on, 54, 96–97
associationist psychology, 96–104, 140, 187; and feminism, 112–14; linked to liberal and radical causes, 99; of Hartley, 100–104; of Hume, 98–100; related to economic issues by Italians, 133

associations, Hartley's doctrine of, 102–4
atomism, revival of ancient, 25, 191; Hobbes and, 38–40
Autome, Bernard, 75; *Comparison of French and Roman Law*, 75

Bachofen, J. J., 186–87
Bacon, Sir Francis, 11, 21, 59, 80, 115; *History of Henry VII*, 81
balance of principles, in Republican theory, 78–79
balance of property, Harrington on, 80–82
barbarian society, defined, 153
Beccaria, Cesare, 67, 114–15, 133; *On Crimes and Punishments*, 114
Becher, Johannes, 3, 13, 27–34, 42, 64, 68, 71, 134, 191; *Political Discourse*, 28–34
Bentham, Jeremy, 43, 67, 115–17; *An Introduction to the Principles of Morals and Legislation*, 116
Bertin, Jean Baptist, 129, 131
Bodin, Jean, 72, 74–77, 139, 148, 151, 190; *Method for the Easy Comprehension of History*, 75; *The Six Bookes of a Commonweale*, 75–77, 139
body politic, 42, 69, 121–22
Boisguilbert, Pierre le Pesant de, 34, 66, 120–25; *A Brief for France*, 120; *Dissertation on the nature of Wealth, Money, and Taxes*, 120; *The ruin of France*, 120; *Treatise on Grains*, 120
Boyle, Robert, 23, 25, 44, 60; *General heads for the natural history of a country*, 74
Brahe, Tycho, 22
Buffon, Louis le Clerck, comte de, 73, 107

Galiani, Ferdinando, 121, 138, 193; attacks Physiocrats, 131–33
Galileo, 12, 52, 53, 109, 121, 191
Gassendi, Pierre, 25, 40
Gay, John, 98; *Dissertation Concerning the Fundamental Principles of Virtue and Morals*, 97
gender, 163; Millar on issues of, 178–88
general good of society, served by factional interests, 158
general happiness, Helvetius on, 109–10
general spirit of a nation, defined by Montesquieu, 148
general welfare, Smith on consistency with individual greed, 169
gentry, 36, 37
geometry. *See* Euclidean geometry; *esprit géometrique*
Gournay, Vincent, 129
governments, Smith on function of, 172
Graunt, John, 58, 60, 66, 71, 188; *Natural and Political Observations . . . Upon the Bills of Mortality*
greatest happiness principle, Hartley's 103–4
Gresham College, 60
Grotius, Hugo, 139, 141, 147; *The Law of War and Peace*, 139

Habit and custom, Hume's emphasis on, 99
happiness, as only end of actions, 97
Harrington, James, 2, 11, 14, 79–82, 148, 159, 162; *Commonwealth of Oceana*, 71, 77, 79–82, 192; economic determinism of, 192; opposition to Hobbes, 80–81; *The Mechanics of Nature*, 80
Hartley, David, 97, 98, 100, 105, 109, 115, 117, 185, 187, 188, 194; associationist psychology of, 100–104; *Observations on Man*, 100–104; *Various Conjectures on the Perception, Motion, and Generation of Ideas*, 101
Hartlib, Samuel, 59

Harvey, William, 44, 60; centrality for Hobbesian psychology; 40–41; Harrington on, 80
Helvetius, Claude Adrienne, 105, 106, 107–12, 114, 117, 132, 138, 143, 185, 187, 188, 192; admired by Bentham, 115; charged with crude materialism, 107; critical of Montesquieu, 107–9; *On the Mind*, 107–10; sensationalist psychology of, 107–12; *Treatise on Man*, 107–12
Henry VIII, 37, 38
Herder, Johann, 77
Hermetic, 21; *see also* Renaissance Naturalism
Hippocrates, 14
historical jurisprudence, 75; as source of philosophical history, 72
Hobbes, Thomas, 2, 24–26, 27, 35–48, 50, 52, 53, 59, 71, 75, 96, 98, 105, 141, 147, 156, 191, 192; anti-clericalism of, 11; *De Cive*, 192; *Leviathan*, 39–47, 192; opposed by Harrington, 80–81; opposes Cartesian intuitionism, 46; pure materialism of, 40; radical implications of his work, 47, 192; relation to Salutati, 19; rejection of empiricist approach to social sciences, 44
homeostatic mechanisms, 69
homeostatic model, 193
Homily on Obedience, 7, 9
homogeneity, methodological, 11
Hornigk, Philipp von, 29, 134
human nature, distinguished from other animals by Ferguson, 157; uniformity of, 155
Hume, David, 97–100, 109, 156, 160, 165, 179, 182, 187, 188, 194; *A Treatise of Human Nature*; 98–100, 115; attacks physiocrats, 131–33; associationist psychology of, 98–100
humoral theory, 76–77, 151
hunting and gathering societies, status of women in, 181–83
Hutcheson, Francis, 104, 160, 162, 170, 171, 179, 181; *A Short Introduction to*

progress, Ferguson on human, 157–58
progressive theory of society, attributed to Montesquieu, 153
propriety, Smith on relation to virtue, 168
prudential knowledge, 190
psychological tradition, 2, 195; and Hobbes, 35–47, 192; and mechanical philosophy, 35–56; and Spinoza, 52–56; related to legal theory of Salutati, 19; transformed by emphasis on passion, 98; used by Glasgow School to analyze virtue, 164–66
Pufendorf, Samuel, 139–41, 147, 162, 164, 171, 179, 181; *Eight Books on the Law of Nature and Of Man*, 12, 139; on perfect and imperfect rights, 170; *On the Duty of Man and Citizen*, 139–41
Puritanism, 38; Hobbes's opposition to, 35
putting-out company. *See* Verlagen

quantification, Hobbesian contribution to emphasis on, 47; Petty on, 62
Quesnay, François, 68, 69, 126, 127–32, 138, 188; opposes historical methods, 132

race, 195
rational actor assumption, 67
realism, 14, 56
reason, as one way of linking ideas, 96; as purely instrumental, 54; as source of pleasure, 53; Hobbes on, 45–47; Hume's distrust of, 99; Spinoza on, 51–54
refinement of manners and tastes, attributed to commerce by Montesquieu, 154
Reform Bill of 1832, 115
reformist goals, of Montesquieu and Vico, 143
relativism, implicit in Aristotelian political perspective, 17
Renaissance Naturalism, 21–22, 25; and cameralism, 27–34

republicanism, appropriated by Royalists and Parliamentarians, 80; classical theories of, 78–82
resolution and composition, 24; Condillac on, 105; *see also* analysis and synthesis
Roman law, 17, 74, 139, 179, 186; treatment of women, 180
Rousseau, Jean Jacques, 108; attack on intellectual women, 113; *Emile, Or On Education*, 113; *Discourse on Inequality*, 73
Royal Society of London, 60, 62; opposed by Hobbes, 44

Saint-Simon, Claude Henri de Rouvery de, Count, 111
Salutati, Coluccio, 18–19, 39; relation to Hobbes, 19
sanctions, 117
savage society, defined, 153
Schröder, Wilhelm Freyherr von, 30, 71, 134
science, seventeenth-century uses of term, 20
Scots Law, 179
Scripture, role in controlling moral discourse, 12
secular character, of early social science, 11
Sekendorf, Ludwig von, 3
self-evidence, theory of truth used by physiocrats, 132
self-interest, 127; assumed by Petty as motivating economic decisions, 66; cameralists suspicion of, 135; Ferguson on expansion of, 160–61; Hartley on limited value of, 103; Helvetius on universality of, 109; linked to commercial society, 154–55; Montesquieu and Ferguson on limits to, 155; refined, 104; Smith relates to virtue, 168
self preservation, 40, 42, 53; Hobbes on relation to civil society, 42; limited importance for Hume of, 99
sensationalist psychology, 104–12; of

utilitarian ideals of Smith, 172
Utilitarianism, 114–17, 177
utility, defined by Hume, 99

value, transformed from moral to economic notion, 47
value of a human life, calculated by Petty, 64; Hobbes on, 47
Van den Ende, Francis, 49
vanity, 167, 169
Verlagen, 32–33
Verri, Pietro, 133
Vespuci, Amerigo, 72
vibrations, Hartley's doctrine of, 101
Vico, Giambattista, 3, 132, 138, 140, 141–46, 147, 153, 158, 195; *Principles of a New Science Concerning the Nature of Nations*, 140–46
virtues about imperfect rights, 170; Cicero on, 163–64; Hutcheson on, 163–65; in republican theory, 78–79; judgments of emotional, not rational,

165; linked by Smith to propriety, 168; not related to law, according to Machiavelli, 19; Smith on, 164–68
vital motions, 40–41, 51; related to pleasure and pain, 41
Voltaire, 84, 108

Wealth, defined by Cantillon, 125; why approved, 167
Wilkins, John, 22
Willis, Thomas, 68
Wollstonecraft, Mary, 101, 185; *A Vindication of the Rights of Woman*, 112–14
women, Millar on the roles and status of, 179; treatment of, under English and Scots law; 180; treatment of, under Roman law, 180
world soul, 22; *see also anima mundi*
Wundt, Wilhelm, 18

Zincke, George Heinrich, 28

The Author

RICHARD G. OLSON was born in 1940 in St. Paul, Minnesota. He received a B.S. in physics from Harvey Mudd College. After receiving his A.M. in physics from Harvard University, he moved into the program in history of science, receiving his Ph.D. from Harvard in 1967.

After teaching at Tufts University and at the University of California at Santa Cruz, he returned to Harvey Mudd College in 1976 and is currently Professor of History and Willard Keith Fellow in the Humanities as well as Professor of History at the Claremont Graduate School.

Professor Olson's publications have focused on the interaction among scientific and other aspects of European culture. They include *Scottish Philosophy and British Physics: The Foundations of the Victorian Scientific Style* (1975), and *Science Deified and Science Defied: The Historical Roles of Science in Western Culture* (vol. 1, 1982; vol. 2, 1990).

Professor Olson has contributed to numerous scholarly journals, including *The American Journal of Physics, Annals of Science, History of Science, Isis,* and *The Journal of the History of Ideas.*

The Editor

MICHAEL S. ROTH is the Hartley Burr Alexander Professor of Humanities at Scripps College and director of the European Studies Program at the Claremont Graduate School. He is the author of *Psycho-Analysis as History: Negation and Freedom in Freud* (1987) and *Knowing and History: Appropriations of Hegel in 20th-Century France* (1988), both published by Cornell University Press. He is the co-editor, with Victor Gourevitch, of the revised and expanded edition of Leo Strauss, *On Tyranny* (1991), published by the Free Press. He is currently writing about contemporary strategies for representing the past in the humanities and about conceptualizations of memory disorders in the nineteenth century.